CLAYESMORE SCHOOL
REGISTER
GW00504139

CLAYESMORE

A Celebration

CLAYESMORE

A Celebration

Written and edited by

Val Horsler

Clayesmore: A Celebration

First published in 2012 by Third Millennium Publishing Limited,
a subsidiary of Third Millennium Information Limited.

2–5 Benjamin Street
London
United Kingdom
EC1M 5QL
www.tmiltd.com

ISBN: 978 1 906507 63 3

British Library Cataloguing in Publication Data.
A CIP catalogue record for this book is available from the British Library.

Editing	Val Horsler
Design	Matthew Wilson
Production	Bonnie Murray
Reprographics	Studio Fasoli, Italy
Printed by	Gorenjski Tisk, Slovenia

Contents

PART 1:
Beginnings / 8
A Beautiful Environment / 40

PART 2:
Iwerne Minster / 46
Living at Clayesmore / 82

PART 3:
Clayesmore Preparatory School / 88
Art, Music and Drama / 104

PART 4:
The Modern Era / 122
Outdoors / 138

PART 5:
The Clayesmore Community / 148

PART 6:
The Present and the Future / 158
by Martin Cooke

List of Subscribers / 172
Index of Names / 177
Acknowledgements and Picture Credits / 184

Foreword

For many associated with Clayesmore, and certainly for those who knew him, David Spinney's 1987 book *Clayesmore: A School History* has a fond and oft-visited place on the bookshelves. I very much hope that this fine new volume, which complements rather than succeeds Spinney's work, will be treasured just as much by Clayesmorians and their families of all generations. It has been produced to celebrate the 80th anniversary of the school's arrival in Iwerne Minster in 1933 and I am very grateful to all who have contributed to it.

There have been times when Clayesmore has struggled to keep going and there have been any number of people since 1896, when it all began, who have made wise and bold decisions, and sometimes leaps of faith, that have ensured our continuity. Many have long since died but I would like to think that they would be very proud of Clayesmore in its current form.

We look back with gratitude and pride, and we look forward with confidence and ambition. As, yet again, the curriculum and the examination system in the UK come under review, there is a strong call for the values and beliefs espoused by Alexander Devine to be given greater prominence. With young people having access to information, knowledge and opinion through the gadgets they carry in their pockets, Lex's cry, 'Think for yourself,' has never been more important. The roundedness of the education he believed in and which Clayesmore continues to provide in its daily life is also of quintessential consequence to each individual as they set out upon life's path.

Clayesmore remains true to its mission and proudly so, and I hope you will enjoy this celebratory volume every bit as much as those of us who have been involved in its production.

Martin Cooke
May 2012

PART 1:

Beginnings

The roots of Clayesmore School lie in the educational radicalism of Alexander (Lex) Devine, born in Manchester in 1865 to a prosperous family of mixed Greek and Irish descent who owned a printing works in the city. He forged a career in journalism, and in due course became the police court reporter for the *Manchester Guardian*. In the 1880s he regularly reported on the vicious gang violence, known as 'scuttling', that had broken out in Manchester, and found himself increasingly involved in the public debate about the reasons for the unrest. The gangs were made up of boys and young men who banded together to wage war on each other using an array of sometimes quite horrific weapons. As court reporter, Lex covered the trials of dozens of scuttlers, and decided to delve into the motivations driving them. His article on scuttlers and scuttling, published in the *Manchester Guardian* in September 1890, identified four causes: lack of parental control, lack of discipline in schools, the influence of 'penny dreadfuls' and the sheer monotony of life for poverty-stricken youths who were either unemployed or toiled at backbreaking occupations during the day only to be faced with nothing to occupy them in the evening.

Lex decided that a two-pronged approach was needed to combat the problem. Always an advocate of corporal punishment, he thought that those convicted should be flogged rather than sent to prison; but at the same time he wanted to establish preventative programmes targeted at younger children and aimed at stopping them from joining the gangs.

Below: Alexander 'Lex' Devine among the Old Boys football team, 1903.

Tommy Cannon and 'the moke'

Tommy Cannon was one of the more unfortunate among Lex's waifs, in that he had a badly cleft palate which made his speech almost incomprehensible. He had been left behind in Manchester when Lex moved to London, but had been given the promise that he would be sent for as soon as possible. Once the new school had begun to take shape, Lex fulfilled this promise and sent Tommy the money for his rail fare, instructing him also to bring 'the moke'. This was a wooden instrument of corporal punishment copied from one used on juvenile offenders at the magistrate's court. No pictures of it survive, let alone the real thing, so how it worked and what it looked like remain a mystery.

Unused to train travel, it seems that Tommy carried this strange instrument into the compartment with him rather than entrust it to the guard, to the great annoyance of his fellow passengers, who complained vociferously all the way to London. Nor could he make them understand his replies. He must have been relieved to be met at the station by Lex, and to be able to hand over his unwieldy charge.

Tommy Cannon was to stay at Clayesmore for almost the whole of his life, making himself useful as a general handyman and outliving Lex himself. David Spinney remembers him as 'a wispy little man with a ragged moustache, and quite incomprehensible to talk to' who when the school moved to Iwerne Minster had the room next to the stable arch, into which no visitors were allowed to go. He had returned to Manchester for a short time in 1923, setting himself up as a chimneysweep, but the venture failed and he returned to Clayesmore. In 1942, when he knew he was dying, he took himself back to Manchester, arriving with only a small suitcase and a photo of Lex, and there he is buried, his gravestone asserting that for 46 years he was 'a servant of Clayesmore School and the friend of successive generations of Clayesmore boys'.

He set to with great energy raising both consciousness and funds among the philanthropists of the Manchester industrial scene, and proved adept at organising and running facilities for these young boys in what quickly became a series of clubs which offered opportunities for relaxation, recreation and the development of skills and interests. The entrance fee was 2d and the subscription 1d a week, and the clubs soon had several hundred members and waiting lists.

Further development of the idea came when a new law allowed magistrates to release first offenders into the care of a responsible guardian rather than send them to prison. Lex took on this role and established a boys' home, named after General Gordon, which saw 200 boys pass through it in its first year. But Lex had a fatal flaw: he was extravagant, not good at managing money and inclined to follow the mantra 'buy now, pay later – if at all'. His management committee lost faith in him, and he was forced to resign from the clubs. He struggled on with the boys' home for a while, but here too the finances overwhelmed him and the creditors stepped in. With a sad little rump of 12 waifs still clinging to him, he decided to move to London.

Never without friends or ideas, Lex came up with a new plan. He realised, as did others, that his strength lay in offering hope and a future to the lame dogs, the misfits who

Below: 'Scuttlers' could find education and apprenticeships in places like the Salford Lads' Club (seen here waiting for the club to open, on the corner of Coronation Street in Manchester), offering an alternative to gang culture.

failed to flourish in a 'normal' environment; he could give them what they needed, and they in their turn liked and trusted him. Therefore he would set up a school – and the pupils would be the boys with whom the mainstream public schools could not cope. Funding would come from parents and guardians who, by sending their troublesome charges to him, would avert both the unhappiness and the disgrace of expulsion. 'Don't expel your hard cases,' was the message he sent to the great public schools; 'send them to me.'

The message fell on receptive ears. Lex's reputation as a kindly disciplinarian who had a way with intractable boys allowed the public schools to deal with their potential failures by employing the convenient half truth that 'he is not getting on as well as he should here, and we feel that he would benefit from more individual attention in a smaller school' – though Lex always insisted that he was not running a reformatory, and would not accept the real reprobates. Edward Lyttelton, headmaster of Eton during Clayesmore's early years, told an old Clayesmorian in the 1920s that Lex had been 'a remarkable man [who] made a great success of more than one boy I sent to him. I could never have kept them at Eton. He had an astonishing

Above: Edward Lyttelton.

Left: Manchester, c1880.

Lex's verdicts on his pupils

The school archive holds a leather-bound register which Lex kept in his own hand right from the start, noting in brief the family and school history of his pupils; it runs from 1893 to 1909, with the entries tailing off in detail towards the end. Very early in Clayesmore's history, as the register makes apparent, the school accepted boys from a wide variety of backgrounds and nationalities, ranging from Europe and the Middle East to South America. Many of the entries follow up a boy's later history, either with attached press cuttings or notes, and several include the sad later annotation in Lex's hand: 'died for his country'.

Lex's comments are uncompromising, and include verdicts such as 'impenetrably stupid', 'incurably lazy', weak and easily led'. One boy, James Graham Adam, is condemned as 'the most absolutely selfish boy I ever met, cold-hearted, full of empty stupid swagger'. Adam appears to have conducted love affairs with a housemaid at the school and with one or two village girls – 'not brains enough to see his own folly'; 'a great relief when he left… latterly his influence was evil and undesirable… not a nice boy in any way'.

The first entry in the register is that of Archibald Stephen Hawardine, who joined the school, aged 14, in April 1893 and who had an unhappy family history: 'deserted by father (gambling and drink); mother bravely set to work to earn her own living; two sisters took situations; the boy left neglected, got with loose boys, spoilt by friends of mother's… plenty of spirit and pluck, inclined to be lazy… strong, passionate temper, keen on matters of £sd… affectionate, wants to do right, weak…'. He appears to have become one of Lex's successes who, after leaving in 1896, kept up his connection with Lex and the school: 'finally settles down – very often at Clayesmore – very affectionate still'.

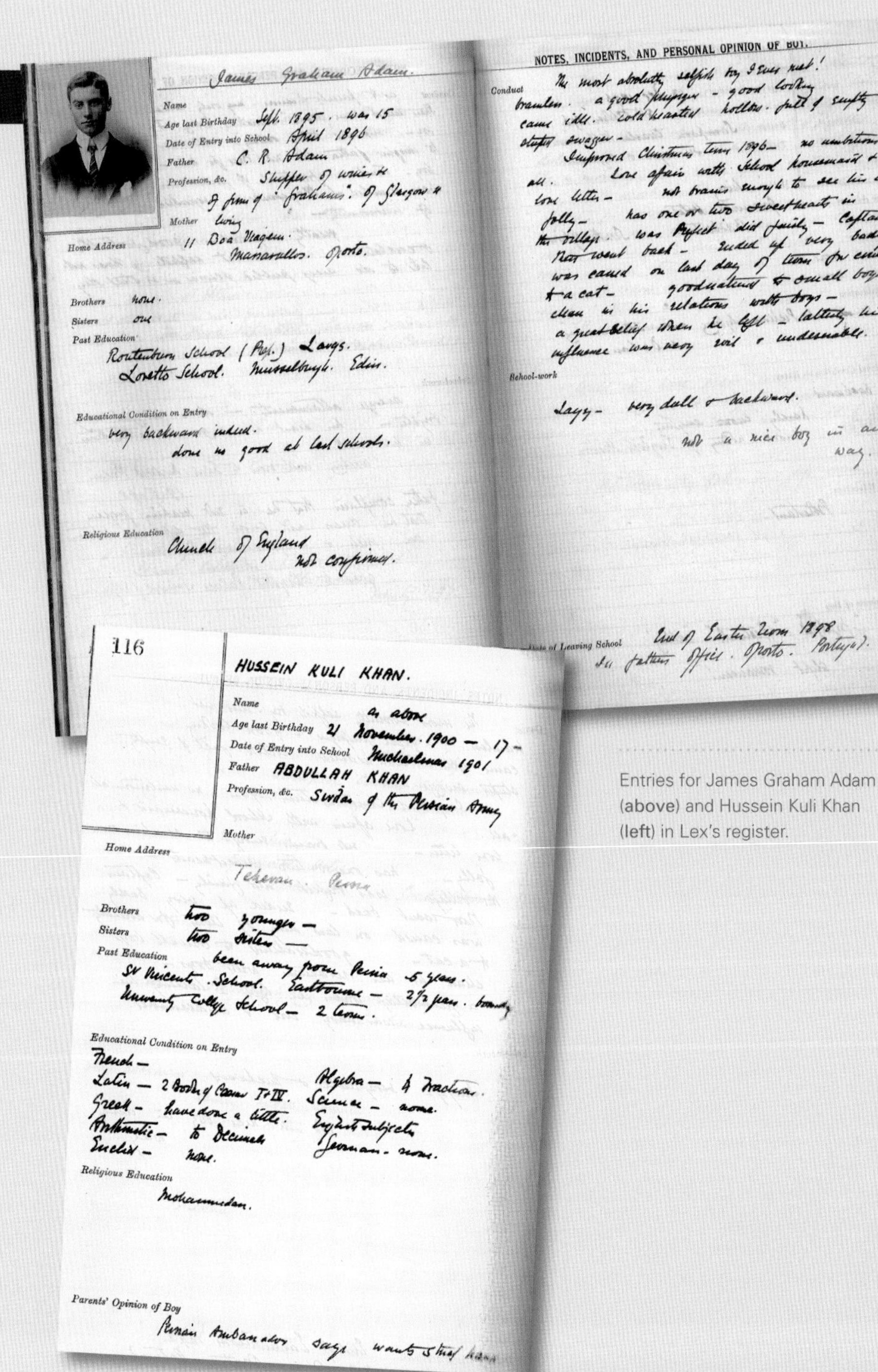

Name: James Graham Adam.
Age last Birthday: Sept. 1895. was 15
Date of Entry into School: April 1896
Father: C. R. Adam
Mother: living
Brothers: none
Sisters: one
Past Education: Routenburn School (Prep.) Largs. Loretto School. Musselburgh. Edin.
Educational Condition on Entry: very backward indeed. done no good at last schools.
Religious Education: Church of England not confirmed.

NOTES, INCIDENTS, AND PERSONAL OPINION OF BOY.
School-work: Lazy – very dull & backward. Not a nice boy in any way.
Date of Leaving School: End of Easter Term 1898

116
HUSSEIN KULI KHAN.
Name: as above
Age last Birthday: 21 November 1900 — 17 —
Date of Entry into School: Michaelmas 1901
Father: ABDULLAH KHAN
Profession, &c.: Sirdar of the Persian Army
Mother
Home Address: Teheran Persia
Brothers: two younger —
Sisters: two sisters —
Past Education: been away from Persia 5 years. St Vincent School. Eastbourne – 2½ years. boarding. University College School – 2 terms.
Educational Condition on Entry: French – Latin – 2 Books of Caesar I to IV. Greek – have done a little. Arithmetic – to Decimals. Euclid – none. Algebra – to Fractions. Science – none. English subjects. German – none.
Religious Education: Mohammedan.
Parents' Opinion of Boy: Persian Ambassador says wants strict hand

Entries for James Graham Adam (above) and Hussein Kuli Khan (left) in Lex's register.

Many are 'not bad fellows', and their faults are often put down to mothers who spoil them. One such is Robert Arthur George Hannington, 'a good boy, not strong in character, with a most foolish and hysterical mother… what his mother will make him I can hardly imagine'. Another with the same disadvantage is Patrick Vivian Harris, who was nine when he joined the school, but 'his mother withdrew him after ten days of incessant communication from home. Not a nice boy – utterly spoilt by a foolish and brainless mother.'

Frank Thompson, on the other hand, is 'a bright, high-spirited boy, clean-hearted, honest and true', Charles Edward

Above: The school's 31 pupils in 1898.

Right: Robert Barbour Whyte (left) with his brother.

Goodyear is 'a thoroughly nice lad, innocent-hearted, stammers badly', and Guy Rutherford Levesley is 'a bright, intelligent boy, very affectionate', despite running away twice and believed to be 'spoilt at home'. Robert Barbour Whyte, who joined in 1908, was another of whom Lex approved. He had a distinguished academic and sporting career at Clayesmore before going on to Balliol College, Oxford, and dying at Loos; there is a memorial to him in the school chapel and he was the author of a short ode to Clayesmore:

Clayesmore this is, bold to the outward view,
Who in her living aims is also bold.
She dares a fresh and manly faith to hold
And blends the older order with the new.

CGR Sydney-Turner, who can be seen in the photo above in the striped blazer, fourth from the right in the back row, ended up as an upstanding and distinguished member of society (*see p15*), but his record at Clayesmore was patchy; as Lex records: 'not a boy of strong will power… breaks into storeroom and steals – ask father to remove him… refuse to recommend to Civil Service commissioners'. But he was academically bright and clearly overcame his difficulties which, according to Lex, were because 'something [is] quite wrong at home; sense of right and wrong not clear with father'.

Lex's notes about several of the boys in the photo make it clear that they were indeed hard cases; even their parents are on record as believing them to be weak-willed, lazy, dishonest and untruthful. Richard Atkinson, the boy sprawled out on the ground at the front, was remanded for theft at Bow Street in 1907, and Gilbert Lindsey Daniell, sixth from the right in the back row, was imprisoned for two years for embezzlement in South Africa. And the young boy on the left with his arm around the neck of the dog, was Ivor King Harvey Locke, later to be the villain in a cruel divorce case after a marriage that lasted only four days. As the divorce petition in 1911 had it, he bullied his wife into marrying him on December 24 1910, having told her that he was wealthy, but immediately announced that they would be living on her money and, at dinner that evening, offered her possessions as security for a bill which he could not pay. He then knocked her about and handled her brutally; she left him on December 28.

Hussein Kuli Khan, who joined the school in 1901 and was later to be Minister of Foreign Affairs in the Persian government, 'wants to be treated differently to the others'. His classmate, Maurice Cecil Alabaster, was later to be tried for murder, under the name Maurice de Fourtalis, after a woman with whom he was associated was found dead. When it turned out that she had died from heart failure, probably after being assaulted by him, he pleaded guilty to manslaughter and was sentenced to nine months in prison.

Michael Wolkonsky, the son of Prince Peter Wolkonsky, had not been to school before coming to Clayesmore, and found it 'all so complicated, but very interesting'. He was at the school with his two cousins, Cyril and Roman Crown, and all three disappeared during the Russian revolution; advertisements after the war failed to locate them.

The entry for Harry Berg (1901) – 'lacking in self-respect, inclined to be servile, one has to be very careful in correcting him' – includes a letter from the boy to a Mr Ovens: 'I have something to tell you that will please you and that is that I am reconciliated (*sic*) to my people and am going home from Xmas. I have not told any lies this term, have read my Bible daily and have said my prayers day and night… I hope you will forgive me if I tell you that I have not once been able to read my magazines because boys of the school burnt them in front of me… but what I wanted to tell you was that I am in want of money. I have had no money for about four weeks but don't think that I am begging.'

Charles Hay Anzeley Moore is considered by his parents as 'dishonest, untruthful and weak', and Lex suspects him of 'pocket robberies from visiting teams', though there is no evidence. In January 1902 his father came to the school and accused him of stealing a diamond tiara, to which he confessed but then said that he did not know where he'd sold it. 'Is he all there?' Lex asks. And Eustace Arthur Anson (1905) is 'dirty, cunning, extraordinarily lazy, vain and "told his father he was quite unfit for school".' Even his mother wrote to 'Mr de Vigne' that 'his great fault is extreme indolence, both mental and physical, and he is very clever at evading excesses either of mind or body'.

Left: Cyril (top) and Roman (bottom) Crown, two boys who disappeared during the Russian Revolution.

way with boys…'. One of those who moved from Eton to Clayesmore was Geoffrey Heneage Drummond, who won the Victoria Cross in 1918; and one CGR Sydney-Turner, who arrived at Clayesmore with a somewhat shady reputation which he did little to dispel while at the school, ended up as Colonel the Reverend Sydney-Turner, DSO, OBE, Légion d'honneur, assistant scout commissioner and vicar of Peartree, Southampton.

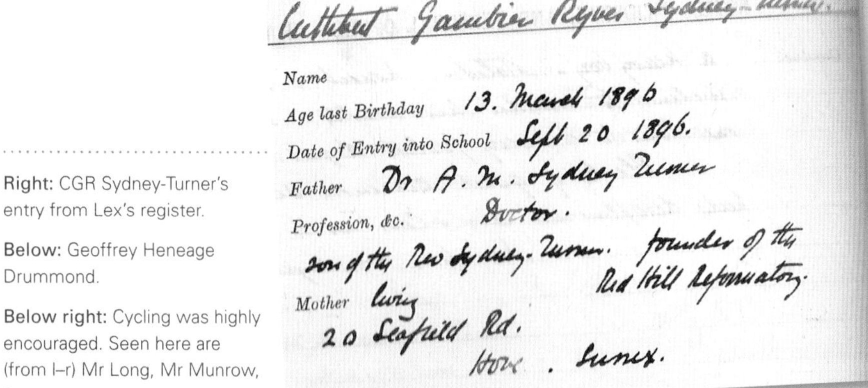

Cuthbert Gambier Ryves Sydney-Turner.

Name

Age last Birthday 13. March 1896

Date of Entry into School Sept 20 1896.

Father Dr A. M. Sydney Turner

Profession, &c. Doctor.

son of the Rev Sydney-Turner. founder of the Red Hill Reformatory.

Mother living

20 Seafield Rd.

Hove . Sussex.

Right: CGR Sydney-Turner's entry from Lex's register.

Below: Geoffrey Heneage Drummond.

Below right: Cycling was highly encouraged. Seen here are (from l–r) Mr Long, Mr Munrow, Powys-Lybb and Kerr.

A friend had lent Lex a house in north London, but as his ideas took root and boys began to arrive at his new school, he moved to a larger house in Edmonton, and then to Glebelands in Mitcham. Here his vision took a clearer shape; Lex was a genuinely progressive educational thinker, and along with others of the time, such as the founder of Bedales, JH Badley, with whom Lex was on friendly terms, he decided that the bedrock of his mission would be to treat the boys in his care as, before all else, individuals – and that his school would be 'a liberal democratic state not a reactionary dictatorship'. The conformism of public schooling at the time was not for his charges, whose perceived faults could be explained by their unwillingness or inability to fit in with the narrow, limited pattern of education normally on offer. 'Think for yourself, boy' was to be the watchword he would drum into his pupils for the rest of his life.

Glebelands became unsuitable for this new venture – not least because Lex was employing his usual cavalier attitude towards paying the bills presented by the local tradesmen – so once again, with the support of friends,

Above: Claysmore House at Enfield.

Right: The rifle range at Enfield, as featured in a 1901 article in *The Navy and Army Illustrated*.

he moved on. Enfield in Middlesex offered a house called Claysmore – with the extra 'e' quickly added to its name at the suggestion of a canny friend to avoid any association with its heavy, damp, clay foundations – and it was made ready to take its first batch of 12 boys in February 1896. Eccentric as ever, Lex decided that it would be good for his charges if they were to make their own way from Mitcham to their new school. He gave them a route – longer than necessary, perhaps to avoid the perils of central London – and it took them five days. At their last stop they sent Lex a postcard: 'Expect us about 6pm tomorrow, in rags, penniless and worn out'. They arrived to find their headmaster stoking the furnaces so that they could have much needed hot baths, and they enjoyed a huge tea afterwards.

The mainstream public schools continued to send him their misfits; but his progressive outlook was also an attraction, and he worked hard to counter the image of Clayesmore as a reformatory and to spread the word

Nov. 23rd, 1901.] *THE NAVY AND ARMY ILLUSTRATED.* 219

A PUBLIC SCHOOL BOYS' RIFLE RANGE.

IT is not at every school for the sons of well-to-do men that physical manual labour is included as an item in the general work of the school, but at Clayesmore School, Enfield, Middlesex, manual labour has, since the foundation of the school some six years ago, been made an important part of out-door work. This experiment has received a considerable amount of notice and interest on the part of many other schools who have been anxious to observe its result. Roughly speaking, the typical English schools in the nineteenth century had, and they still have, a twofold aim in scholastic work and success in games, and it is difficult to say which of the two commands the most respect. The result is that, in the stress of competition, school life alternates between violent study and violent exercise, and it is a very grave question as to whether this is a full or satisfactory life. There is obviously something wanted to complete the balance; hence the athletic prig, no less nauseous than the pedantic prig, and intellectual over-pressure, with muscular strain and many dangers moral and physical. Now, in instituting manual work as part of the school life at Clayesmore, an attempt has been made to provide some remedy. Not only John Locke, the philosopher, but the great men of all ages—from Plato and Rabelais to Carlyle and Ruskin—have seen and told us that if we want to make boys capable men, as well as scholars and gentlemen, we must put them in touch with the simplest conditions of life; and not the least important element in a liberal education is a practical acquaintance with manual labour.

A PRACTICAL ACQUAINTANCE WITH MANUAL LABOUR.

Making the embankment

Amongst the various enterprises undertaken by the boys of Clayesmore within the last few years, they have erected a range and rifle-butts on the school estate, which have been affiliated to the National Rifle Association, passed as a sound range by the War Office inspector of musketry, and has been declared to be one of the most complete miniature ranges in the country. It is 200-yds. in length, and in order to ensure perfect safety it has been found necessary to erect behind the mantlets an embankment, which has necessitated the excavation and embanking of over 600 tons of earth. This has been carried out entirely by the boys of the school, from careful plans and survey made by them beforehand; and as an instance of how far rifle shooting in the school goes to produce a rifle-shooting district, shortly after the beginning of the war the boys placed the range on two days of each week at the service of the working-men and tradespeople of their locality, which resulted in the formation of the successful Enfield Rifle Club. The range was formally opened last week by Mr. H. O. Arnold-Forster, M.P., Parliamentary Secretary to the Admiralty.

SCHOLARS, LABOURERS, AND RIFLEMEN.

Some boys of the Clayesmore School.

Right: The summer term at Enfield, 1899.

Below: The Duchess of Wessex opens the kennel club, 1899.

Bottom: The school at Pangbourne, December 1903.

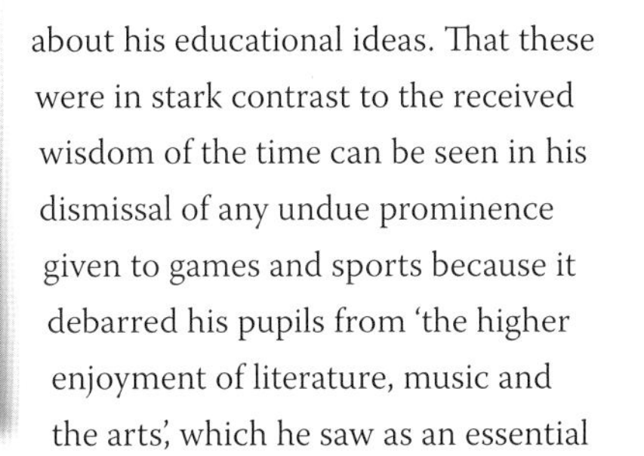

about his educational ideas. That these were in stark contrast to the received wisdom of the time can be seen in his dismissal of any undue prominence given to games and sports because it debarred his pupils from 'the higher enjoyment of literature, music and the arts', which he saw as an essential part of the curriculum; he was also insistent on manual labour as vital to every boy's education. He was against early specialisation, and believed that 'studies calculated to awake interest' were just as important as those taught for their 'value as a mental discipline'. Above all, every encouragement should be given to independence of thought.

Numbers rose. The original 12 in 1896 became 31 in 1898, and by 1902 had reached a respectable 50 or so. Influential people sent their sons to Clayesmore, including several newspaper editors, the Regius Professor of Surgery at Edinburgh and the last British Governor of Heligoland. In June 1899 the Countess of Warwick distributed the prizes and formally opened the new kennel club. The small school had become established. But the house at Enfield was now too small; Lex looked round for a more suitable property, and found it at Pangbourne in Berkshire.

Pangbourne, 1902–14

This splendid house, set in 100 acres of park and woodland, had been built for a man who died before it was completed, and the executors wanted it off their hands. Although it had the disadvantages of having been designed as a home, not as a school, it had electricity, central heating, outbuildings and plenty of space for games pitches once the ground had been cleared and levelled. Lex agreed to rent it – and then came a bombshell. A clause in the owner's will decreed that the estate had to be sold and the proceeds distributed among his family. Renting the house was no longer an option, and Lex was in no position to buy it. But his characteristic folly in financial matters took over and, although it was totally beyond his means, he agreed to buy in half-yearly instalments. The school moved in at the end of 1902, and Lex soon had the boys organised into manual labour squads to dig a swimming pool and level the grounds for games pitches. In June 1903 there was a formal opening; but by the middle of the following year the hopeless financial situation began to bite, and bailiffs arrived to take away all the furniture.

Yet again, Lex's irrepressible optimism, good luck and the bounty of friends came to the rescue. A complete stranger, who had received a prospectus and was taken with his ideas, asked Lex to visit and discuss them. The lack of even the train fare to Yorkshire meant that he had to pawn his watch in order to buy the ticket – but he returned with a cheque for £2,000. A further £1,000 was donated by a fellow headmaster who thought Clayesmore 'an amusing stunt'. But it was clear that there had to be some sort of financial control. A management committee was set up, chaired by a Clayesmore parent, a bursar was appointed and Lex continued as salaried headmaster. He hated the loss of total independence and referred to this time as 'my years of slavery'. But the school thrived, with a roll about 60 strong – including one day girl, Jean Black, who lived locally and whose brother Harry was a boarder.

Progressive though Lex's educational philosophy was, there was nothing soft about his regime. 'The modern tendency to pamper the boy should not exist at school,' he wrote in the prospectus, and he did not allow a tuck shop, since 'the diet is liberal... and there is therefore no necessity

THIS BUILDING WAS DECLARED FORMALLY OPEN
ON SATURDAY, JUNE 27th. 1903
BY
THE RIGHT HON. LORD REAY, G.C.S.I. G.C.I.E. LL.D.
PRESIDENT OF THE LONDON SCHOOL BOARD
LATE GOVERNOR OF BOMBAY AND UNDER-SECRETARY
OF STATE FOR INDIA.

Above: The opening day plaque.

Left: Pangbourne College, as it is known now, is a small boarding school founded three years after Clayesmore moved out.

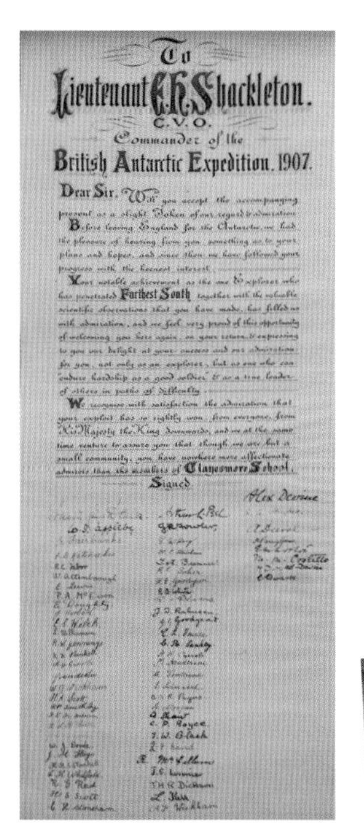

To
Lieutenant E. H. Shackleton.
C.V.O.
Commander of the
British Antarctic Expedition. 1907.

Dear Sir. Will you accept the accompanying present as a slight Token of our regard & admiration.

Before leaving England for the Antarctic, we had the pleasure of hearing from you something as to your plans and hopes, and since then we have followed your progress with the keenest interest.

Your notable achievement as the one Explorer who has penetrated Furthest South together with the valuable scientific observations that you have made, has filled us with admiration, and we feel very proud of this opportunity of welcoming you here again, on your return, & expressing to you our delight at your success and our admiration for you, not only as an explorer, but as one who can "endure hardship as a good soldier" & as a true leader of others in paths of difficulty.

We recognise with satisfaction the admiration that your exploit has so rightly won, from everyone, from His Majesty the King downwards, and we at the same time venture to assure you that though we are but a small community, you have nowhere more affectionate admirers than the members of Claysmore School.

Signed

Alex Devine

Top: Manual labour at Pangbourne.

Right and above: Ernest Shackleton visits as part of his lecture tour in 1909.

Below right: Lex plays croquet.

for supplementing the school food with extras.' Exeats were only permitted in cases of absolute necessity. And he was no shrinking violet when it came to corporal punishment. Lex did not, however, revel in his reputation as a disciplinarian; as he wrote to an old boy in 1911, 'My dear Ian... First let me thank you for your generous contribution to the games fund... The only part of your letter that I want to kick you for is where you say I love the cane! That is a libel, and if you say this to your young brothers no wonder they are frightened, poor boys, to come to an English school. I think the stick is very good for *some* boys whose names I won't mention except that one begins with a 'J'...'

An early diagnosis of dyslexia?

The archives hold a short series of letters from June 1904 about Lewis Jones, the son of Canon Jones of Chichester, whose progress at school was causing concern. The canon wrote to Lex, 'I think our interview with Dr Shuttleworth yesterday was very satisfactory, though it only confirmed my own impressions of the case. He gave a long time and the uttermost care and attention to Lewis, testing him in every way. I was very glad that he emphatically dwelt upon the advantages of leaving him in school with other boys, and not devising for him any specialised treatment of private superintendence and tuition... I am anxious that the arrangements should not contract his playtime – for the more he is actively engaged in the open air the better.' An eight-page letter from Dr Shuttleworth to Lex suggested that the boy could be suffering from a mixture of 'word-deafness' and 'word-blindness'. Practice was part of the answer and 'I advised Canon Jones to get a holiday teacher for him who has experience in the oral teaching of the deaf... Of course his general health should be well looked after and games like cricket and golf which help coordination between eye and hand are good for him – also carpentry and other manual work.'

Spring 1908 saw me deposited by my father as a new boy at Clayesmore, Pangbourne, after a two-mile drive in the station 'growler'. For the first time I came face to face with Alexander Devine, and my first memories of that meeting are still very vivid. A large, bright and airy room, every wall of which was lined with books, a long brass-bound table with, at one end, a reading desk behind which stood, dominating the whole, a shortish dark man whose smiling face and merry eyes immediately made one feel welcome. In front of the fireplace lay his beloved Aberdeen terrier Jock, who was his constant companion.

Life at Clayesmore in those days was a great deal tougher than it is today. The day started off with a cold shower, summer and winter, standing under the spray while one's dormitory captain counted one to ten which at times seemed so very slow. Chapel was held morning and evening in the large white-painted dining hall. Sundays for the Juniors meant dressing up in Eton suits with, of course, Eton collars. These ghastly things had to be worn every day of the week until one became a 'Middle' when one was promoted to a stiff turn-down collar and Sunday dress was black coat and waistcoat and striped trousers. At one period for several terms the whole school used to walk the two miles down the hill to the parish church at Pangbourne for Sunday morning service. After lunch on Sundays all bicycles had to be paraded for inspection by Lex for cleanliness and roadworthiness. At the same parade all boys with dogs, and there were many in those days, had to bring them up for inspection. Sunday evenings were generally spent lying on the floor of Lex's study complete with one's pillow and rug, listening to stories told by him in the flickering firelight.

Some memories: trips up the Thames in steam launches; lectures of all sorts, many illustrated by magic lanterns; plays – yes, Clayesmore had its budding actors even in those days. I believe Clayesmore was the first school to have its own golf course, even though it may have been a very rough one, with sheep hurdles as bunkers. Huts in the woods on terra firma and, for the more ambitious, up in trees, all built by their owners in their spare time. Scout camps in the woods, and the great gathering of all the Berkshire scouts held in the grounds, which was one of the first jamborees. And the many nationalities one met at the school: boys from Australia, Canada, India, Newfoundland, New Zealand, Argentina, Belgium, Brazil, Holland, France, Greece, Portugal, Russia, Siam, United States and even a German.

Frederic St K Anderson (1908–14),
included in a jubilee-year pamphlet, 1946

Clayesmore School
1896–1946

Jubilee Memento

Top: Jubilee memento pamphlet, 1946.

Bottom left: Scouts Edwards and Macmillan in the woods at Pangbourne, 1912.

Below right: Scout camp in the woods at Pangbourne, 1911.

Right: Junior dormitory relay race at Pangbourne.

Below right: The Lorimer Memorial Window.

Bottom: One of Elizabeth Scott Lorimer's letters to Lex Devine.

The school day began with a cold shower, summer and winter, and the afternoons were given over to football or cricket as well as the activity that made Clayesmore different from nearly all other public schools of the time – 'manual.' The importance and value of manual labour as part of a rounded education system was a cornerstone of Lex's approach, both as a healthy alternative to the cult of games and as an elevating educational experience which moreover

John Scott Lorimer

The archives hold a series of letters between Lex and the recently widowed Elizabeth Scott Lorimer in August and September 1908. The contact had been facilitated by one James Grun, who wrote to Lex on August 30: 'My dear Devine, Joy and gratitude quite overcame Mrs Lorimer when your wonderful news arrived that the boy might come to you. I had not encouraged hope – feeling very little myself – so your extraordinary kindness struck home with double force. Indeed, had I known to begin with exactly what Mrs Lorimer's income amounted to – and also remembered Clayesmore's school fees – I should not have ventured to trouble you at all. The added generosity of reducing the fees another £5 completes your good deed... Well – I wish you could have seen "the smile that won't come off" with which Jack swaggered about on learning that you'd take him. Child as he still is, he understands that a big stroke of fortune has come his way. Adversity has sharpened his understanding... and he feels that it devolves upon him to put up a good fight on behalf of his mother as well as for himself. I am sure that you will find the lad alright: plastic enough to receive your impress, firm enough to retain it. School life will be new to him...'

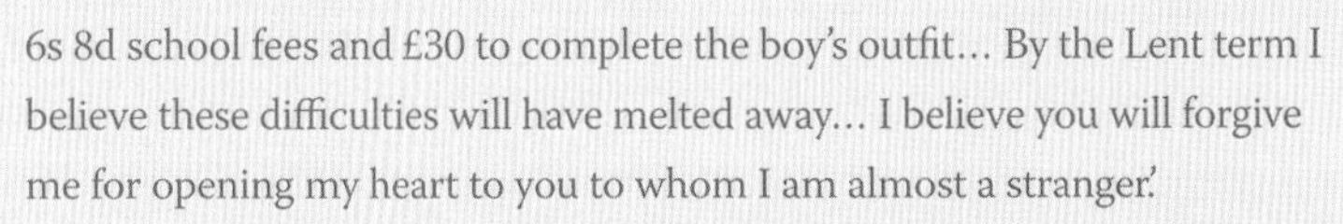

Eversleigh
St [illegible] Road
Clacton-on-Sea.

Sept 6. 08.

Dear Mr Devine.

I thank you from my heart for your most kind & sympathetic letter. Unfortunately the manager of the Bank does not see his way to advance me £30 of my allowance as I asked him to. This means that I am obliged to ask if you would kindly consent to take the boy for the Lent Term instead of now – Mr Grun kindly suggested

The boy & I have come through much tribulation, but we have neither of us been allowed to lose our faith in his Father's goodness, though we have come very near to it –

I believe you will forgive me for thus opening my heart to you to whom I am almost a stranger

& Believe me
With many thanks
Yours sincerely
Elizabeth Scott Lorimer

Alex: Devine Esq.

Mrs Scott Lorimer herself wrote: 'I am extremely anxious to be able to put my laddie in your care. I am anxious that my boy should use his life for the good of others and do not think my mother love is entirely bewitching me when I say I believe he has the making of a fine man in time if he is influenced and guided in the right ways now.' But there were still financial obstacles to overcome, and on September 6 Mrs Lorimer wrote again: 'I am obliged to ask if you would kindly consent to take the boy for the Lent term instead of now... I find it impossible under the circumstances to tell Mr and Mrs Grun that I lack the difference between the £23 6s 8d school fees and £30 to complete the boy's outfit... By the Lent term I believe these difficulties will have melted away... I believe you will forgive me for opening my heart to you to whom I am almost a stranger.'

The financial difficulties appear to have been overcome, since John was able to join Clayesmore before the end of September. But the school Roll of Honour records the sad news that he died in the First World War. The *Clayesmorian* for June 1918 carried the following tribute: 'Last on the list in which sorry struggles with pride for a first place, we record the death of Captain John Scott Lorimer MC, who was killed in action last November... It is difficult to pay full tribute to one who amongst all Clayesmorians was so affectionate and loyal a son of the school, hiding all the sentiment so deeply felt under a manner of chaff and fun that, disguise it as he might, crept out at times and exhibited its deep seriousness. A good son to his widowed mother, a faithful Clayesmorian, a man of high principle and a brave soldier. What nobler praise can be given. It was pleasing to us to read in a letter from a friend at the front, as a memory of his last visit to us: "Jack Lorimer was so touched at his last visit to his old school, and the fuss that was made of him."'

Manual in the rain

When it's dig, dig, dig,
And your boots are full of dirt,
And the mud and dye are mixing
On your soaking, sticky shirt;
And it's pick, pick, pick
Till you feel a perfect wreck
Dropping half your load of gravel
Down another fellow's neck.

– *Clayesmorian*, March 1911

Left: Bicycle inspection on the terrace at Pangbourne, *c*1908.

Inset: *The Clayesmorian*, 1911 edition.

Below: Manual training.

Left: Lex – 'alone I did it'.

Below: The narrow gauge railway at Pangbourne.

Cricket in summer and football in winter, limited tennis and boxing when the school had an ex-army drill sergeant. Manual work was one of the great themes of Devine's educational policy. He thought that all boys ought to be able to use their hands, and not be shy of doing hard physical work. We were therefore formed into groups to do this on one or two afternoons a week, usually under his own personal supervision. We rather enjoyed this when some definite scheme was put in hand, but resented it when we were assembled and nothing particular had been planned, and we were put on some 'ad hoc' job like sweeping up autumn leaves. Two good schemes: covering the central courtyard, which was laid to grass and could turn into a quagmire, with a good strong cement and stone surface; and repairing the public road to Winchester, which in wartime had been pretty well worn by army vehicles going to and from Salisbury Plain.

Graham Mervyn (1914–18)

had the effect of getting things done. An early installation at Pangbourne was a narrow gauge railway with tipping trucks which could carry the soil excavated from the site of the new swimming pool to the field being levelled for cricket; visiting teams got used to seeing squads of sturdy Clayesmorians working nearby, stripped to the waist in hot weather, filling the trucks, pushing them along and dumping the soil. Manual was what most old boys of Lex's time remembered best about Clayesmore, as their later letters indicate, and many of them wrote with pride that their proficiency with tools gave them a huge advantage over the products of other public schools in the trenches of the First World War.

The house system at Clayesmore was unusual, in that boys started in the Juniors, moved on to the Middles and finally became Seniors. The boys therefore remained with their contemporaries during their entire school career while their housemasters stayed behind. As for uniform, one boy remembered it as not particularly prescriptive, and that Lex was one of the first to allow less formal dress

Left: Francis Beresford Katinakis, a pupil from 1905–12, seen here in his Norfolk suit. On leaving, he went to Sandhurst before joing the Dragoon Guards. He was awarded the MC in 1915 and died of his wounds in 1918.

Below: Boys in the trademark Norfolk suits in the woods near Pangbourne – (from l–r) Buckhurst, Scott, Couvelas and Stewart, 1912.

for everyday wear. However, as usual he had his views: 'For Sunday use, all wear Eton jackets in the Junior House, in the Senior House black jackets are permitted, black or white waistcoats (the latter in summer only) and cloth trousers of a quiet design and colour. For daily use, Norfolk suits. These should be of Harris tweed or homespun (not serge). No waistcoats should be worn. Knickers are preferable to long trousers, and should be of the same material. Trousers must be made without pockets. Tall hats are used on Sundays in the Michaelmas and Lent terms; in summer straw hats, with a band of the school colours. A school cap is also provided for everyday use. Boys' wardrobes should contain as few unnecessary articles as possible. Boys usually bring too many clothes and

Above: Lex with staff and boys in their Sunday best, June 1904.

lumber of all sorts to school, which leads to untidiness and inconvenience. The headmaster... will gladly receive any suggestions on the subject, so that what is worn in school by the boy shall not be wasted at home, and vice versa.'

School rules, which started with the injunctions that 'Ignorance of a school rule is no excuse for breaking it, except in the case of new boys within their first two weeks' and 'A breach of common sense is a breach of a school rule', were augmented by the headmaster's 'golden rules'; a sample:

- *Never believe anything because I tell you it is so. Find out for yourself!*
- *A gentleman is a 'gentle' man. Always appreciate the other fellow's point of view.*
- *Let your home be a perching place... rather than a bird's cage.*
- *It's no use grumbling. Keep your temper. I can't remember having asked for it.*

Alongside all these normal accoutrements – manual perhaps excepted – of a public school of the time, Claysesmore reflected Lex's reformist, idealist zeal for a new path in education. He campaigned hard – though without success – to introduce a new school examination system which was decades ahead of its time. Unusually, he allowed the boys to keep their own dogs at school and formed a kennel club (see box for his tract on the subject). Always a self-publicist, his letters to the national press provoked

Above: Junior House, 1912.

Dogs at school

At most of the public schools the privilege of dog keeping is not allowed; but boys often keep dogs all the same, and with undesirable results, for they do so 'on the sly' at some outside stable or at some small cottage... The novel experience of keeping dogs at school has now been in progress at Clayesmore for nine years, and the result has been altogether good... The value of the kennels is found to lie partly in the fact that dogs provide an interest for leisure hours, for those odd times of day when the boy has nothing particular to do – periods, as every schoolmaster will attest, that cause the greatest anxiety and often present a serious problem... If a boy has nothing else to do, he can go to the kennel and busy himself with cleaning it up, or grooming, exercising and talking to his own dog. It is necessary that each boy shall care for his own dog; he must not be allowed to transfer his obligation to any other boy or to any paid servant. The work must be attended to by the owner as the price of permission to keep the dog... Of course, it is quite clear that dogs at school without management would mean pandemonium... therefore it has been found necessary to constitute a properly organised kennel club as one of the departments of the school. The president is one of the masters, and the boys take part in all the concerns of the dogs and their kennels.

Above left: Lord Buckhurst (9th Earl de la Warr).

much debate about the future of education, and people were becoming increasingly interested in his methods. He was establishing himself as rather more than just someone who had 'an astonishing way with boys'.

Perhaps the best tribute comes from a letter written to him by a boy who left Clayesmore in 1913 to go to Eton, and was bitterly disappointed with his new school. This was Herbrand 'Buck' Sackville, later to be Earl de la Warr: 'I absolutely agree with all your ideas about originality. There is not a single boy here with any individuality whatever. They are most of them very good fellows and I like them very much, but not one of them has any ideas of his own. They all think exactly what is the proper thing to think and do exactly what everyone else does... We learn nothing but Latin, Greek and maths. We have no geography and next to no history... The French is pitiful... it seems to be the proper thing also to despise anything French or foreign as un-English. Music and drawing come under this heading and are therefore most despicable... and science is considered extremely low. Then there is the religious question... abstruse theological and dogmatic points which are really quite inconsequent. I am sure it breeds a very narrow-minded kind of religion.'

Northwood Park (**above**) and its surroundings (**below**).

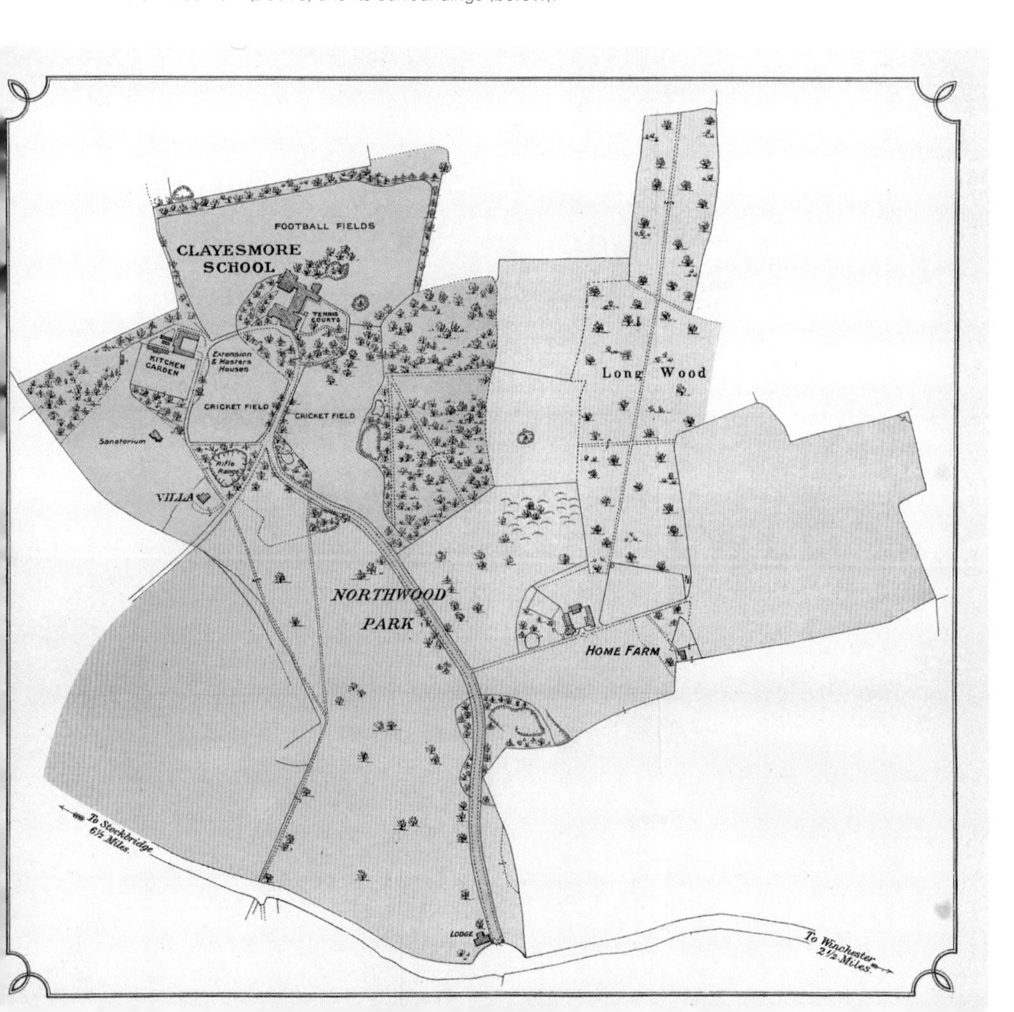

Northwood Park, 1914–33

Lex's impulsive nature revealed itself again during the Easter holidays of 1914, when the opportunity came to move the school to a more advantageous site. This was Northwood Park, north of Winchester on the crest of the Downs, which had the benefit of being a school already, with playing fields, a swimming pool, a gymnasium, 150 acres and much else to recommend it. Owned and run by the Eastman family as a naval school, it had fallen on hard times and was very run down. Mrs Eastman negotiated a rent highly favourable to her family, and both schools announced to the surprised parents of their pupils that the new term would start in a new place (for the Clayesmorians), and with a new name and a new headmaster. On the first night of the summer term, the Eastman boys slept in their usual dormitories while the Clayesmorians dossed down on the floor of the hall and the billiard room – and were more than upset to find that, rather than enjoying the comforts of electricity and flushing toilets as in their old school, they had to deal with smoky oil lamps and primitive earth closets.

Lex set to with his usual energy to begin work on modernising the facilities and turning this new school into a facsimile of the old; for one thing, he quickly abolished the tuck shop. That summer term was one of glorious weather, and much adaptation and change took place. But when the new school year started in the autumn of 1914, war had broken out.

Graham Mervyn, who joined Clayesmore at the beginning of that autumn term, records of the war that 'At first it was hardly noticeable in the school, tucked away, as we were, on the Downs, two miles or more from the nearest village. But then news came through of one old boy killed, or another wounded, or another missing. We followed the progress of the armies by marking the fighting lines in France with tapes and flags on pins, and we read the news and studied the pictures in the *Illustrated London News*. It was remote, though some said they could hear the guns when the wind was in the right direction.' Staff left to join the army, the electricity and plumbing contractors had more important work to do, which put back the improvements to facilities, and refugee pupils arrived from Belgium.

Old Clayesmorians wrote to their headmaster about their experience of trench warfare; one of them was Alexandre Ambert who, with his two brothers, Henri and Léon (also an OC), fought in the French army at the front from the beginning. Lex was later to receive a letter from their grieving father telling him, 'Léon est maintenant le seul qui nous reste'.

The first OC casualty occurred in January 1915, and by the end of the war 37 old boys had lost their lives, many of them having been decorated for gallantry. Edward Fairlie was the only boy who featured in the first school photo to die in the war; a major in the King's Royal Rifles, he was killed in March 1918, aged 36. One who survived was William Humphrey Meyrick Weinholt, who joined the school in 1900 and ended the war as acting colonel of the 9th Royal Lancashires, with a DSO and bar and three mentions in despatches. Even more distinguished, and another survivor, was Geoffrey Heneage Drummond, who joined Clayesmore in November 1900 after just over a term at Eton, and received the highest honour of all, the

Above and right: The school prospectus at Northwood Park, highlighting the aesthetic importance of the estate.

Below: The school in 1929.

Victoria Cross. His award came in 1918, when he was a lieutenant in the RNVR in command of a motor launch whose job was to follow a block-ship into Ostend and take off whatever crew he could after it had scuttled itself. Despite murderous enemy fire, which badly wounded him and killed two of his own crew, Drummond managed to take off two officers and 37 men, and then back his sinking boat out of the harbour before being rescued. As the vice-admiral's despatch recorded, 'It was due to the indomitable courage of this very gallant officer that the majority of the crew of the *Vindictive* were rescued.'

Clayesmore had little difficulty maintaining its numbers during the war, and was augmented in the autumn of 1915 by nine boys from Letchworth School, which had recently closed; its headmaster, JHM Stephenson, joined in January 1916, having been promised the vice-mastership, a post already held by Edgar Dodd, who protested; in the event, Stephenson became bursar. Two other staff members who arrived during the war were the Count di Balme and Desmond Coke, who had joined in 1914 but then left for the army before being invalidated out in 1917, having served with distinction. A man of substantial private means as well as a reputable author, he was a great benefactor both to the school and to individual pupils. He built a new library for the school in memory of his OC nephew, Gilbert Burney, who had died in the war, and although he did little classroom teaching, his love of fine arts and connoisseurship were an education in itself for many of the boys of his time. There was an idea that he would eventually replace Lex as headmaster, but ill health forced him to retire in 1925.

In other areas the school suffered from a lack of good staff; scientists were particularly transient, and it did not help that Lex was inclined to find a great well of humour in the bad time given to incompetent staff by the boys. One unfortunate teacher, known as 'Little Willie' and soon dismissed, was lampooned by the headmaster at the next school concert in a song with the refrain 'So I murdered Little Willie in his little velvet suit.' The boys loved this sort of thing about Lex, but it led at least one distinguished old boy, John Plamenatz, to pass the severe verdict on him that he was 'not a gentleman.'

Thirty-odd feet below Belgium

For some years Clayesmorians on history trips visiting the battlefields of the Western Front have laid a wreath on a simple monument near Railway Wood, just outside Ypres. It is to honour the remains of 2nd Lieutenant Geoffrey Boothby OC, a sapper in the 8th South Staffordshires, which lie 30 feet below. We know something about him because he is listed in the original school register – a small boy who joined Clayesmore at the age of nine in 1904. There are also two entries in the *Clayesmorian*, one, in the April 1916 edition, a letter from him with a cheery account of mining and working in the tunnels under No Man's Land. It ends with the poignant 'Otherwise, mining is a peaceful business. We dig a bit, and listen a bit, and everything is very nice… until we hear the Bosch digging too.' Just after that letter was published, on April 28, he failed to hear the Bosch soon enough and was killed in an explosion.

Seventy-five years later, after the death of his mother, Arthur Stockton, a retired professor, found a bundle of letters in her attic. They told of an early love affair about which he knew nothing. Edith Ainscow had met Geoffrey Boothby briefly in 1914, probably through Edith's brother Arthur, and they had started to write to each other when Geoffrey left medical school for officers' training camp. The correspondence starts with Geoffrey telling Edith what his surname is, and that she has no excuse not to write as she now has his address. The first letters are signed off with just 'Cheero!', but over the next 15 months, as their love develops, they are writing to each other as 'dearest' and 'darling'. They fell in love simply through their correspondence; although Geoffrey had some home leave, they were unable to meet and were in fact never to see each other again.

Professor Stockton has edited and published the letters, and the result is a remarkable glimpse into the lives, hopes and thoughts of two young people gradually falling in love against the grim backdrop of the First World War. Lex describes Geoffrey turning up to visit the school in 1915 'in his characteristic casual way and with the same humorous air and friendly attitude as in the old days.' These characteristics come across in his letters. There is a lot of banter between Geoff and Edith about his moustache, her hair and even dysentery. But there are also more sombre short insights into the trenches, the tunnelling, gas and artillery.

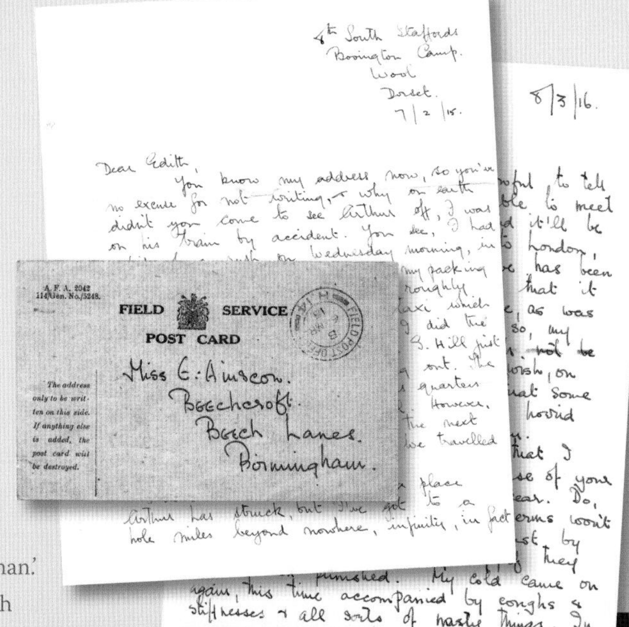
8th South Staffords
Bovington Camp.
Wool
Dorset.
7/2/15.

Dear Edith,
You know my address now, so you've no excuse for not writing, & why on earth didn't you come to see Arthur off, I was on his train by accident. You see, I had … Wednesday morning, in …

A. F. A. 2042
114/Gen. No./5248.
FIELD SERVICE
POST CARD
The address only to be written on this side. If anything else is added, the post card will be destroyed.
Miss E. Ainscow.
Beechcroft.
Beech Lanes.
Birmingham.

8/3/16.
… My cold came on again, this time accompanied by coughs & stiffnesses & all sorts of nasty things. In

Though there is an apparent casualness in his writing, presumably so as not to alarm Edith about the realities of war, there is also deep sadness mixed with patriotism. 'Nearly all my friends in the Staffords have been killed in the fighting… It's a horribly sad thing how many friendships have been made and broken by this war. But it does make one feel really proud to be an Englishman.'

Edith comes across as both romantic and practical. She writes about 'a distant future' with 'the sweetest little house that ever was', sends him poetry and asks for a badge as a keepsake. In all the letters, behind the cheerful accounts of trivial incidents, there is a longing to

Above: Edith Ainscow.

Left: 2nd Lieutenant Geoffrey Boothby OC.

Top: Pupils lay a wreath (above) at the memorial to 2nd Lieutenant Geoffrey Boothby at the Railway Wood monument near Ypres as part of the annual school battlefield trip.

see each other again and, as is evident in Edith's last letter to him, a fear that they might not be reunited: 'I can't really believe that you're coming yet but I hope and hope and hope. Do, do be careful; just for a week and let's hope the Fates will be indulgent for once.' This letter is dated May 4 1916; but as she wrote, her Geoff was already dead.

A fellow officer wrote to Geoffrey's mother, Alice Boothby, with an account of the explosion that killed him and its aftermath: 'I found the gallery entirely blocked... with earth and broken timbers, and was almost immediately made insensible by the fumes. From the severity of the explosion and the fact that he was so near the seat of it, your boy's death must have been immediate.' His body was not recovered but left buried where it lay, and it is tempting to imagine that, as the preface to the book speculates, 'Edith's photograph lies with him, in the tunic pocket closest to his heart.'

Tony Chew

Left: King Nicholas I of Montenegro.

The Montenegro connection

Lex's foreign holidays in the years before the outbreak of war increasingly took him to Montenegro, a country he grew to know well and to love, and where he made many friends, among them the king, Nicholas. When the war overwhelmed Montenegro and the rest of the Balkans, refugees began to arrive at Clayesmore, and boys who were there at the time remember much internecine strife between Serb, Croat and Slovene – except on the football field, where communication in the various Slavonic languages could baffle the opponents and prove to be an advantage.

At the end of 1915, with the king in exile and the country overrun, the Montenegrin Red Cross invited Lex to visit and report on conditions for exiles in the various European relief centres. Lex departed on this mission during the Easter holidays of 1916, and when he returned continued to fundraise for Montenegro, particularly among charitably inclined individuals and organisations from the United States. But his involvement soon deepened, as it became clear during the war years that British and American attitudes towards the postwar future of Montenegro and its king were ambivalent. As he wrote in 1918, 'I never let pass a single chance of defending and championing the cause of the country, or of obtaining friends to her cause and refuting the attacks of her traducers, in season and out of season, in a hundred different ways.' In doing so he made enemies in the British Foreign Office, and was regarded with distrust as 'to all intents and purposes the agent of King Nicholas in this country'. In 1917 indeed, when the Montenegrin government in exile approached the British government about the appointment of accredited representatives to the Court of St James, Lex Devine was the man King Nicholas wanted. The Foreign Office was having none of it: 'We must exclude Mr Devine at all costs.' But he continued to act 'in an unofficial manner as [Montenegro's] "friend" in Britain and elsewhere', and portrayed himself as the 'honorary minister' to the Court of St James and as Montenegro's de facto representative in Britain.

Lex also involved himself in Montenegro's relationship with the United States, and was instrumental in the appointment of a man sympathetic to the country's cause as its consul general in New York. Once this was achieved, he began a long correspondence with President Woodrow Wilson, describing himself as 'probably regarded by the king and people of Montenegro as their chief English friend', and submitting for Wilson's consideration a balanced appraisal of the Montenegrin question. When it became clear at the end of the war that the king's return to his country would be postponed, if not completely blocked, Lex bombarded both the American president and the British Foreign Office with letters defending Nicholas's government in exile and calling for justice and fair play. He sought an interview with Wilson while he was in Paris for the peace negotiations, and was indefatigable in attacking the 'perfidy' and 'barbarism' of the Serbians, who by then were, as he put it, 'military occupiers' of Montenegro. Wilson initially took the time to reply to Lex's letters, sometimes personally, but after a while ceased to interest himself in the matter and did not grant Lex the interview he wanted. King Nicholas, in the event, was never allowed to return to his country, and died in exile in 1921; Montenegro was eventually subsumed into the new Yugoslavia.

Lex's efforts on behalf of Nicholas and Montenegro had been rewarded in the summer of 1915, when Montenegrin ministers in exile visited Clayesmore and announced that the king had made him a Commander of the Distinguished Order of Danielo I. He wore the decoration with pride whenever he could, and some of the staff and boys took to referring to him as 'His Excellency the headmaster'. When the portrait of Lex at the school was cleaned recently, it was discovered that a medal had been painted on his chest, presumably his Montenegrin one, but that it had been almost immediately overpainted and obscured; why this happened is not known.

One of Clayesmore's most distinguished old boys was himself a Montenegrin. John Plamenatz (1912–75), who was born in Cetinje and sent to Clayesmore in 1919, two years after the family fled their native country, was at the school until 1930, when he left to study philosophy, politics and economics at Oxford. His father had been foreign minister and his mother was the daughter of one of the king's advisers and god-daughter of Queen Elena of Italy. Their son went on to be a Fellow of All Souls and a notable political philosopher, becoming a Fellow of the British Academy in 1962 and Chichele professor of social and political theory in 1967.

Count di Balme

Graham Mervyn writes: 'It must have been sometime in 1915 that a tall, slender, greying, military figure walked into our classroom to take French. There had been a series of misfits, and French teachers were normally figures of fun for English boys: there was the occasion when some bright sparks led a real farm horse into the classroom just to prove that they knew that 'cheval' meant 'horse'. We soon learned that no such liberties could be taken with the Count di Balme. He had been a captain in a crack Italian cavalry regiment and was now retired. He meant business and we were shaken to the core. If we were inattentive or stupid he would fly into a rage: 'I vill cane ze to ze blood', though he never did. The Count stayed many years and became a revered figure, putting many boys on the road to a good knowledge of French and in many cases an interest in other languages.'

I think the attraction of Clayesmore to my father was that manual work was included in the school calendar. I can see dear old Lex now with a black and grey check coat, stiff winged collar and bow tie, plus a trilby, plus a large cigar, marching at the head of a gang of boys pulling a handcart full of stones to repair a hole in the drive. My particular job was to look after the chicken that lived under the chapel, which sometimes allowed me to miss roll call.

We were all expected to have a swim in the pool next to the gym before breakfast, which I hated as I couldn't swim, and my friends had a great deal of fun ducking me. I later learned to swim and proudly displayed my new skill by swimming the length of the pool. We bathed in the nude, which meant that those who had paid a visit to Lex's study the previous evening could demonstrate the results.

I wore a dark green Norfolk suit with a belted coat and breeches secured by two buttons below the knee. For manual work it was football gear, shorts and shirts. On Sundays we wore black suits with a stiff collar, and I remember many struggles to get my tie properly knotted. For OTC we were issued with khaki uniforms, and it was an art to learn how to wind puttees correctly round ones legs so that they stayed put.

Tom T Miller (1915–17)

When I went to Northwood Park in the autumn term of 1914 the accommodation was for about 100 boys. There was a beautiful dining room, oak panelled, and a splendid gymnasium attached to an indoor swimming bath with (slightly) heated water. In other respects the arrangements were primitive: old-fashioned washbasins in the dormitories with icy water to wash in during winter, and oil lamps; as for the toilets, they were equipped with what we called 'thunderboxes'. Mr Devine lost no time in having things altered, and within a year electricity had been installed, new washbasins were supplied with hot and cold water and the unmentionables were made to flush.

It was undoubtedly the personality of the headmaster that made Clayesmore different from other schools – though we did not see much of him. He made announcements from the top table after dinner, gave talks in chapel and made an occasional tour of the dormitories before lights out. Our main contact was the Sunday evening gathering in his study. This was a much looked-forward-to occasion for the Juniors; clad in pyjamas and dressing gowns they would file in before bed and he would tell tales of mystery or horror. For the Seniors it was an optional event when a more adult book would be read. He was a natural story-teller and could read aloud in a way that made it seem not like a reading at all. He was also, despite not being able to read a note of music, able to play a whole piece on the piano after hearing it only once.

He was a kindly uncle figure to the Juniors – although a summons to his study might spell trouble – and relations became more formal as one progressed up the school. However, there were plenty of opportunities for him to indicate his views. 'Think, boy, think. What would you do? Think for yourself. Reach your own conclusions.' He laid great stress on a sense of humour, and was keen for boys to go into professions that suited them rather than following what was expected.

Graham Mervyn (1914–18)

It was on May 5 1917 that I first entered Clayesmore, complete with my new bowler hat (regulation) and the company of my cousin Carl Wilter, who had entered the school a year or two previously as one of the contingent brought from Letchworth by Mr Stephenson… At my age, 13, I was in the Middle House, Lex's arrangement being to divide the school into Juniors under Mr Wood, Middles under Mr Dodd and Seniors. There was an initial ceremony for new boys, who had either to sing a song to satisfy the audience or chew a piece of soap. I have never been able to sing and was later rejected from the choir, but fortunately remembered the words of 'Black-Eyed Susan' well enough not to have to eat the soap. After that I settled down to a happy first term.

I was looking forward enormously to getting back to my Southport home, but before the end of the holidays I was looking forward equally to returning to Clayesmore, and after that there was never any doubt of my happiness all the time I was there.

There were two occasions when I felt a grievance. The first was when I was reading a book as I returned from the field, walking behind a priv, and I inadvertently followed him through a door that was allowed to him but not to me. The other was on my birthday. I had received some foreign stamps and had taken my album early into the Big School room in order to arrange them before prep started. I had put the album away on the bench beside me and was getting on with my work when a prefect spotted it. Against the rules to have anything but one's work in prep.

Miss Hazledene taught art when she was not playing tennis in an ankle-length skirt and with a swinging underarm service. Ted Ardizzone was her best pupil, but I think his later work owes nothing to her. The science masters were the most difficult to obtain, and none stayed more than a term, often not so long. They never seemed suitable for the work, and we ragged the life out of them. We thought that Lex did not give enough time to finding suitable replacements, being already too involved in fighting the hopeless cause of Montenegro; and in any case his sense of humour made him all on our side, as he seemed to get as much enjoyment out of our foolery as we did.

We all loved Lex; we knew him and he knew us. One of his all too rare habits was to get us all out of our beds about a quarter of an hour after lights out on a summer evening to go for a walk with him along the country lanes. At other times, also after lights out, he would bring visitors into the dormitory. On one occasion it was a group of Serbian officers among whom, as he told us afterwards, was a regicide, a man who had taken part in the assassination of King Alexander in 1903.

John W Jevons (1917–21)

Water Supply

The abundant supply of excellent spring water, shown by analysis to be of exceptional purity, is drawn from a depth of 320 feet from the School well.

School Farm

The School Farm on the Estate supplies the School with milk, butter, eggs, and dairy produce generally.

Sanatorium

There is an excellent Sanatorium in the Park, situated at a distance of 300 yards from the main buildings; it is specially constructed and equipped for its purpose, and is in charge of a duly qualified trained Nurse.

Rifle Range

There is an open-air Rifle Range in the grounds. Instruction in shooting is given by a competent Instructor.

Drainage

The Drainage has been tested and approved by sanitary experts as excellent in every way.

Gardens

There are excellent Kitchen Gardens, well stocked for the supply of fresh fruit and vegetables all the year round, as well as a fine range of glasshouses.

Swimming Bath

There is a covered Swimming Bath, 50 feet by 30 feet, specially constructed, and the water kept at a proper temperature. Swimming is taught to all boys by a competent Instructor.

Playing Fields

There are fine Playing Fields for Cricket and Football, both for Senior and Junior boys.

Senior House Arrangements

The Senior House is in charge of a House Master, but is also under the direct supervision of the Head Master.

The general government of the Senior House approaches that of a Public School: personal responsibility and self-government under reasonable direction forming a distinct feature of the system. Meals are taken in Hall with the House Masters, at separate tables. This arrangement ensures a certain amount of supervision in the matter of table manners and the discouragement of hurried feeding.

4

Above: Lex relaxes on the terrace with his dogs.

Below left and opposite: Pages from the school prospectus at Northwood Park.

'Two men looked out through prison bars
One saw mud, but the other saw stars.'

That's what Lex wrote in my autograph book below a watercolour sketch. I still have the book. I perhaps saw what he meant then only in a general way, but it made an immediate and lasting impact on my mind and I have since quoted it times out of number. For in fact it embodies the whole philosophy which Alexander Devine sought to teach to his boys, and was what he meant when he said, as so often he did, 'Think, boy, think!'

He certainly was a remarkable man. Maybe all the things that have been said about him in terms of extravagance and carelessness about money were true, but he had a dedication that amounted to genius in his knowledge and understanding of boys, which inspired in them a deep, if unspoken, affection and confidence, and no fear whatsoever. So I for one am conscious to this day, and acknowledge, the debt I owe to him and to Clayesmore as the place where I learned to ask questions and not be satisfied with glib answers.

And of course it wasn't only Lex. It is true that in those days masters came and went. Of those who went I recall that on departure they were as unlamented by the boys as they presumably were by Lex. But not all were such – especially not the Count; and also Dodd, Saunders, Yeomans, Desmond Coke, Hughes. All these had the boys' affection and respect. The fact is, there was no place at Clayesmore for anyone who was not prepared to give all that he could in the service of the school and the boys; and in that regard, as in all others, Lex's word was law.

The summer term was always idyllic for the beauty of the place, the woods, the fields and above all cricket, which was the game I loved. Never shall I forget the bitterness of my feelings when, batting for the first time in the First XI, I was given out caught at the wicket when I knew I hadn't touched the ball. It was nearly as bad when the vicar's team was one short and I was sent out to field for them and had to catch out Laurie Lock, the captain of the school XI. He later told me not to worry and that he would have been very cross with me if I had missed so easy a chance.

All this and nothing about lessons. Well I was no good at them. I was one who had to be interested to learn, and so I developed an abiding love of the English language, history and the fascination of the French language, unpicked from the Count while perhaps being technically abysmal and in fact absorbing more than I (and certainly he) thought possible. But geometry was meaningless, and it was only later that the fascination of figures became clear to me. I don't think Lex really minded if one did poorly in the classroom, and probably blamed the master as much as the boy, but he did mind lethargy of mind and body; and when in contact with him he saw to it that no such state existed.

I loved Clayesmore when I was there. I have loved it ever since. But I didn't know for quite a few years afterwards just how much it has meant to me and how much I owed it.

Sir Dennis Pilcher (1918–21)

Station and Train Service

WINCHESTER, L. & S.W.R. and G.W.R. :—

WINCHESTER (Hants), from Waterloo, 66 miles; from Paddington, 79 miles. *Fares* : 11/0*a*, 7/0*b*, 5/6*c*; R. T. for six months, 19/3*a*, 12/2*b*, 10/6*c*; Week-end, 15/0*a*, 9/6*b*, 7/6*c*.

	Waterloo.			Winchester.
A.M.	5 35	...	...	7 14
	5 50	...	...	7 29
	6 10	...	...	8 17
	7 10	...	...	9 37
	7 40	...	...	10 2
	8 55	...	...	10 23
	9 25	...	...	11 10
	9 40	...	...	12 31
	10 35	...	...	12 44
	11 40	...	...	1 11
P.M.	12 50	...	...	3 2
	1 5*e*	...	...	3 52
	1 10*d*	...	...	3 52

	Waterloo.			Winchester.
P.M.	2 10*e*	...	...	3 39
	2 13*d*	...	...	3 42
	2 20	...	...	3 59
	2 55	...	...	5 1
	3 5	...	...	5 52
	4 50*r*	...	...	6 13
	5 0	...	...	6 42
	5 30	...	...	7 44
	6 0	...	...	8 6
	6 55*r*	...	...	8 20
	7 15	...	...	9 55
	8 15	...	...	10 6
	9 50	...	...	11 21

Sunday.

	Waterloo.			Winchester.
A.M.	9 20	...	...	12 1
	10 5	...	...	12 25
	11 50	...	...	1 10
	12 0*r*	...	...	1 25
P.M.	5 45	...	...	7 57
	6 40*r*	...	...	8 9
	9 15	...	...	11 36

a First Class. *b* Second Class. *c* Third Class.
d Saturdays only. *e* Saturdays excepted. *r* Restaurant Car.

Telegrams

Telegrams should be addressed to "Devine, Northwood, Winchester," and are received by private wire from the Post Office, Winchester, to avoid delay.

Telephone

No.: 14 SPARSHOLT.

Conveyances

to the School may be ordered from Pettit's Garage, George Hotel. Telephone 0491 Winchester.

Hotels

"George Hotel." Large Garage and Repair Shops.
"Royal Hotel." "Ye Olde Hostel of God-Begot."

14

Clayesmore. The School Buildings are approached by a winding drive of half a mile.

15

Richard Milroy Clarkson

The school archives contain a copy of a letter written in 1915 by Lex Devine to Richard Clarkson's mother, clearly in reply to one from her enquiring what Clayesmore could do for her son. After telling her that religious education was at the heart of what the school offered, Lex went on to reassure her that 'we are very keen on games here, but frankly we believe in boys having other interests as well…' After thus countering any worries she might have had about Clayesmore's progressive reputation, he confirmed that his school could offer help in 'a matter you refer to'; this appears to have been Clarkson's weak chest, from which he suffered all his life.

Richard Clarkson went on to study engineering from a school not noted for its teaching of science. Aged 21 in 1925, he joined the de Havilland Aircraft Company and gained his pilot's licence in the company's Moth. He soon took responsibility for de Havilland's fledgling aerodynamics section which, from small beginnings, became increasingly vital as aircraft flew faster and higher and became more sophisticated. When he started he had a single assistant; when he retired in 1968 his department employed 200. He always remained ahead of the game, and his work made a major contribution to the development of every major aeroplane of the period, from the Moth to the Comet. But his enduring reputation – recognised to this day by Boeing – is founded on the Mosquito, the most efficient bomber of the Second World War, which could carry the same bomb load to Berlin as a Boeing Flying Fortress, using half the power and a fifth of the crew. It was so fast that it could make two round trips a night from Britain to the German capital, and could outrun Messerschmitts. Nearly 8,000 were built.

Awarded the OBE in 1951, Clarkson lived to the great age of 91 and was the oldest OC present at the service in Salisbury Cathedral for the school's centenary in 1996. He died in the October of that year and the Prep School Chapel Choir sang at his memorial service at Sherbourne Abbey.

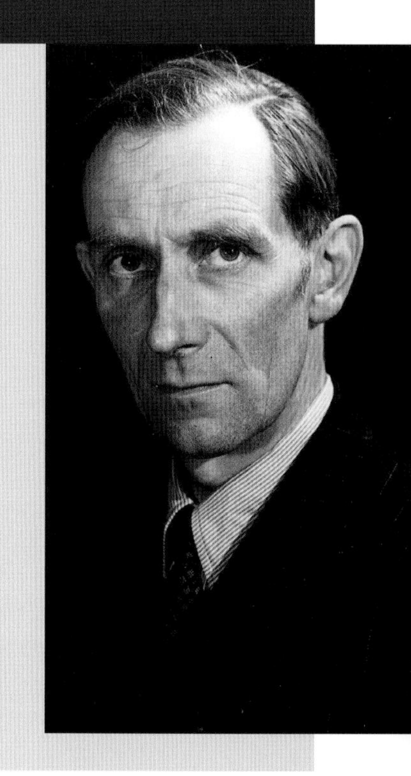

Above: Richard Milroy Clarkson.

The submarine blockade in 1917 brought food shortages and memorial windows went up in the chapel. When the end finally came in November 1918, Lex was too upset by the high death toll among OCs to feel like celebrating; but the boys thought otherwise, and staged a rebellion on Armistice Day until a holiday was granted. The school's alumni had indeed suffered an unusually high proportion of casualties, a fact recognised by the War Office when it presented Clayesmore in 1919 with a small piece of artillery. This trench mortar now stands in front of the school gates at Iwerne Minster.

The immediate post-war years at the school felt lacklustre: the OTC (never very effective) was disbanded, scouting died out, no issue of the *Clayesmorian* appeared, cricket and football were played unenthusiastically and one year there were no athletic sports at all. Lex himself was much taken up with the affairs of Montenegro, and it was only the continued loyalty of the Count and Miss Colson – officially the headmaster's secretary but in effect the bursar and much else besides – that kept Clayesmore going at this time. And Lex was also embroiled in a dispute with his landlord, Eastman, who took him to court over the unauthorised ploughing up of part of the estate for food during the war. The case, when it came to court, was settled in favour of the landlord but with such a nominal penalty that it was in effect a defeat. The relationship continued prickly.

Yet the later careers of many of the 1915–20 intake are a monument to the high quality of academic and sporting standards of Clayesmore at this time. Richard Clarkson went on to be a power in aeronautics, Adlard Coles became a distinguished yachtsman and writer on the sport, JWA Stephenson was to be probably the best amateur fast bowler of his day and Eric Fernihough held for a time the world motorcycle speed record. John Plamenatz went on to academic heights at Oxford and Marcus Cheke became Vice Marshal of the Diplomatic Corps. For such a small school the record is remarkable; as a pupil of the time later said, 'I do not say that we learnt a great deal, but what we did learn we learnt well, and it was good, solid stuff, and much more serviceable than the large amounts of superficial work done at some of the schools.'

Above: The trench mortar outside the school's gates.

Below: Evelyn King.

But Lex was beginning to fade, there was no obvious successor after Desmond Coke had been forced by ill health to retire, negotiations with the landlord to buy the estate failed and numbers, during that decade of depression, were slumping badly. Then in 1929 a new face came on the scene as vice-master.

This was Aubrey de Selincourt, scholar, double blue, musician, writer, translator of Herodotus, a friend of Sybil Thorndyke and a man of enlightenment and charm. Moreover, he had a rich father, Martin de Selincourt, who bought the school and its good will and went to law with the landlord to achieve a substantial reduction in the rent. But the younger de Selincourt nevertheless faced an intimidating task. Faithful old staff had retired, the Count was getting old and the devoted Miss Colson, who had done her best to keep on top of the administrative work, now spent much of her time nursing an increasingly frail Lex. Graham Mervyn, an old boy with business experience, volunteered to lend a hand in sorting things out, and reckoned that in 1930 the school was losing a massive £1,000 a term.

Lex, however, gave the school one last gift. In the summer of 1930 he interviewed a young Evelyn King for what King expected to be a short-term teaching post before taking up a scholarship at the Inner Temple and a career at the Bar. Writing in March 1981, in his 74th year, King recalled the occasion: 'I was interviewed at the Royal Thames Yacht Club in Knightsbridge. Lex was then 65 years of age. He explained, in a soft and attractive voice with a touch of Irish in it, that he had founded Clayesmore, that it was his life's work and he spoke of his love of it. He said he had not been fortunate in his staff. Before we left the club he had offered and I had accepted a post on the teaching staff with a salary of £300 a year to commence in September. I was to teach history throughout the school and coach the rugby XV.'

On arriving in September King was told that Lex was ill – he was never to see him again – and after being shown his room by Miss Colson, he went to see Aubrey de Selincourt who, to his bewilderment, announced that since there was no one to teach maths, 'I want you to do so throughout the school'.

King again: 'That was the end of history for the remainder of my teaching life. He told me Lex was dying upstairs. He, Aubrey, was to take over the school. This, it seemed, was not easy. He wanted to modernise. Corporal punishment was to be abolished and prefects stripped of their powers. Lex's ideas were out of date and repugnant to him.'

Unfortunately, most of the staff and boys were deeply devoted to Lex and resentful of this new regime. Events moved swiftly, as King recalled: 'Within three weeks Aubrey asked me to become a housemaster and I accepted. Within five weeks the masters, one morning, came down to their classes and found the classrooms empty. A schoolboy revolution had broken out. The boys, all of them including prefects, were huddled together on the playing fields giving three cheers for Lex… The boys returned to a rather late lunch which Miss Colson, fiercely loyal to Lex, had prepared. Prefects sought an interview and resigned collectively. For a while Alister Mackenzie and I and a junior housemaster named Bluett, with the Count and Miss Colson as persuaded allies, more or less ran the school. Aubrey gave us a free hand. Then Lex died [on Boxing Day 1930].'

His obituary in *The Times* acclaimed him as 'a pioneer who lived to see his ambitions largely consummated' and that 'above all he was loved, and any boy in real trouble

Aubrey de Selincourt

Aubrey de Selincourt was Clayesmore's second headmaster, who took the reins when Lex Devine was in failing health. Aubrey had already led a colourful life. In the First World War he took part in the Gallipoli landings, and later transferred to the air service as a reconnaissance pilot until he was shot down in 1917 by the top German flyer, Werner Voss; he spent the remaining months of the war as a POW. A scholar of University College, Oxford, he was already established as a classical authority; his works on Alexander the Great and Herodotus are still highly regarded.

Long before I went to Clayesmore I was a devotee of Aubrey de Selincourt's seven children's novels, in which his connection with Clayesmore can be strongly seen. The first, *Family Afloat*, was written in 1940 in the darkest hour of the Second World War. Like all his children's novels, it is built around one sailing family living on the Isle of Wight – as a genre, the books are a bit like Arthur Ransome's *Swallows and Amazons*. Aubrey used his own children, Lesley (Elizabeth in the books) and Anne. These two make friends with two brothers Anthony and Robin, based on boys whom Aubrey had taught.

There is no doubt about the identity of Anne and Elizabeth's parents, Mr and Mrs Rutherford. Aubrey's wife Irene was Irene Rutherford the poet, the fictional Mr Rutherford is a schoolmaster and they live in the de Selincourts' own house on the Isle of Wight; and finally the last character in the stories is the de Selincourts' sailing yacht *Tessa*, a two-masted yawl that had once been a fishing smack, with an engine that never works. In *Family Afloat* they all sail to France and en route rescue the crew of a French fishing boat. The children have convinced themselves that another yacht is a smuggler, and the amused adults do nothing to correct the illusion. We learn subsequently that the other yacht is really crewed by a cheerful group of schoolmasters, one of whom I suspect to be Clayesmore's David Spinney – something he himself admitted might be the case.

The novels appeared one a year throughout the 1940s. *One Good Tern* describes how the children build their own stout sailing boat, *Tern*, during the Christmas holidays. In *Three Green Bottles* they holiday at Burnham on the east coast and it is there that they meet their friends Anthony and Robin. The four are well matched. Anthony is a hearty, sports-mad teenager and Anne is a no-nonsense practical child of the same age. The growing relationship between these two is something that de Selincourt handles with skill, and in so doing is way ahead of his time. In *One More Summer*, the children find and explore what they believe to be a ghost ship. Then in 1947 de Selincourt published *Micky*, a novel years ahead of its time in that the children rescue a little boy, Micky, an abused child who has fled a foster home.

How do these books relate to Clayesmore? Mr Rutherford teaches in a school that is transparently Clayesmore. The book's illustrations were drawn by Aubrey's brother Guy, who had a short spell as Clayesmore's bursar, and some of the illustrations in *Family Afloat* are by Carl Verrinder's wife Eleanor. And there is the David Spinney connection with *Family Afloat*.

Aubrey de Selincourt wrote over 40 books, including the seven children's novels as well as standard works on classical Greece and Rome, some of them still in print. Others are biographies of Captain Cook and the explorer Nansen, and he also wrote of his love of the Dorset countryside.

James Morley (1953–6)

Above: Aubrey de Selincourt.

Left: *One Good Tern*, first published in 1946.

turned instinctively to him'. On the other side of the coin were the creditors who remained unpaid, the bursars driven to distraction by his cavalier approach to financial management, the staff whom he often failed to support against the ragging of the boys. But his funeral and burial in Sparsholt churchyard were attended by a cavalcade of Claytesmorian boys and staff, old and new. As *The Times* said, he was undoubtedly much loved; and his approach to teaching is admirably summed up in a letter he wrote in 1928 to John 'Jack' Jevons, an old pupil who was then teaching at Seaford School: 'I am sorry you don't like French, and if you will let me scold you I don't like to hear you say that your school certificate candidate who had a poor chance caused you to take no trouble over him. He might have done better if you had. I hope you will never degenerate into the type of schoolmaster I know so well who takes no interest in any boy unless he is clever and likely to do him credit. That is of course all wrong, isn't it?'

Verdicts on his life's work and his approach to the education of sometimes difficult boys included the Anglo-Catholic cleric Dr Dearmer's view that 'He disclaims any rule of thumb and works by personal influence, common sense and an infinite capacity for taking pains.' Frank Whitbourn in his biography, *Lex*, says that he 'saw that the true aim of education was to help the individual to achieve his individuality; to develop all his faculties that he might become a harmonious personality and body, mind and spirit.' And four years after his death, JL Hodson wrote in the *News Chronicle*: 'I am tempted to say that this is the sort of school that schools ought to be; and then I wonder whether it is too agreeable, whether the wrench of leaving it for a rough and tumble world will not be too severe! On the other hand, should not happiness build up reserves of strength?'

Aubrey de Selincourt asserted his authority with speed, and the school rapidly settled down within the new regime. But problems remained, with which he was unequipped to deal. He was a man of letters who could be a brilliant teacher, but he had no idea how to be a manager, how to promote the school to potential new parents, how to run an office. He avoided his problems by practising the cello in an upstairs room. Moreover, the lease of Northwood Park was at the point of expiry and relations with the landlord remained frosty. He therefore decided to move, and started to look for a new property in the west country. The choice fell on a lovely house at Iwerne Minster in Dorset. Martin de Selincourt approved the purchase and Aubrey's brother Guy, known as Bob, became bursar. At the beginning of the summer term of 1933 the school moved.

Below: de Selincourt's letter to parents announcing the school's move to Iwerne Minster, January 1933.

Bottom right: One of the last photographs of Lex, along with the tablet that honours him and hangs on the wall in the Ismay Room in the main house.

CLAYESMORE SCHOOL
NORTHWOOD PARK
WINCHESTER

A. de Selincourt, M.A.
Headmaster.

Telegrams:
Clayesmore School
Winchester

Telephone:
Sparsholt 14.

January 19th, 1933.

DEAR

It has for a long time been felt that the estate at Northwood Park has certain serious disadvantages, and that it is in many ways inadequate to the needs of the School. The School House is somewhat dark and very inconveniently arranged, and as regards heating, ventilation and lighting has never been properly brought up to date. Moreover, as the estate is not the property of the School, but is held on lease only, it has been difficult to make satisfactory alterations and improvements.

It is with great pleasure therefore that I am able to inform you that the Governing Body have been able to purchase for the School the magnificent house and estate known as Iwerne Minster, and to these new premises Clayesmore will move at the beginning of the Summer Term.

I need hardly stress the advantage to the School of owning its buildings and land—an advantage which it has never before enjoyed. And apart from this, the change will greatly benefit the School.

The house at Iwerne Minster is in every way suitable to our needs. It was built at the end of last century by the late Lord Wolverton at a cost of £175,000, and was bought subsequently and brought thoroughly up to date by Mr. J. H. Ismay, who lived there until his death in 1930. The gardens and playing fields are excellent, and there are, in addition to the usual grass tennis courts, a hard tennis court and a squash court, and a lake of three acres in extent for boating.

The village of Iwerne Minster lies between Shaftesbury and Blandford, on the main road, and is 22 miles from Bournemouth. The situation is open and healthy, and the climate of Dorsetshire is well known for its mild and healthy quality which has, indeed, made that county a favoured one for schools.

The acquisition of the Iwerne Minster estate is a great step in the history of Clayesmore, and one which I confidently believe will be for the great and lasting benefit of the School.

I will send you shortly some photographs of the new buildings, and the details of our ceremony of inauguration, which will be held in June.

Believe me,
Yours sincerely,

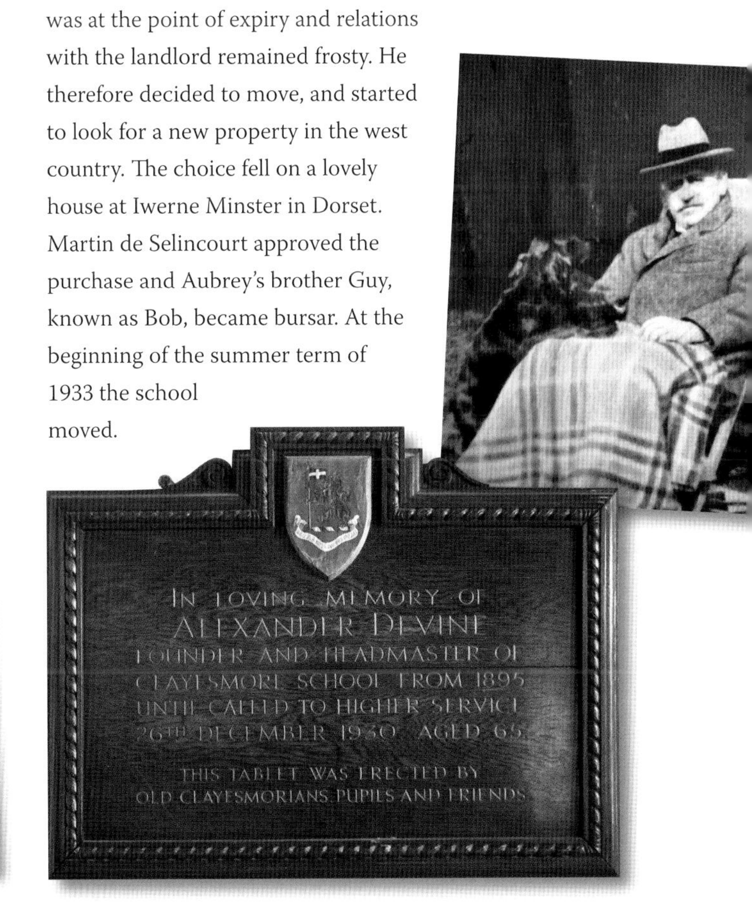

A Beautiful Environment

The village now known as Iwerne Minster is referred to in a Saxon charter as 'ywen' and in Domesday Book as 'Euneminstr'. When Domesday was compiled it was a prosperous possession of Shaftesbury Abbey, with three mills, 18 hides (areas of land) and a total of 50 tied peasants. *TRE* (*tempore regis Edouardi*, in the time of King Edward) it had been worth £10 but was now worth £14. It remained in the hands of the church until Henry VIII's Dissolution, when it passed to the Bower family, who are first recorded as landowners there in 1552. Thomas Bowyer Bower built an elegant house at Iwerne at the end of the 18th century, but this was demolished when the estate was sold in 1876 to the 2nd Lord Wolverton who, before inheriting his title, had been Liberal MP for Shaftesbury.

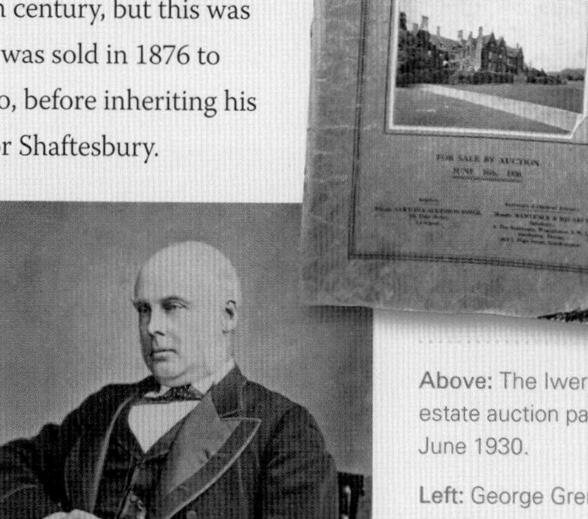
The
Iwerne Minster Estate,
DORSETSHIRE.

Above: The Iwerne Minster estate auction pamphlet, June 1930.

Left: George Grenfell Glyn, 2nd Baron Wolverton.

Far left: Alfred Waterhouse.

Right: The Manor House at Iwerne Minster.

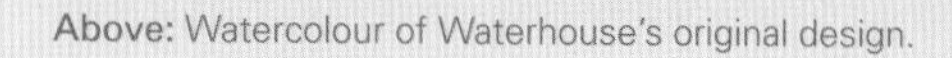

Above: Watercolour of Waterhouse's original design.

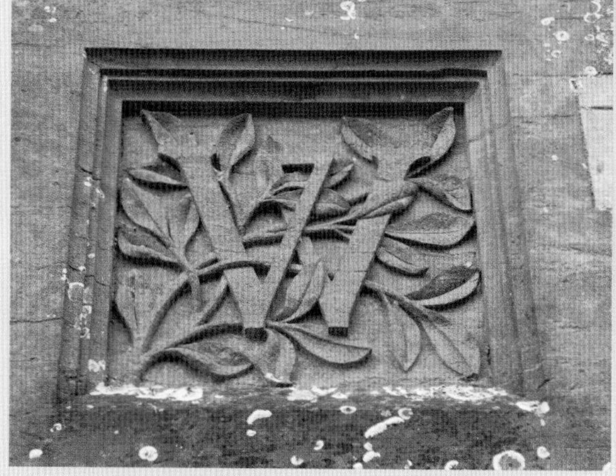

Above: The entwined W monogram (**left**) and double-headed eagle crest (**above**) of the 2nd Lord Wolverton.

He commissioned Alfred Waterhouse to design a larger and more fashionable mansion, which cost £80,240 and was built in 1878. Wolverton's double-headed eagle crest and his entwined W monogram can still be seen around the building, and the timber staircase in the hall along with the panelling in the headmaster's study are relics of the original Waterhouse design. A rather tenuous Waterhouse connection with Iwerne is the possibility that John William Waterhouse used the lake as the scene of his painting of the Lady of Shalott.

Wolverton died in 1887, and the house was rarely visited by the family thereafter until, in 1908, it and its 2,612-acre estate were sold to James Ismay, son of the founder of the White Star Shipping Company and brother of Bruce Ismay, chairman of the company at the time of the sinking of the *Titanic* and a survivor of the disaster.

Left: The walled garden ('The Ladies' Walk') in the 1940s.

Far left: The trophy room.

The Hardy letter

Ismay's interest in his property extended to the village of Iwerne Minster and included the building of a village clubhouse. In this hung a signed Augustus John print of Thomas Hardy (left), donated by the author in recognition of the enterprise, 'affording a nucleus for local centralisation in opposition to the tendency towards the towns.' The print and accompanying handwritten letter are now in the possession of the school and hang in the Ismay Room in the main house.

TELEPHONE: DORCHESTER 43.

MAX GATE,
DORCHESTER.

22 : 4 : 1924

Dear Mr Ismay:

I shall have much pleasure in signing the portrait for your village club-house if the members care for me to do it. These village clubs which have sprung into existence of late years seem thriving very hopefully, & to be affording a nucleus for local centralization in opposition to the tendency towards the towns: if so, it is a good thing.

Sincerely yours
Thomas Hardy

James Ismay built a billiard room and a smoking room on the site of the Wolverton conservatory (now the Burney Library), and created Adam-style ceilings in the main reception rooms. He lived in it until his death in 1930, after which it stood vacant until Clayesmore moved in. The house – now listed Grade II – remains much as it was, internally and externally, allowing for the inevitable alterations that conversion to a school originally involved, and in more recent years the essential addition of new technology.

Those of the original outbuildings that survive mostly date to the 1880s. There are two entrance lodges, the second of which was built when the drive was rerouted to create a more sweeping approach to the house. A trophy room in the grounds became a squash court and is now the centre of the music school. The boarding house known as Gate was originally a stables courtyard incorporating a fire station. The landscaping of the

Above: The lake.

Opposite: Aerial view of the school and grounds, pre-Second World War.

estate, by Edward Milner, combined formal gardens and terracing close to the house with more rugged natural features further away. A 'fine old avenue of majestic elms', which led from the house down to the lake and beyond, survived until the 1970s.

The prep school now sits on what were the magnificent walled kitchen gardens, described in the 1930 sale documents as 'three vineries and two peach houses; two carnation houses; propagating house; greenhouse in two sections; melon and cucumber house'. All that now remain are parts of the once heated walls.

There was a speedy programme of conversion and building under Evelyn King, most of which has been replaced – the 1930s classroom block as the result of a

Below: Gate boarding house.

Bottom right: Devine House.

fire in 1979. The new chapel, dedicated to OCs who died in the two world wars and funded by donations made in their memory, was built in 1956, marking the school's 60th birthday. The new buildings made necessary by the move of the prep school from Charlton Marshall in 1974 entailed the demolition of the kitchen garden and its buildings, and the arrival of girls led to the purchase of the old vicarage in the village as a boarding house for them; now named Devine, it has been given back to the boys. Another village building taken over by Clayesmore is the former school, which is now an art centre. King's House, a purpose-built girls' boarding house, opened in 1984, and the same era saw the new classroom block, the Sports Centre and the Peter Burke Theatre.

The late 1980s also saw a new lease of life granted to the lake, which tended to dry out over the summer

Only Fools and Horses – the chandelier episode

Claysemore's main house hall and the courtyard outside were the setting for one of the most famous episodes in *Only Fools and Horses*. 'A Touch of Glass', originally screened in 1982, later came second in a vote to find the most popular moment in the sitcom.

The story goes as follows: after Del Boy and Rodney give a stranded Lady Ridgemere a lift home, they overhear her husband haggling on the telephone over the cost of cleaning two priceless Louis XIV chandeliers in their stately home. Del convinces his lordship that chandeliers are the Trotters' speciality and agrees to do the work at a knock-down price. They return a week later with Granddad, who is sent upstairs to undo the holding bolt while Del and Rodney climb stepladders below and hold a blanket under one of the chandeliers to catch it as the bolt is released. Granddad undoes the bolt and hammers it down – and Del and Rodney can only watch in disbelief as the chandelier on the other side of the hall comes crashing to the floor, to be followed by Granddad sauntering insouciantly down the stairs.

The original ending was to have been Del and Rodney staring at each other over the priceless ruins. Nicholas Lyndhurst later said that that the director, Ray Butt, threatened him with the sack if he ruined the scene by laughing – though many of the cast and crew could hardly contain themselves, and Butt himself had to stuff a handkerchief into his mouth and leave the room. The actual ending has Del finding out from an indignant butler that Lord and Lady Ridgemere are away from home and don't have the Trotters' address, after which they make a hasty exit in their yellow Robin Reliant, shedding stuff out of the back as they career across the school courtyard and out of the gates.

The prop chandelier was an expensive piece of kit costing £6,000, and as only one was made, the scene could be shot once only. The school did not give permission for its floorboards to be raised, so Granddad in the room above was filmed elsewhere.

months, leaving an expanse of mud and rubbish with plants struggling to survive. An arrangement with Wessex Water and Roger Daltrey (of The Who), who owns a nearby trout farm, allowed the installation of an electric pump in the River Iwerne, underground water pipes and an overflow system. The result has been a much more consistent water level – though dry periods can still see it struggling – as well as the flourishing of wildlife living and breeding in and around the lake and a great increase in the number and type of flora there. A gift by Roger Daltrey of 200 trout added to several other species which were introduced to stock the lake, on which boating and angling now regularly take place.

More recently the Social Centre has been built, and the new century, after the arrival of Martin Cooke as head, has witnessed a flurry of building: the Jubilee Building, for the sciences, opened in 2002 and the Spinney Centre, for the humanities, in 2004. The prep school opened a new pre-prep and nursery in 2007 and the Everett building in 2008.

Top: Pre-prep and nursery.

Above: The Everett Building.

All weather pitch

PART 2:

Iwerne Minster

Claysmore's new home had not previously been a school, but its flat parkland was eminently suitable for games pitches, and the main house and its many outbuildings were ripe for conversion. The move did not, however, bring an immediate rise in the school's fortunes. The talented and energetic Evelyn King had decided to develop his own career by buying and becoming headmaster of a school called Craigend in Edinburgh, and took with him to Scotland another stalwart of the school staff at the time, Alister Mackenzie, as well as Miss Carver, the hard-working matron. Despite his scholarship and his care for his pupils, Aubrey de Selincourt could not make his headmastership work, and his father finally, in 1935, decided that he could no longer throw good money after bad. Clayesmore would have to close.

As a final desperate throw of the dice de Selincourt approached Evelyn King, who was making a great success of Craigend and had achieved recognition in the national press as the youngest headmaster in Scotland. When this was misreported in the *Daily Mirror* to the effect that he was the youngest in Great Britain, media interest was such that he held a lengthy press conference in which he expounded his educational ideas to an eager audience. One of the reporters asked him whether he could encompass his vision in just a few words, to which he replied that his would be a school that would 'produce good husbands'.

King agreed that he would at least talk to Martin de Selincourt. Asked over lunch whether he had a proposal for the future of Clayesmore,

King came up with one. In summary, he would set up a new company, Clayesmore (1935) Ltd, which would purchase the goodwill of the school for a nominal sum and buy the premises for £12,000 on a 100% mortgage provided by Martin de Selincourt. He would provide new pupils for the school from Craigend, and he and Aubrey would run it together, though King would be responsible for all major decisions. 'What guarantee have I that you will succeed?' asked Martin. 'None' was the reply. 'Do you think you will succeed?' 'I don't think I will succeed. I know I will succeed.'

To which confident assertion Martin said, 'Do you know, I believe you will.' And the deal was done.

There followed months of intense activity: finding a buyer for the Edinburgh school, telling the staff, pupils and parents of the decision, trying to persuade some of the Edinburgh boarders to move to Clayesmore and at the same time finding new boys. King's reputation was such that he was able to persuade 30 Craigend boys to transfer their education 400 miles south, and he also took back with him not only Alister Mackenzie and Miss Carver, who clearly now thought the school had a future, but five more of the Craigend staff, including George Dobie, chauffeur/handyman, and his wife Ivy, who remained at Clayesmore for the next 50 years, and David Spinney, who taught at the school for the rest of his working life and was the author of the major history of the school published in 1987. Miss Carver also remained until she retired, when she was replaced as matron by Ruth Dear, who in her turn stayed for over 40 years.

King again: 'If Lex had regarded himself as unfortunate in his staff, the wheel had now turned full circle. Joining me at this time were David Spinney and John Appleby, Humphrey Moore and Reggie Sessions, all of whom stayed on the staff until retirement and often beyond. Carl Verrinder, appointed a term or two before me, was there until he retired 45

Below: The staff at Craigend School relax at breaktime, 1935.

I recall DS [de Selincourt] as sensitive, gentle, helpful and understanding. He taught me Latin – not much but enough to give me a taste for it 50 years later. My writing then showed all the shortcomings which now dismay my readers… Even then there was a (very) small school orchestra, probably five strong, and while I scraped my three-quarter-size fiddle he played the cello, but he grasped it oddly, not between his knees like a jockey tackling Becher's Brook but with one leg stretched out in a leisurely fashion. He may have had some infirmity going back to the Great War; I never knew. We Juniors were often invited to the drawing room to play with his daughters Anne and Lesley [later married to Christopher Robin Milne]. They would turn cartwheels to please – to tease? – us and later there would be tea and cakes. Naturally Mrs DS was not far away.

He took a conscientious interest in all our (orthodox) activities… Looking back now I wish it had been DS who'd had the job of telling me of my father's death – though I might have cried, and one didn't cry in front of King. But to give King his due he'd arranged for that old reprobate Ken Scholefield to be waiting for me outside that dreaded DOOR OF THE HEADMASTER'S STUDY, and I remember so well how my old friend offered comforting words.

1930s pupil in a letter to David Spinney

Right: George Dobie, faithful retainer.

years later. And Peter Burke, my successor as headmaster, eventually retired 30 years after first appointment. No school had a more devoted or more dedicated staff – and they were working for practically nothing. We were, I think, to an unusual degree, a band of brothers, conscious of the past, intent on a better future and willing to devote every minute of the working day to that end; and working days in boarding schools did not end until lights-out. They bore it all bravely.'

The new regime began to take effect at the beginning of the autumn term of 1935, with 40 original Clayesmorians squaring up to 30 Craigenders and 30 newcomers. The summer holidays had seen a frenzy of activity, converting outhouses into classrooms, common rooms and dormitories. Evelyn King was determined to start as he meant to go on – and two early casualties were Aubrey de Selincourt and his brother Guy, who lasted only one term under the new ordinance. King also set up a new governing council under the chairmanship of Sir Harold Bellman, father of two Clayesmorians, who was to chair the council for the next 25 years.

There was a flurry of building over the next few years, much of it financed by a generous bequest by Desmond Coke, who had died in 1931. The old tradition of manual persisted too, mainly to be seen in the digging of a new swimming pool. Work started in January 1936, and such was the enthusiasm – despite the heavy Dorset clay – that it was finished by the summer. David Spinney's *History* has an anecdote about that enterprise. On a dark February evening the school was being treated to a lantern lecture in the library, of such prodigious dullness that it appeared to be accompanied by much more shuffling and foot scraping than normal. When the lights went up at the end King and the lecturer found themselves facing an almost empty room – the boys had melted into the darkness and were to found digging away at the swimming pool by the light of bicycle headlamps.

A new chapel, a new dining room, new classrooms – all were complete by the time war broke out in September 1939, although much of the work was necessarily flimsy. A teacher who leant incautiously against one of the rickety partitions between classrooms could find himself precipitated into the next room, to the huge delight of both sets of boys. But these improvements were vital to the continuing prosperity and success of the school during those increasingly tense and depressed years. Within a year of King's assumption of the headmastership, numbers reached 150 and there were now four boys' houses; and a further highly important development at the start of the 1936/7 academic year was the forging of a link with a nearby preparatory school, Charlton Marshall (for which see Part 3).

Claysmore during the Second World War

The declaration of war on September 3 1939 had an immediate effect on the school. David Spinney disappeared into the navy and other masters were quickly called up. King himself, aged 33 when war broke out, was immediately commissioned and so rapidly made new arrangements for school governance through a transfer of power and ownership from his own company, Clayesmore (1935) Ltd, to a registered charity; admission to the Headmasters' Conference quickly followed. He also had to seek a new temporary headmaster: 'I found Frank Fletcher, who had been headmaster of both Marlborough and Charterhouse (and was a little inclined to talk about past glories). He had every qualification – high intelligence, academic distinction, twice chairman of HMC, administrative ability, a lifetime of boarding school experience – and, at the start, enthusiasm for his new job, his "war work" as he called it. But he lacked the ability to adapt. There was, on the surface, no trouble but he never understood Clayesmore. As his friendly, sad and apologetic letter to me made clear, it was I who had made the mistake, not he.'

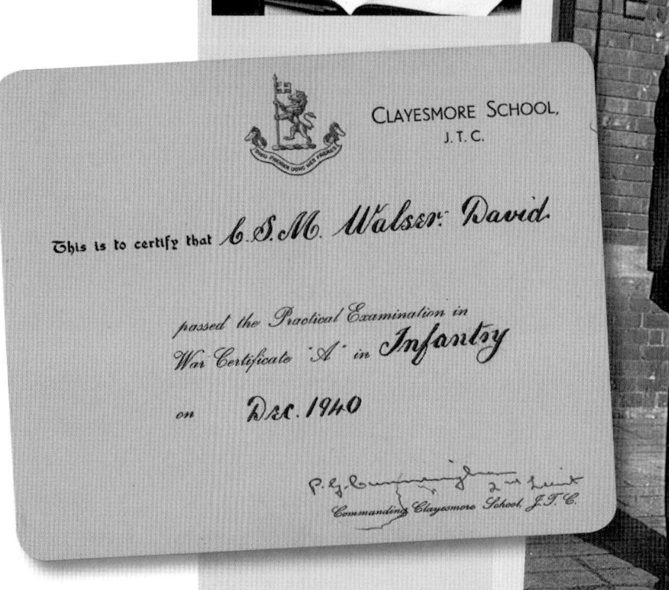

CLAYESMORE SCHOOL,
J.T.C.

This is to certify that C.S.M. Walser: David.

passed the Practical Examination in
War Certificate 'A' in Infantry

on Dec. 1940

2nd Lieut
Commanding Clayesmore School, J.T.C.

Above: The swimming pool at Iwerne Minster – a product of the manual regime.

Left: John Appleby, acting head during the Second World War years.

Below left: David Walser's JTC certificate.

Below: Cadet Officer Walser *c*1942.

'Think for yourself, boy'

Lex's legacy showed itself still alive at Clayesmore during the war in the resourcefulness of boys looking to relieve the rigours of rationing. For those who were prepared to walk eight miles each way, and who had sufficient funds at their disposal, the Anvil at Pimperne *(below)* was a mecca, dishing up ham, bacon and eggs, toasted cheese and fruit cake; never mind that the supplies came from the black market and that the establishment was regularly raided by the authorities. More personally ingenious was the reaction of John Gold (1939–41) to an extra ration of milk, which he loathed. Making sure to be the first to arrive in the kitchen where the jugs of milk were waiting to be collected, he would gather the accumulation of cream on top of the milk into suitable containers borrowed from the chemistry lab, jam them between the spokes of his bicycle wheels, toil to the top of Iwerne Hill and then freewheel down, arriving at the bottom with his butter ration gloriously augmented.

Oliver Bott (1938–46) 'yearned for privacy, as a Middle – perhaps the most difficult age – and for the length of a winter achieved it, to share in secret with friends. Through an arched entry a narrow yard flanked the north side of the stables, leading to a small range of outbuildings above which stood a miniature tower with a small lancet window but no visible entrance. A search revealed the only way in – through a never-opened trapdoor above the shower room. A private den could be made there, but it must have the comfort of a fire; the floor was of concrete and the walls plain brick, but there was no chimney. A small square hole could be made in the eastern wall beneath the eaves, invisible from the school grounds; the bricks removed would make a hearth. There was a pile of large old slates in the deserted yard below which could form a flue in the corner of the den leading up to the new hole; all that had to be found was a little cement and sand. The job was completed in a fortnight and a makeshift stool or two knocked together for furniture. The ensuing warm, happy evenings were to shape my future life, for I had decided to become an architect. Smoke, however, was our undoing: one evening in early spring a master noticed it issuing from the hole in the wall. The den was discovered, with its rafters unprotected from any upward-flying sparks. The fire must be lit no more, but to our utter surprise no punishment followed.'

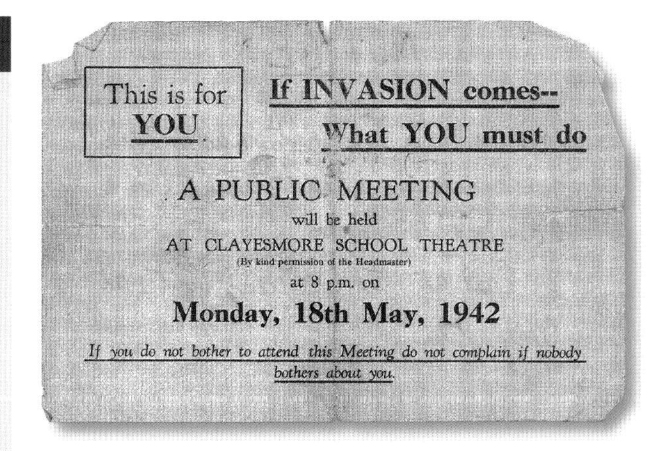

This is for **YOU**

If INVASION comes--
What YOU must do

A PUBLIC MEETING
will be held
AT CLAYESMORE SCHOOL THEATRE
(By kind permission of the Headmaster)
at 8 p.m. on
Monday, 18th May, 1942

If you do not bother to attend this Meeting do not complain if nobody bothers about you.

John Appleby agreed to take on the acting headship, though he was a rather other-worldly man to whom the outreach elements of a headmaster's role were anathema; but he held the fort successfully until, after the Battle of Britain had seen off the immediate danger of invasion, headmasters became eligible to return to civilian life and King came back to Clayesmore.

The school was in a state of flux. The teaching staff were almost all in uniform. New appointments had to be made from the elderly, the medically unfit and conscientious objectors. Oliver Bott (1938–46) remembers 'the idiosyncrasies of teachers which gave life to the school, and childish delight to the boys. Mr Hillier taught biology with such Celtic enthusiasm and fervour that he won a personal following among his pupils; those who were to take their First MB seemed a race apart. Mr Daniels taught physics with the wearisome precision of Parliamentary draughtsmen, dictating a qualitative and a quantitative definition of each term he used. He would walk to class leaning slightly backwards and holding his books balanced on his right hand in front of him, as a waiter carries a tray – a demonstration, we thought, of unstable equilibrium. Traditionally, teachers at public schools had been as segregated by sex as their pupils. The war began to alter things.

Top: Public Meeting Notice from 1942. Iwerne Minster had its own Home Guard and published a pamphlet about the war effort.

Left: The Anvil pub at Pimperne, a mecca for those prepared to walk the 16-mile round-trip.

Food – and expeditions – in wartime

Food and fuel for its cooking were short, so school meals were dull and monotonous: 'national' bread, grey in colour; 'full fruit standard' jam, mostly made from turnip pulp and plum-red dye; a tiny ration of butter, more precious than gold; stewed mutton, as tough as old boots; Spam; ground rice; tapioca; suet puddings almost devoid of fruit boiled in long cylindrical tins from which they emerged wet, white and slimy – we knew them as 'Arbuckle', for a reason not to be asked. Walking and cycling offered a bonus, the chance to have a meal out of school.

For walks we usually preferred the chalk downs behind Iwerne Minster and the woodland of Cranborne Chase beyond, rich with groves of coppiced hazel. This offered a choice between two contrasted ports of call for tea. Nailed to the fence of a thatched cottage at Tarrant Gunville was a tiny hand-painted notice announcing 'Teas'. Two old women lived there, with grey hair severely pinned back in buns and with wrinkled brown faces like winter-stored russet apples. On the single mahogany table in the cramped front room they served an old-fashioned plain tea – bread and butter and home-made jam, wedges of rather heavy fruit cake and tea in a great white porcelain pot with a knitted cosy. A café on the main road from Salisbury to Blandford at Pimperne offered a wider menu – everything (almost) with chips. The proprietor, whose sharply pointed nose twitched between a chin and forehead which receded acutely, we knew as the Anteater.

Stourhead (then still in private hands) was a favourite destination for long summer days. We would climb the wall, wriggle through the encircling shrubberies and cautiously enter the fabulous gardens. The serpentine, wood-shaded valley, with lakes, temples, statuary, grotto, bridge and hermit's cell, were to our eyes fit for Kubla Khan; and through the adjoining park on the high ridge to the west was King Alfred's Tower. The door was locked, but a great fallen branch could be dragged across and leant against the stair turret so that we could scramble up and through the lowest lancet, then climb 200 steps to gaze across Somerset to Glastonbury and the Vale of Avalon. Stourhead was the Arcady which we sought on the holiday, a glorious day in May, which was declared to celebrate Victory in Europe. We ended our visit in the picturesque thatched pub opposite the garden gates, then still managed by the People's Refreshment House Association.

Oliver Bott (1938–46)

Left: Members of Spinney's House with bikes, a valuable means of exploration in July 1937.

Below: Cranborne Chase.

Above: The gardens at Stourhead.

Clayesmore during my time there had many shortcomings, but one great advantage. It lay in the heart of Dorset, quiet, unchangingly rural, unaffectedly beautiful, and all at our disposal. On summer Sundays we were given packed lunches and told to disappear, which we did as far as our legs or bicycles would take us. It is hard to remember that during the war the motor car became almost extinct, and that for a few short years the landscape was not far removed from Hardy's picture of it. To one of my suburban background, the Dorset countryside was a revelation.

It has to be remembered that Clayesmore was founded as a sort of private reformatory, and in my day much of the original atmosphere still lingered. Nobody could have called us civilised, but in addition to our preference for the eccentric and the unusual we maintained a lively interest in art, music and drama. Scadding's art room was always full of activity and experiment. NAS himself, immersed in a picture of his own, presided to the extent of preventing outright chaos but usually refused to do more than raise a weary eyebrow when approached for advice. His policy, if so it could be called, was to provide the opportunity and example and leave the rest to us. A glance at the art produced at that time certainly shows his inertia to be justified.

Clayesmore aroused in me a love of music for which I can never be sufficiently grateful. Much of this was acquired in Reggie Sessions' room on Saturday nights listening to records on his gramophone, which was ancient and used fibre needles which required sharpening with a special clipper every time the record was turned over. Since in those days of 78s each side lasted about five minutes, listening to a symphony required considerable patience.

Drama was in the Bohemian hands of CHP Verrinder, who came close to the ideal of what a theatrical producer should be. The productions were conjured out of chaos on a shoestring and generally in the face of the headmaster's disapproval, but they never failed to delight, largely because of a happy knack of appropriate casting. The first production of my time was *The ascent of F6*. I doubt if many people on the stage or off it had the faintest idea what it was about, but it remains a memorable theatrical experience.

John Gould (1940–5)

A wooden hut was erected on the roof of the Library by, inter alia, Hogarth and Gibb, who hauled the sections up by rope and constituted a comfortable 'snug' for the duty observer. On an 'air raid warning red' the observers were alerted by intercom phone. On one night I was i/c Obs and we reported the flaming descent of – as it happened – an enemy bomber. Congratulations were later received from the local Observer Corps or some such body. Nearer home, the bursar's office was occupied at night by one master and one boy (in separate beds); the former was O/C ARP and the latter his runner. It was very cushy for the latter because he also was brought a cup of tea while still in bed on the morning which followed his duty night. I know! I used to enjoy it.

1930s pupil in a letter to David Spinney

Right: Evelyn King (centre with arms folded) along with house staff and prefects in 1938.

At Clayesmore, Mrs Mackenzie pioneered the change; she had the ability and the presence to teach boys successfully, to hold their interest and (where possible) to get them through their exams. The school now recruited two other women to teach – Miss Joscelyne, formidable in aspect and evident capability, and Miss Thomas, equally knowledgeable and cultured but slighter in figure and more diffident in manner. They lived together in a cottage at Donhead St Mary, ten miles away, using all their petrol coupons to drive in each day in a very small old car. With the sixth forms they were excellent, teaching in the manner of university lecturers; socially they suggested a slender bridge to the outside world, hinting at communities other than school.'

John Gould (1940–5) also remembers the advent of 'Jos and Thos' (pronounced Toss), with whom he remained in touch for the rest of their lives: 'In 1943 the announcement that Miss V Joscelyne MA and Miss KM Thomas MA would temporarily join the staff aroused considerable speculation and some concern in an all male establishment, and for some days we eyed them warily while we came to terms with this unknown quantity. We soon realised, however, that the headmaster had struck gold. As they told me later, their recruitment was suitably idiosyncratic, the interview running as follows:

'HM (briskly): Have you ever taught boys before?

J&T (nervously): Well no, as a matter of fact we haven't.

HM (keenly): Have you ever taught French?

J&T (realising that all was now lost): Well no, I'm afraid we never have.

HM (heartily): Well that seems very satisfactory. Can you start next week?

'They remained at Clayesmore for many years, to the delight and benefit of generations of boys to whom they became the personification of the school itself. Learning without pedantry, a proper scepticism without cynicism and an informed interest in all our doings were the gifts that Jos and Thos brought to Clayesmore, and at a time when they were sorely needed. Visits to their wonderful cottage perched high above the Nadder valley were

Plane crashes near the school

The official entry in the Upper Heyford squadron log records: 'At about 10.00 hours on June 13 1940 Hampden P4297 was seen to stall on a turn while circling round a boys' school at Iwerne Minster near Blandford. The aircraft crashed into a wood and burst into flames, the three occupants, P/O JES MacAlister, P/O EAE Sedgeley and 634958 AC2 Lennon J being killed. As the exercise being carried out included practice in changing seats it is not certain which of the officers was piloting the aircraft.'

Lionel Pimm (1938–41) was quickly on the scene, as he recalls in a letter to Gordon Chubb (1942–6), who researched the incident in 1987: 'As far as I recall, and it was over 45 years ago, Huntley, Priestley (who died in 1943 in the landings in Italy) and myself – being the three second-year science sixth of the time and all working for a medical career – were in the chemistry lab with Verrinder. We heard the plane low and a sickening crump, and needed no telling that it had crashed. We more or less downed tools regardless of Verrinder and rushed out and across the fields towards Hambledon Hill to the pall of smoke. I seem to recall that someone optimistically took a fire extinguisher.

'I think we were the first boys to arrive. The plane was ablaze, there was nothing we could do and no sign of crew needing help. Later a crew member was extricated, which I remember clearly because he was the first dead human I had ever seen. I believe we may have gone back to class (First MB was imminent for me and also Higher Cert) and then later gone out again to study the remains. Lots of younger and junior boys – probably indeed the whole school – went out during the day and souvenirs such as bullets were recovered – someone claimed a burnt human finger bone… Of course at the time we thought it was the crash of a bomber limping home from a bombing raid on enemy troops or ports, whereas I believe in fact it was a training flight.'

Gordon Huntley (1937–40) also remembered the incident, though slightly differently, as he acknowledges ('ask any policeman!'): 'The aircraft came in from the north-east in a low fast turn and did a half-circle round the school – the best view of a Hampden I had seen to that date – and then veered off towards Hambledon, disappeared behind a copse and bang – which shook the

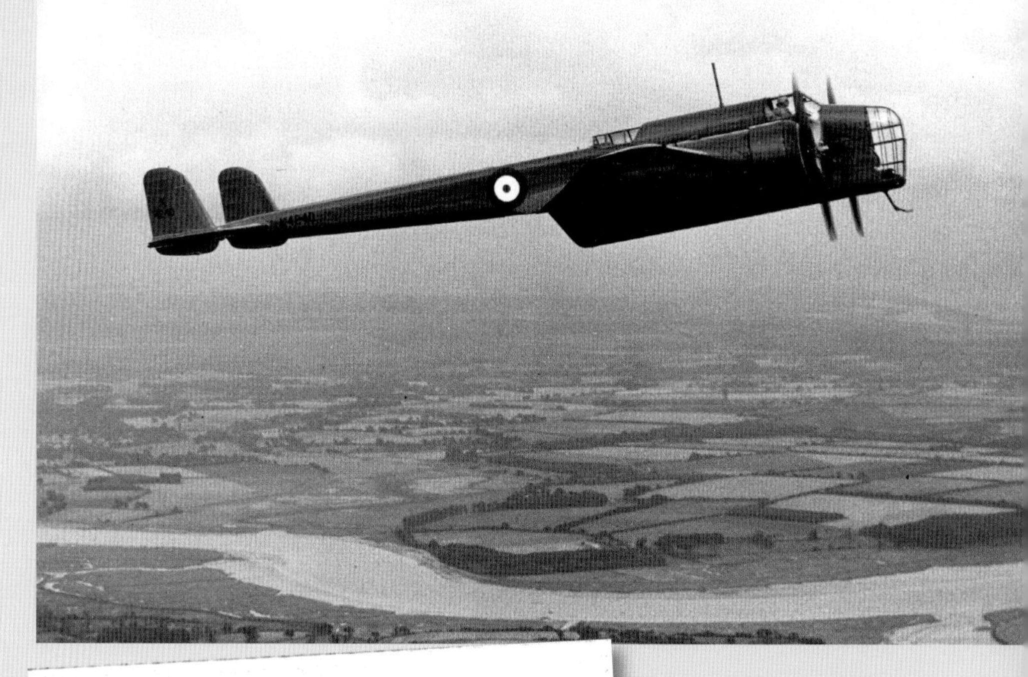

Above: The Handley Page medium bomber, the 'Hampden', which during the early years of the war proved inadequate.

IWERNE MINSTER PAGE THIRTEEN

AIR RAID PRECAUTIONS.

THE A.R.P. organisation was one of the first to be established in the village. Amongst its first duties was the issue and fitting of gas masks to the public, and these were constantly inspected throughout the war, to see that they were kept in order properly.

A check had to be kept on the numbers of people in each house, and of schoolchildren in case of incidents occurring. In company with the Police, a watch had to be kept on the inadvertent showing of lights during the hours of blackout.

There were frequent "alerts" during the war, both by day and night, particularly between 1940 and 1942. Many incidents occurred in the near vicinity, but the village suffered neither casualties nor damage.

In the early days, a voluntary system of Fire Watching was organised, and for 18 months one of seven parties (one for each day of the week) kept watch during the hours of darkness each night, prepared to dash to the possible scene of a fire at a moment's notice, with stirrup pump, buckets and axes.

The personnel kept themselves efficient by constant practices in conjunction with the First Aid Post, and the Police, with whom relations were most cordial.

The organisation of the A.R.P. was used for other purposes too, such as the collection of information for the use of the Military in case of invasion, etc.

The Wardens' Post was first at Lloyds Bank (Mr. Dyson), and then at The Cottage (Miss Pratt and Mrs. Nicholls). There was an Observation Post on the roof of Clayesmore School House.

IWERNE MINSTER A.R.P.

Controller, Shaftesbury R.D.C., A.R.P. : Lt.-Col. Norris.
Deputy Controller, No. 3 Group—Mr. T. F. Cox.
Head Warden : Major J. M. Randle Ford, O.B.E., M.C.

Sector Wardens : Mr. W. Dyson, Mrs. N. H. Nicholls, Miss E. N. Pratt

Wardens : Mr. Appleby, Mr. G. T. L. Chittenden, Mr. Churchill, Mr. G. L. Cruse, The Ven. Archdeacon, H. J. Edmonds, Mr. D. Hillier, Mr. Minns, Mr. Moore, Miss Priddle, Mrs. W. J. Rich, Miss Souden, Mrs. F. E. Whitbourn, Mrs. Woodhouse

Messengers : A. Arnold, Miss V. Browning, John Brooks, Tom Brooks, John Davies, Miss M. Fletcher., G. Gray, C. G. Hawes, Miss A. Mogridge, D. Pike

Rescue and Decontamination : Mr. W. Gray, Mr. John Wareham, Mr. W Wareham

Report Post : Mrs. T.F. Cox

Left: Page from the Iwerne Minster War Effort Pamphlet concerning air raid precautions.

Right: A Messerschmitt Bf 110 shot down over the fields of Dorset during the Battle of Britain, 1940.

school. David Walser and I were walking outside Spinneys looking up at the aircraft, and immediately ran inside for a stretcher, a heavy wooden one which we lugged the half mile or so across the field in case someone had been thrown clear. By a narrow margin we two were the first on the scene. All very foolhardy for us and the great crowd of chaps behind us – it might have been cooking a bomb load for all we knew and the ammunition was exploding like firecrackers. I picked up a few rounds of .303 which was used later for potting foxes on Home Guard duty in the half light of dawn. With hindsight, the pilot was probably distracted and sideslipped on the turn into the trees. Hampdens were notorious, I later heard, for doing this, unless corrected very smartly…'

Two German aircraft also crashed near the school during the Second World War, as recalled by Malcolm Gordon (1939–44) in a letter to Gordon Chubb in 1985: 'Two ME110s came down at about the same time of day on September 27 1940. One crashed in woods near the top of the Blandford/Shaftesbury road, killing both crew members, who were finally buried in the Brookwood Military Cemetery. The other made a forced landing on the forward slope just below the wooded crest of Preston Hill… The ME had been winged while returning from a raid on Bristol and was chased at tree-top height around Iwerne by one of our fighters; they made at least one pass over the lake field on the far side of the lime trees, witnessed by myself and others from the zigzag ARP trench alongside the classroom block. My recollection is that the Lewis AA gunner at the searchlight unit near the watercress beds loosed off a few rounds, as did RSM Charlie Banfield, using an OTC .303 rifle from a position by the mounting block near the stable archway. Meanwhile, Cadet Lt/Col Allan Wilson and his section, without even a blank cartridge between them, took cover in the ha-ha. They were not to know that the ME was on the run and about to make a forced landing, and a very skilful one. The pilot was unhurt, but had landed in an effort to save the life of his badly wounded rear gunner who did, it is believed, receive first aid from the school's nursing sister, Maud Edwards.'

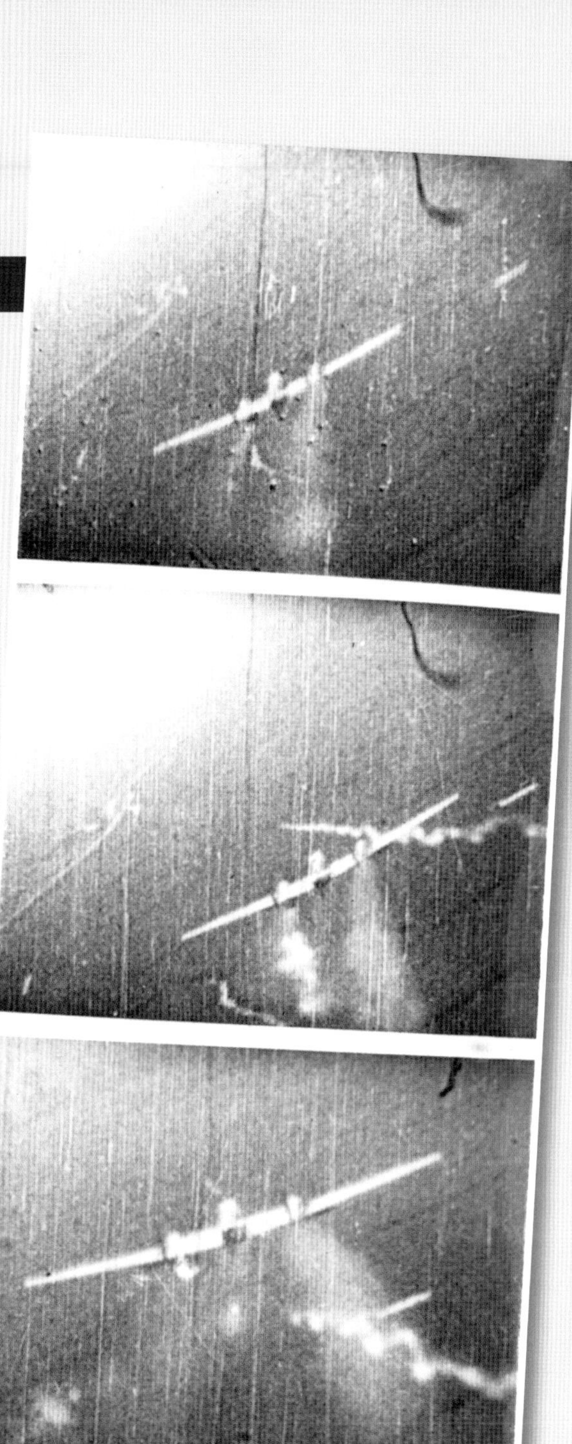

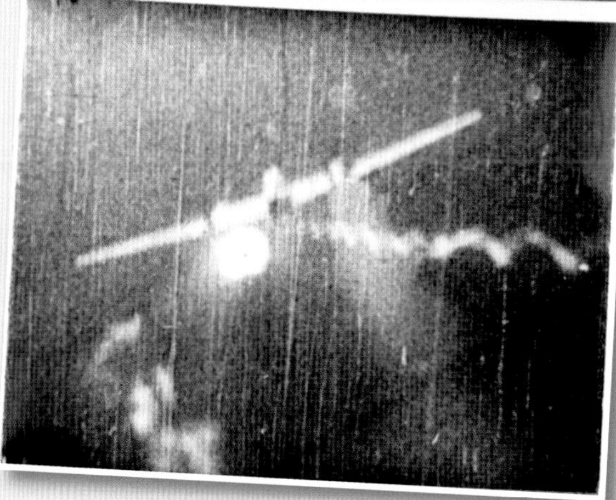

I came to the school in 1940. I suppose school routine then was essentially rather standard for those times, but the background was distinctly different and rather sombre. In the early days it was the threat of invasion; the immediate concern to us inland was the anticipated arrival of German paratroops landing ahead of the expected invasion. Seniors in the army-based Junior Training Corps, which we all joined, took turns at night to guard the Corps' armoury across the courtyard from the chemistry lab. This was stocked with up to a hundred serviceable rifles, together with other army equipment including Bren light machine guns. This was no charade; the boys were armed but as we know, there was no invasion, even though one was anticipated.

The school had its own air raid warning siren, presumably linked in some way to public ones. When they went off at night, those of us in the main building collected our gas masks and went down to the basement and slept on palliasses – straw-filled mattresses that were extremely uncomfortable. Later, in the summer of 1940, came the Battle of Britain, when we often saw aerial combat followed by the aftermath of crashed aircraft; strangely my recollection is of the many crashed German planes. I never saw 'one of ours', though many must also have been shot down. We used to cycle to visit the wrecks, which were usually unguarded, allowing us to pilfer 'souvenirs'. As we progressed through the school, career choice was overshadowed for most of us by the certainty of call-up. There was an element of choice between army, Royal Navy and the RAF, and the latter, in spite of our army orientation through so many hours spent in the Corps, of which I became the Company Sergeant Major, was the goal, among my friends at least, with the ambition to become pilots. Never for a moment did any of us consider the relative chance of survival dependent upon our choice, which I now find strange; fighting in the war was something that one just accepted, indeed even looked forward to. I wasn't to join my friends, for it was very soon detected that, quite unknown to me, I was colour-blind.

Two incidents stand out in my memory. First, one night after lights-out, when we prefects were still up, a Lancaster bomber crashed across the main road from the playing fields. Six of us rushed towards this monster in the dark. Both wings were on fire with intermittent small explosions. For me, discretion was the better part of valour and, anticipating an even bigger explosion, I went no further and lay face down on the ground a hundred yards away. Two others, however, ran on and hearing calls from inside got through the broken fuselage, only to be beaten back by the heat.

The second also concerned a crashed plane, but this time a troop-carrying glider, which I suppose had been cast off from its towing aircraft in the fog. This time it was in the afternoon, and lots of us went to see it moments after it landed in the mist. As we arrived 30 or so fierce-looking

NOTICE

Anyone who has not had their Gas Mask re-fitted recently, is advised to do so.

Call at the Warden's Post at any time.

Left: Notice regarding gas masks.

Below: John Simpson's glider on the lawn at Clayesmore. John was a nonconformist maths master from 1939–42 who flew from Hambledon, Win Green, Winklebury and Whitesheet Hill.

scholarship, got a first, and am now an honorary fellow of my college, Peterhouse. Teaching standards in wartime aside, there are other things that make a good school, so thank you Clayesmore for preparing me so well for my career.

Sir Rodney Sweetnam (1940–5)

Above: ACF Cadet camp, summer 1943.

soldiers carrying their rifles with their faces smeared with camouflage and speaking in a foreign tongue confronted us. It took us just sufficient time to be thoroughly frightened before it transpired that they were a Highland regiment with unrecognisable Glaswegian accents. Finally, in the early summer of 1944, we witnessed the invasion forces on their way to the coast; a memorable and quite remarkable sight. For weeks before D-Day there was an uninterrupted day and night and nose to tail convoy of men and military hardware moving south. The sheer scale of this military might along just one of many roads that must have been used was unforgettable.

For me, as the European war ended, it was Cambridge to read natural sciences and start my career in medicine. My call-up was deferred because doctors were urgently needed. My turn came soon after I qualified, and it was off to the Royal Navy to spend two years in our last battleship, HMS *Vanguard*, where the need for my newly acquired medical expertise was largely concerned with the treatment of one condition amongst the sailors!

I am not quite certain how I got into Cambridge because the standard of wartime teaching at Clayesmore was, to say the least, variable. However, I managed to be awarded a

V+1 Oh whizzo prang ho. I've been having a most glorious time. Last night we lit a tremendous victory beacon 12 feet high and best of all we were all supplied with fireworks, oh I don't think I ever felt so happy or enjoyed myself more. On t'other pages I will give you a description of what I did.

Monday: Had the usual morning, all the papers said it would probably end tonight. We were given a half holiday in honour of the day, that is we did our prep at 4.30 instead of 6.30. I wrote a letter home but I was feeling browned off, after tea at six wild rumours started going round then we had it officially. Oh boy, at about 8.00 the school went mad, everyone shouting and rushing about, I had made up my mind to beat the big gong in the hall and I did. Other boys switched on the siren then bust the switch off so that the siren couldn't be turned off. Then I climbed up the fire escape on to the roof (out of bounds) and helped other boys hoist a union jack.

There was tons of ragging and singing but we were told to shut up as tomorrow (Tuesday) was to be the official VE day. At last we quietened down, on the horizon we could see glows…

Tuesday: The first bell went at 8.30 instead of 7.00, then at 10.30 we went to chapel and had a short service, then for the rest of the day you were free, at 3.00 I listened to Churchill and then at 9.00 to the King. I liked Churchill best. Then at 9.30 we went down to the V beacon. It was wonderful, there was a terribly good guy of Hitler, his fingers were fireworks and his nose and all his body was stuffed with them, and the fire was then soaked in petrol.

Then (this is the best part) we were all issued with millions of fireworks, as many as I could hold, then as the shadows fell we threw fireworks and danced round the fire, then when it was completely dark we sat round the fire and sang. We stopped at about 11.00 and came to bed.

Peter Wightman (1944–8)

A Bevin Boy

Two old boys met again for the first time in 53 years at the Clayesmore Centenary Fair in 1996: Tony Hart and Ian Ferguson. We were both in Scadding's art class while at the school. In no way could I compete with Tony on TV. But I did get on BBC ten-o'clock news for ten seconds on March 25 2008 when I received the Bevin Boys Veteran Badge from Gordon Brown at 10 Downing Street.

Illness kept me at school till I was 19 and I went straight into the mines. I'd been called up and hoped for the Indian Army, but I was sent to Bamfurlong mine in Wigan. After being toughened up above ground, I became the junior member of a team sent to 'drive a road' – seek out and tunnel new seams of coal. The biggest shock going down the mine for the first time was the speed of descent in the cage. The sound of coal hitting the metal of the tubs was like gunfire. 'That's another one for the enemy,' we'd shout, in the knowledge that we were helping to keep our ships afloat as well as providing for the home front. Official recognition for our war service came late, with the issue of special commemorative badges on the 60th anniversary of the date when our work ended.

Ian Ferguson (1940–3)

Left: Ian Ferguson with Tony Hart.

Below: Ian Ferguson and former comrades collect their Bevin Boys Veteran Badges from 10 Downing Street in 2008.

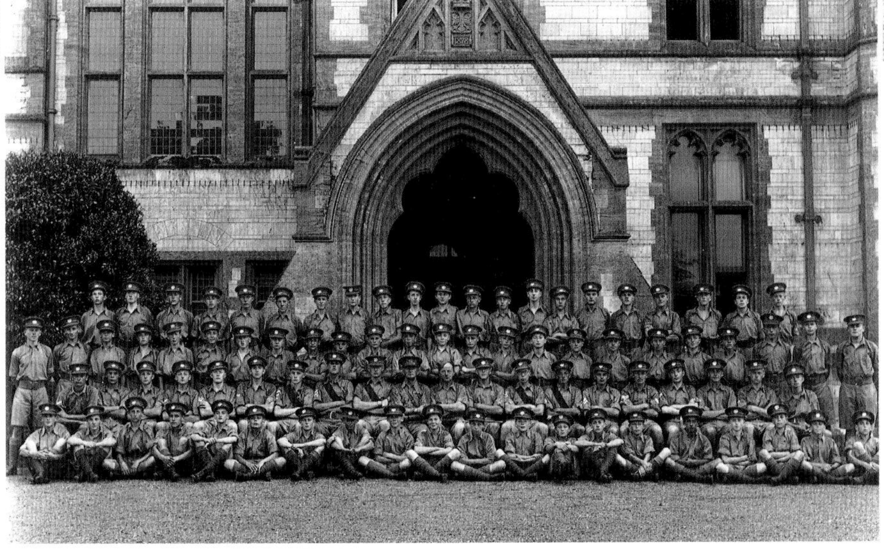

Above and top: The Clayesmore JTC, 1941.

delightful in themselves and frequently enhanced by surreptitious calls at the Rising Sun on the way home. Jos was sometimes accompanied by Rudolf, a fearsome looking Alsatian of great intelligence. During lessons he dozed peacefully in a corner, but if Jos should for any reason leave the room, he would immediately assume her place on the dais and sit with ears pricked, gazing steadily at the class. It needed only one short sharp bark to convince the most hardened malefactor that no liberties were to be taken.'

During the war numbers increased steadily. When the new school year began in September 1942, the combined strength at Iwerne Minster and Charlton Marshall was larger than it had ever been. But as the war progressed heavy casualty lists began to come in. As King recalled, 'In morning chapel we stood for a moment in silence as I read out the names of Clayesmorians killed in action. It happened too often; and when the name was of one who but months before had been a schoolboy, it was poignant. Letters of sympathy to grieving parents, letters of congratulation to the decorated and promoted seemed to fill the day.' A total of 43 OCs lost their lives during the war, many of whom had been at the school when the war began, but also at least two who dated back to Pangbourne or Northwood Park days and had served in the First World War. Others survived major actions in every theatre of the war, and yet others played their part in different ways, like Edward Ardizzone, official war artist.

Oliver Bott remembers the preliminaries to D-Day: 'At the beginning of June 1944 we knew that the invasion of Normandy was at hand. For three days and nights convoys of Bren-gun carriers, tanks and army lorries packed with troops followed each other, southward bound for the landing craft concealed from seaward view in Poole Harbour. We watched, happy and excited, from the gabled dormitory windows overlooking the road. The news of

VBH (Bruce) Venour

At the end of August 2011, VBH (Bruce) Venour, aged nearly 88, visited the school. He is a veteran of the Second World War, Burma, Korea, Malaya and Palestine, and has written the following poem about the Battle of Britain. His name is on the prefects' board as are those of the two boys to whom he refers in his poem: Harris, 'who died in flames above the German countryside', and Craig, who 'died beneath the sea, drowned for his country'. His two companions are also on the Clayesmore Roll of Honour.

Remembrance of a day

Let that gold autumn in my memory stand
As held in amber on a Baltic strand.
The sun that shone upon those Dorset hills
The vapour trails, the count of kills
My friends and I were young.
No work to do that day, we thought we will
Go where the mushrooms grow on Iwerne hill
And gather, cook and eat them then and there
And that we did and laughed all unaware
My friends and I, what web was spun.
Within two years one died beneath the sea,
Drowned for his country, leaving Craig and me;
And in another year he too had died
In flames above the German countryside.
Now I am old and they are young.

Lawrence William Harvard Craig

Flying Officer Lawrence William Harvard Craig, a member of the Royal Air Force Volunteer Reserve, died on November 22 1944. He entered the school in 1937. The *Clayesmorian* records that 'An inimitable speech hesitation added point to his very ready wit, and his qualities of brain and physique, allied to exceptional courage, more than once manifested at the school, made him a person outstanding in his generation.' He was flying a four-engine bomber, and it appears that two of the engines cut out owing to an air lock in the engine feed. When he realised that the plane was going out of control he ordered the crew to bail out. Three did so and landed safely, but the remaining six were killed. Craig was aged 20 and is buried in St Peter's church, Little Rissington.

Keith Vivian Frank Harris

Sub-Lieutenant Keith Vivian Frank Harris, a member of the Royal Naval Volunteer Reserve, died on July 26 1944. One of the many Scottish boys who joined the school after Evelyn King took over as headmaster, he was head prefect in 1941. The *Clayesmorian* reports, 'He revisited the school many times after he left and was last here a few months before D-Day, when he had just been appointed to the command of a landing craft. He met his death by accident while aboard a submarine, being killed instantly.' Also aged 20, his name is on the Portsmouth Naval memorial.

Tony Chew

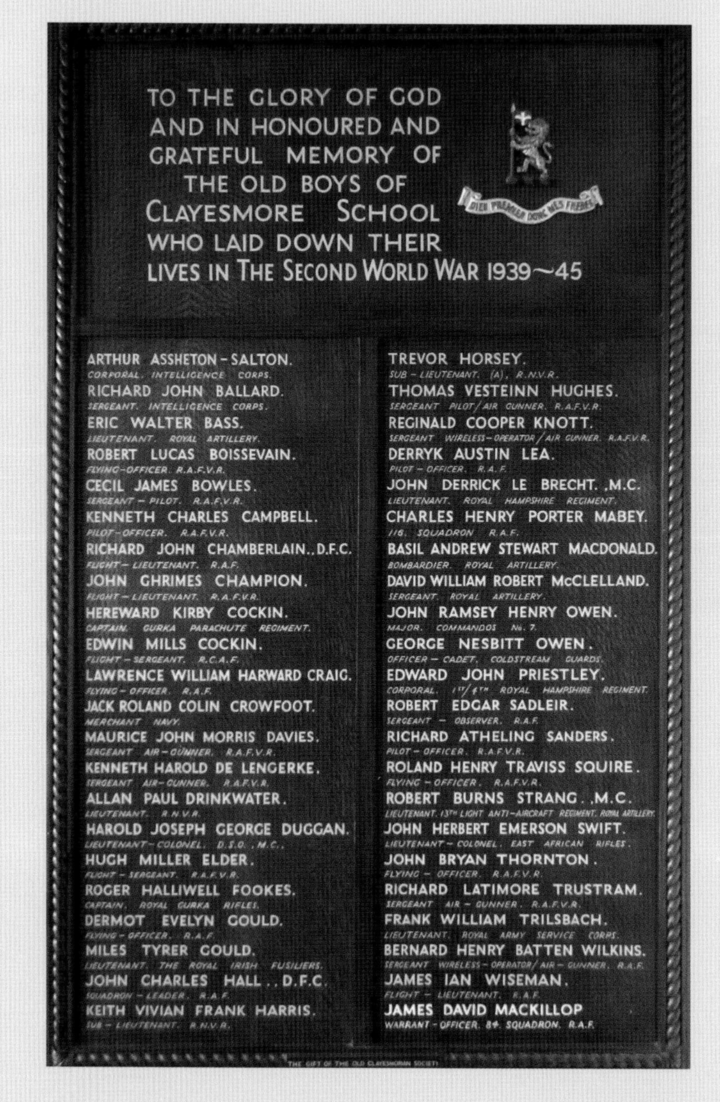

Below: Roll of Honour for the the Second World War in the Memorial Chapel at the school, a gift from the Old Clayesmorian Society.

Above: Victory Day march in London, June 8 1946.

Right: Peter Burke, the 'master' of the school from 1945.

the landing came in the evening of June 6.' VE Day was celebrated on the lake field with a bonfire and fireworks.

Perhaps the strangest, and most idiosyncratic, incident of wartime years was the decision of three adventurous members of the JTC, Bob Homan (1942–7), Michael Turner (1942–6) and Ernie Whybrow (1941–6) to represent Clayesmore at the Victory Day march through London on June 8 1946. Taking advantage of a special holiday exeat, they hitch-hiked to London and there, in battledress and forage caps, and sporting 'Clayesmore JTC' shoulder flashes, they casually fell in behind the Malta contingent assembling in Hyde Park. Explaining, quite truthfully, to stewards that they had become detached from their unit, and further explaining that 'JTC' stood for 'Jungle Training Corps', they completed the whole of the exhausting march from Marble Arch right across to the south bank of the Thames and up the Mall before slipping away from the Maltese as they reached Hyde Park again. Their reward was the privilege of giving a smart 'eyes left' to the royal family on their dais in the Mall, which also held the Prime Minister, Clement Attlee, the Canadian Prime Minister, Mackenzie King, Winston Churchill and General Smuts. None of the marshals along the route questioned the unlisted contingent just three abreast, when everyone else was in lines of twelve abreast, but seemed to regard them as just another part of that grand international military jamboree.

Post-war years

Towards the end of the war Evelyn King decided to change direction: 'By then, to me at least, the joy of morning was gone. Here was a different world, inspiring in me different ambitions, and in 1945 I put Clayesmore behind me as my principal job in life.' He was selected as the Labour candidate for Penryn and Falmouth, and duly won the seat. But his connection with Clayesmore did not end. He was asked to serve as 'warden' of the school, living there most weekends and with financial and administrative responsibility but no salary. In that capacity he worked with Peter Burke, who had joined Clayesmore in 1936 and was now to be the 'master', whose function would be the control of the school, its discipline and its teaching. King acted as warden until he lost his Parliamentary seat in 1950, when he became a governor of the school, and during his later career as a Tory MP he represented Clayesmore on the Governing Bodies Association and became a member of their inner council. When Harold Bellman retired he became chairman of the School Council, and during his later years continued his connection by becoming president.

An interesting, through short-lived, initiative immediately after the war was the establishment by the Education Committee of Dorset County Council of a bursary scheme which would allow boys from less wealthy backgrounds to attend Clayesmore, and the other Dorset public schools, as boarders. This was the result of a report commissioned by the government in 1942, 'to consider means whereby the association between the public schools and the general education system of the country could be developed and extended'. The report was submitted in June 1944, and the council held a meeting with the Dorset public school headmasters in October 1946 to consider how it might be implemented. King and Burke attended from Clayesmore, and the meeting concluded that 'able and suitable boys from less wealthy homes could be happily absorbed into public schools and attain positions of authority and responsibility… as easily as fee-payers'. It was agreed that the council would be responsible for full boarding fees for five years for a quota of boys – though

As one of four Dorset bursary boys joining Clayesmore in September 1948 (the others were Tim Hardyment, Andrew Mills and David Walton), arriving was quite a shock. I only vaguely knew one other boy at the school – John Taylor, who had entered in the first Dorset bursary intake a year earlier. I was on a full bursary from the County Council, which met board, lodging, education and books, and I enjoyed this for the whole of my five years at Clayesmore.

My family background seemed far removed from that of the other, fee-paying, boys. Both my parents had died five years earlier and I, with my elder brother, had been living with aged grandparents in Weymouth. I applied for the scholarship because my best friend, who was a year older, had succeeded a year before in getting a scholarship to Sherborne. I had not studied Latin at Weymouth Grammar School, which was required for Sherborne, so because I knew John Taylor's family slightly, I decided to try for a place at Clayesmore. My grandparents just seemed to accept my decision, although they must have been very surprised by it, as they came from the typical agricultural labourer and domestic servant family background. Going to a private school must have been beyond their comprehension.

I recall receiving the list of clothes, towels and bedding that I would need, and the instruction to get them all name-taped using Cash's tapes. I was given the school number 21 and often wondered who had been '21' before me. The next problem was a trunk and how to get it to Iwerne Minster. I think we used Pickford's to do this, but I still had to get there for the first day. By a stroke of luck a member of the local community in Weymouth, Miss Macfarlane Watt, who ran a private infants' school nearby, volunteered to drive me in her car. This was only my second ride in a car.

I seem to remember that the weather was dull but not raining when we reached the front entrance. I was greeted by Ruth Dear and then taken to meet John Appleby, the Juniors' housemaster, and then Brian Baggett, who would be the dormitory captain. Our dormitory in the main house on the second floor was for six boys, if I remember correctly; one of them was Jeremy Spoor with whom I became (and remain) friendly.

The first few days are blurred, though I recall learning where everything was: the junior common room, the chapel,

Name . . . . Number . . . .

CLAYESMORE SCHOOL.

Clothes List - Summer Term.

No. sent

1 Waterproof and/or Overcoat
1 Best Suit
Black coat and waistcoat and striped trousers (Tails for Seniors) (These are now compulsory)
* 2 School Blazers
* 2 prs. Standard Navy Shorts
* 3 Standard Grey Sports Shirts
* 2 School Pullovers
2 White Shirts without Collars
3 prs. Pyjamas
3 prs. Pants
3 Vests
12 Handkerchiefs
3 Soft White Collars
2 prs. Black Socks
* 4 prs. School Stockings
* 1 School Tie
* 1 Black Tie
* 1 School Cap
* 1 pr. Dungarees
1 Dressing-gown
* 1 Shoe-cleaning Outfit
1 pr. Bedroom Slippers
1 pr. White Gym. Shoes
1 pr. House Shoes
2 prs. Walking Shoes
1 Bathing Suit
6 doz. Cash's Name Tapes (1st Term only)

No. sent.

Hair brush and comb; clothes brush, tooth-brush and paste, nail scissors, face flannel, sponge bag, studs in stud box, garters.

For GAMES, etc.
* 1 Blue Kit Bag
* 1 White Sweater
* 2 White Running Vests
* 2 prs. Running Shorts
1 pr. Cricket Shoes or Boots
1 pr. Grey Flannel Trousers
1 pr. White " " (3 prs. if likely to be in Junior Colts or 1st XI)
* 3 White Sports Shirts
3 prs. White Socks

LINEN
2 prs. Sheets
3 Pillow Cases
3 Bath Towels
2 Coloured Towels for Games
1 Rug

* Items marked thus are obtainable from the Matron, and in the case of new boys, will be supplied on arrival.

School Scarves are also obtainable, but these are optional.

EACH ARTICLE MUST BE PLAINLY MARKED with Cash's Name Tapes (full name and number. This particularly applies to hair-, clothes-, and tooth-brushes, face flannel, sponge bag, etc. as, unless marked, it is impossible to identify these. BOOTS & SHOES MUST BE MARKED with the boy's NUMBER in brass brads underneath the shoe.

OPTIONAL: Tennis, Badminton and Squash Racquets (useful to boys who wish to take part in these games).
Rubber Wellington Boots ; Tuck Boxes with lock and key.
Bicycles are permitted and are entirely the owners' responsibility.

Each boy should carry with him a HANDBAG containing what is necessary for the first night, i.e. pyjamas, bedroom slippers, washing materials, hair-brush, comb.

This List should be accurately filled in and placed on top of the clothes in the trunk.

EVERYTHING NECESSARY FOR THE TERM IS INCLUDED IN THIS LIST AND IT IS REQUESTED THAT NO EXTRA CLOTHING BE SENT.

Above: A summer term clothing list from the 1940s.

Above: The clear-up begins in the Burney Library following the fire in 1947.

with the hope that means-testing their families might make some contribution possible – and that they would select at age 13 on the basis of intellectual capacity, character and 'future value to the community'. The scheme started in 1947, in which year four boys went to Clayesmore with bursaries, followed by four in 1948, two in 1949 and one in 1950.

The total number of places on offer when the scheme started was 22, including two places at Eton. This was a remarkable commitment by Dorset County Council in those years of post-war austerity, when fees were £200 a year at the four Dorset schools and £350 at Eton. The scheme was lamented when it ceased in 1950; Blandford St Mary Parish Council is on record as having minuted its deep disapproval of 'the fact that the public school scholarships were ever discontinued. They think that economies could have been made in other directions and trust that the present policy will be rescinded and the scholarships in question renewed.'

The divided responsibility at the top did not last many years, and Peter Burke as master was to reign over a period of gentle stability until his retirement in 1966 – although his tenure started with a sensational fire in the library that could have had a considerably worse outcome had not the

the dining room and the various classrooms. Clayesmore quickly became my real home and I enjoyed the five years at Iwerne. Naturally there are some criticisms, but what I gained from Clayesmore outweighed these. The school was not good academically in those days; life was too easy. If you had natural ability you could achieve great things, but with no parents to push me I think I innocently assumed that the masters would ensure I achieved as much as possible. This was not so. Alec Coles, the senior maths teacher, could teach only at the speed of the brightest pupil; in my case that was Chengi Kuo, and the rest were left floundering in his wake. A further example of this lack of pressure was my housemaster's report for the spring term of 1953, just before my final term and my A levels. Humphrey Moore wrote, 'I am not sure he works hard enough', which was surely too little too late, and passed responsibility for my prowess to my 78-year-old grandmother, who anyway cared only that I got a good behaviour report. When, in my senior year with David Spinney as housemaster, my report read 'A pillar of church and state and a shining example of unimpeachable rectitude', she was overjoyed. What she did not know was that Spinney had three standard housemaster's reports, and we all got one of these a term.

Clayesmore at that time bestowed on its boys one really great virtue – tolerance. Leaving in July 1953 was a real wrench; the school had been my home for five years and I was ill-equipped to go out into the world. It had also shielded me from some of the realities of life. For example, the language I encountered during my National Service was a great surprise to me; I had never heard such words and did not know what they meant, which was a great source of amusement to those sharing my billet. In some ways this summarises Clayesmore, Iwerne Minster and north Dorset in those early post-war years. It was an idyll; the nation was in a poor state, food was rationed until 1951, but I, for one, was never really conscious of this. I still consider Iwerne Minster one of the most beautiful places on earth.

John Dukes (1948–53)

Right: Lloyd, Beryl and Brian Arpel, mid-1950s. Brian Arpel, an OC, went on to set up the first Australian reunion *(see p150)*.

Ruth Dear (1945–87)

Born in 1913, Ruth Verling Dear always wanted to work with children and so trained as a nanny. Her first post was with the Robertson family, of jam fame, but she wanted to travel, so accompanied the young children of the Fleming family to India. Her association with the Flemings was to last many years, and the children she looked after 60 years previously were at the memorial service held for her at St Mary's, Iwerne Minster, after her death in 2011, aged nearly 98.

Her first post as a school matron was in Darjeeling, where she worked for several years, before returning to Britain at the end of the war armed with a letter of recommendation from the Anglican vicar of St Andrew's, Darjeeling, to his brother, Evelyn King, the headmaster of Clayesmore. Here, the letter said, was a matron of superlative quality who must be snapped up immediately. She was to spend the rest of her working life at the school, 42 years in charge of all the non-catering domestic staff, and was to live after retirement at Iwerne until her death, still involved with Clayesmore and all its doings.

Roger Kingwill, a new boy in 1945, maintained a close friendship with Ruth until her death, and gave an address at her memorial service: 'For her first 22 years Clayesmore had a bachelor headmaster and no other female member of staff resident in the school. Showing prudence and absolute loyalty at all times, she was the feminine influence in the community, to the great advantage of its members. She never exceeded her position, and had a special "way with men" (the words give quite the wrong impression!) – never arch, never intrusive, always respectful of the privacy of the misogynists. She brought grace and composure, firm opinions but never challenge. Her deep loyalty led to deep friendships with an extensive family of Clayesmorians, and her own dedication inspired that of her staff. She was respected by the academic staff for her judgement and her intellectual and cultural contribution, with her interests in poetry, porcelain, painting, music and furniture.'

New pupils remember meeting her on their arrival, often with her large black and white cat, Andy, draped round her shoulders, and being made to feel immediately welcome. She was responsible for laundering and mending all the pupils' clothes and for the general housekeeping, and she and her team were also always on hand to help with social functions. She was a noted seamstress and was an integral part of Carl Verrinder's drama productions. Most male costumes were hired, but all the female dresses were designed and made in the school sewing rooms, using Ruth's library of books of period costumes. She was also responsible for the make-up, and was particularly skilled at 'making scruffy boys look like beautiful women.'

She carried on looking after her former Clayesmore colleagues when they retired. Roger Kingwill paid tribute to her enormous capacity for hands-on help and devotion to, among others, Norris Scadding, John Appleby and David Spinney in their new homes near Marlborough and at Shroton and Iwerne. She was the first female Honorary OC ever, and he remembers parties celebrating her 70th birthday, 50 years at Clayesmore and her 90th birthday.

Below: Ruth Dear turns 'a scruffy boy into a beautiful woman'.

boys in the Junior dormitory smelt smoke and raised the alarm. This was during the exceptionally cold winter of 1946/7, and it was probably the embers of the huge log fire in the library fireplace that ignited the floorboards nearby. The school's water pump was away being repaired, and anyway the lily pond, from which the water would have been drawn, was frozen over; moreover, tins of polish stored in the library were emitting a vile, greasy smoke, and the school telephone line was down. Typical Clayesmore resourcefulness took over. Some boys flagged down a car and found a telephone from which they alerted the fire brigade. Those shivering outside at the roll call were found to be short of a few Juniors, who were located, safe but cut off by smoke on a balcony, whereupon a senior boy led a brave rescue equipped with props from the theatre. Meanwhile, amid all the noise and chaos, a tall, dressing-gowned figure was seen to emerge from a first-floor window on to the library roof and then to a fire escape ladder; it was the master, who had somehow been overlooked.

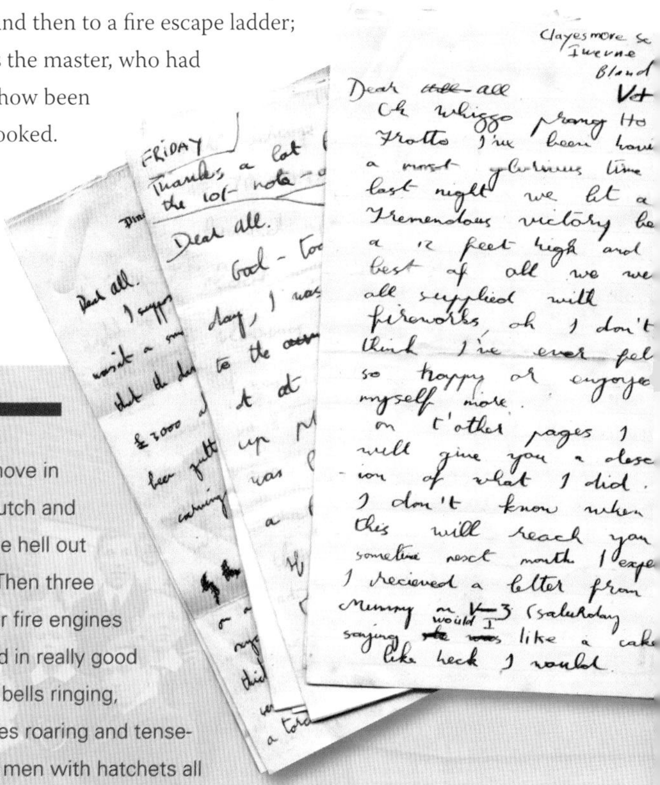
Clayesmore Sc
Iwerne
Bland
Dear all
Oh whizzo prang Ho Frotto I've been havi a most glorious time last night we lit a tremendous victory bo a 12 feet high and best of all we we all supplied with fireworks, oh I don't think I've ever fel so happy or enjoye myself more. On t'other pages I will give you a desc-ion of what I did. I don't know when this will reach you sometime next month I expe I recieved a letter from Mummy on saying would I like a cake like heck I would.

Right: Letters home from Peter Wightman.

Letters home

I suppose Father told you about the fire we had… It wasn't a small one, by God! Capt Cunningham has said that the damage done is estimated at something like £3,000 at the very least. The whole library has been gutted. All the irreplaceable oak panelling, carvings, and books, have gone. Several juniors and seniors were cut off, and our PT instructor, Sgt Aldworth, put on an oxygen mask and rescued them by taking a bag of oxygen with him. You see they were only cut off by the thick black smoke.

First thing I knew was when Hart, a Senior, came running in my dormitory and shouting for a torch at half past four in the morning. He gasped out that the library was on fire. I, and several other Middles, darted up to Tower Dorm, and from there we could see, sure enough, that the library was just one mass of flame.

I ran back to my dorm, shoved on a pair of trousers and a pullover, and with half of the Middles, sprinted over to the other side, and Denny Mi and myself grabbed a stirrup pump and sweated out our guts for about an hour – or so it seemed. Actually, it was only 33 minutes. I had always longed to smash a big window, and brother! when Burke goes around in his dressing gown and asked me to, I don't say maybe.

However, I wasn't in the library long as a few little details like chunks of roof coming down, and bits of floor giving way, coupled with the tremendous heat and smoke, made me shove in my clutch and get the hell out of it. Then three or four fire engines arrived in really good style; bells ringing, engines roaring and tense-faced men with hatchets all over 'em, clinging like grim death to the running boards.

By now dawn was breaking and all the Middles had been sent back but for me, I must have escaped notice. When I got back I found there had been a roll-call, and Karren had gone looking for me. I dived into bed and didn't get up till almost 10.30. We did no work that day except help clean and wash the walls of the main building which were covered with soot. I didn't get hurt except for a couple of burns on my hands.

***

Oh God yes, this is rather important, I've given my name into Mr Karren to go to Switzerland with him in the summer holidays, with a couple of other Clayesmore boys. It's a sort of hiking trip right through Switzerland. The total cost, everything included, that is boat, train, hotel, food, etc, is about £18. Jolly reasonable, isn't it?

Peter Wightman (1944–8)

David Spinney recalled that there was 'something pleasantly stable and permanent about Clayesmore in Peter Burke's time. Year after year the same familiar events came round – the carol service, the usual sporting fixtures, all with their places in the yearly cycle, and their prescribed routine... Year after year there were the same faces on the staff... and year after year there was an endless supply of boys, only more and more of them, until there was no room in the school and the overflow had to be bedded out at Oyles Mill down the road.' There were clubs and societies, some the usual offering covering stamps, photography, films and jazz, others more specialist such as the Archaeological Ramblers or the Society of Heraldic Antiquaries founded by John Brooke-Little, later an eminent herald. Roger Kingwill established the Young Farmers' Club in 1947, and there were several sailing and nautical societies. Generations of boys acquired a lifelong love of music through hours spent sitting on the floor in Reggie Sessions' room before he retired in 1957 (and died only a few months later in Tasmania).

Above: The Ship Club, *c*1947.

Opposite: Poetry Club minutes.

The printing press

One of the activities much enjoyed by the post-war generation was the school's own printing press, which was used to produce small booklets and other material. Modest though the output was, it gave a great deal of pleasure both to the writers and printers and to their readers. John Appleby oversaw the operation, and it was he who wrote the introduction to one of the surviving booklets, *Shadows and Reflections by the Fourth and Shell Forms, 1944–1945*: 'These reflections from behind the bars were written during the Christmas term of 1944 by small carnivorous mammals placed here in captivity – most of them – in the September of that year. They are I think genuine reflections of the wild animal, and present a true picture of what he sees and feels before the close of the prison house doors... If a copy of this book should come into the hands of an Authority, I hope he will read it with sympathy and intelligence. He was perhaps once rather like that. Remembering, he may be more understanding... It is set in Eric Gill's Perpetua type, and was hand set and printed at the Clayesmore School Press in 1945.' There follows an example of the many short entries in this small booklet (with its original spelling): 'It is very perculiar but in a few minutes after Grace I always want to say something and I can hardly wait till the bell gos to say it. I suppose the reason is that you notice it more than you woud if you could talk when there is nothing unusual in it.' The entry is signed *Godfrey* & Teed, the italicised name being the writer of the piece and the other the compositor.

There was a meeting of the Poetry Club on Sunday, 21st November. Members read their own compositions. For the second week in succession the reading of our poems did not take as long as usual. Mr Appleby, however, continued his "Saga of Saint Winifred's" with three more enlightening satires on school life, and these evoked a discussion upon the nature of satire and its limitations as works of art. The absence of Mr Moore was universally regretted — especially in this connection. The following members were present:

Whittaker; Bushen; Elliott who read "An Ode to Wayman" — the second one on this subject; Fisher; and Mr Wayman; Criswell who read "The Castle"; and Appleby who read "Girls Will Be Girls" and "The Padre".

It was decided in addition to hold a business meeting within the near future to consider the question of the election of new members. For next Sunday's meeting it was agreed that the Secretary should ask Mr Richardson to read extracts from Chaucer's "Canterbury Tales". The meeting adjourned at 9:10 pm.

signed [signature] (sec.).

J. Appleby 20/xii/48

The Rules of the Poetry Club.

Rule of Entry: If any vacancies occur new members shall be admitted if approved by all members of the Poetry Club. The number of members is limited to the seating accomodation of Mr Appleby's room.

Purpose of the Club: To read write and criticise poetry. Meetings shall be held for these purposes according to the wishes of the members. The quorum for a meeting is four. Published poems and members' compositions shall be read alternately.

On the resignation of the Secretary the club shall elect another to write the minutes and do the general business of the club.

(Drawn up on Sept 25th).

A. Bright-Paul.
(Hon. Sec.)

The thirteenth meeting of the Poetry Club was held on Sunday 4th March 1945 at 8 p.m.

At this meeting members read their own poetry which showed a marked improvement on any previous work. The work has been collected, and has been placed with the other poems in the custody of the President.

It was decided that no meeting would be held if less than four members were present.

Brooke-Little promised to read, at the next meeting, some poetry by Swinburne; and after partaking of some tea, kindly provided by the President, the meeting was adjourned at 9.25 p.m.

(Signed)

CAS Wood. Hon. Sec.

J. H. Appleby
18th March 1945

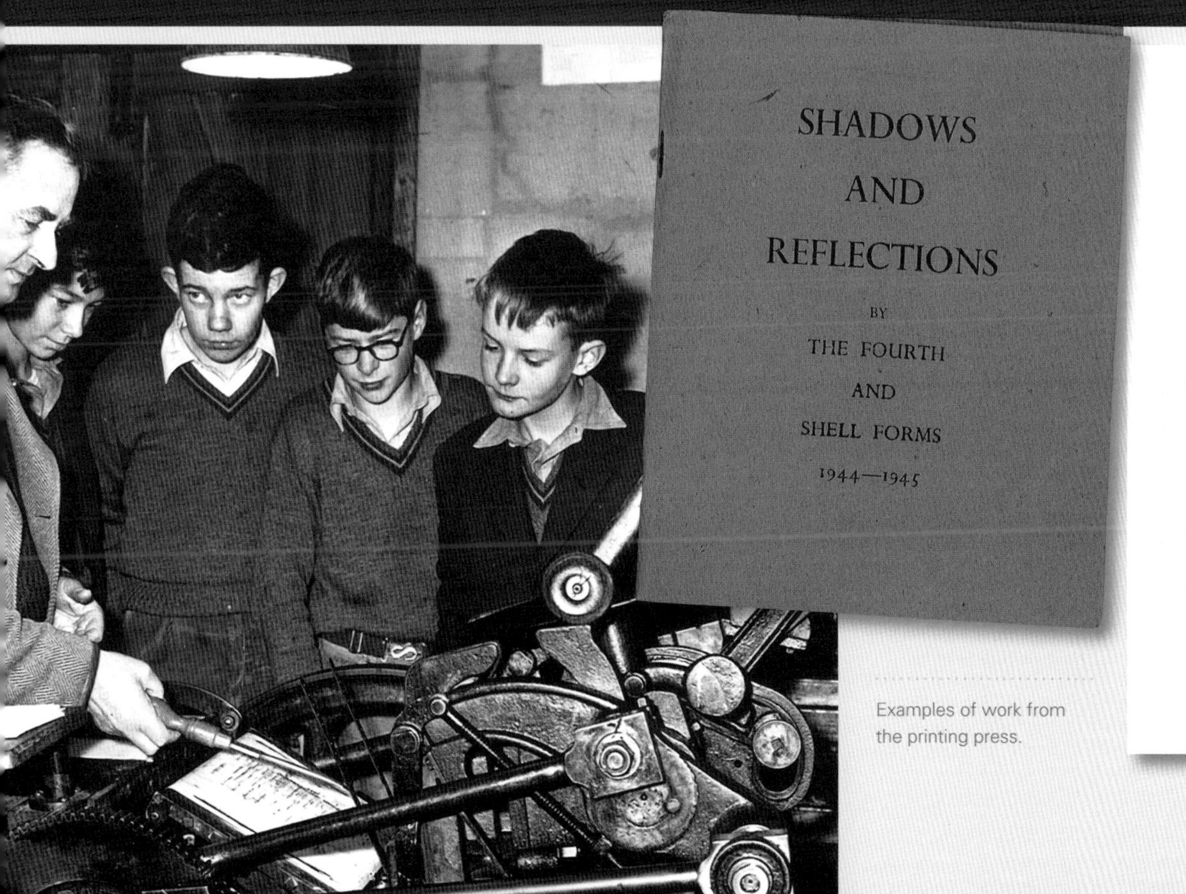
SHADOWS
AND
REFLECTIONS
BY
THE FOURTH
AND
SHELL FORMS
1944—1945

The Clayesmorian

EDITORIAL

THE publication of this issue of the CLAYESMORIAN marks the end of the first year of printing it on the School Press. We cannot, and do not, claim to have reached perfection in printing the CLAYESMORIAN, but we shall go on trying. We are especially anxious not to revert to the old plan of having our printing done for us, as very few other schools have printing presses of their own, and Claysmore has always been a pioneer. Everyone enjoys printing who knows how to print; even those who don't sometimes amuse themselves with a composing stick—but we are very grateful for all the help we have received in the printing of the CLAYESMORIAN and would be loth to turn away offers.

☘ ☘ ☘ ☘

Examples of work from the printing press.

Extracts from Lake Warfare: A Complete History

September 1948–February 1953

To that great generation of fighters that made Lake Warfare possible, this book is dedicated (Spittal, Seddon, Rathbone, Farrow, Sutcliffe-Hey, Wilkins, Rogers, Swan).

Greatest fighters of Lake History (*not* in order of merit)

Rathbone	24 battles to his credit
Farrow	23
Rogers	17
Kelly	16
Sutcliffe-Hey	15
Wilkins	12
Wilmot	11
Spittal	10
Seddon	9

The author took part in 29 lake battles.

When I arrived at Clayesmore for the first time, on Monday September 20 1948, the lake was slowly recovering from a long period of domination under the tyrannical George Goldie. It appears that his activities centred for the most part about Swan Island (now named after Goldie). On this island he built a hut with the aid of his nefarious henchmen. They were equipped with two rubber dinghies… and had contrived to obtain a couple of rifles (.22) and ammunition. They fortified Goldie's island with barbed wire and terrorised the lake from there. Farrow once ventured into the Willow Copse, but soon left when a bullet zipped past his ear and thudded into a tree. This crew were slightly mad…

At 20.30 Gillett and I went down to the lake. It was not long before I spied a large force on the north shore of the Haven in a very threatening position to our base on Scout. Accordingly I went forward and the enemy prepared to resist our attack. Farrow and Raphael discharged their bows at us before retiring past the Boat House to join the remainder. We noticed that the enemy had retired to their base at the willow tree, where lay *Erebus*. I shelled them for a few minutes, but the gathering gloom compelled me to retire. This little skirmish was to have grave results – total war.

[Lake Warfare went on until November 9 1952, when the author described the final operations against the Rathbonians.] Towards 14.00 the rival forces started to gather. I had no fears concerning my men, who all arrived at the appointed hour; I doubted however that all of the enemy would turn up owing to the rain. This was so, but enemy opposition was strengthened by the cooperation of a fairly large force of Juniors. The battle about to take place proved unique since for the first time it was commentated upon and broadcast by portable wireless sets (walkie-talkies)… [There followed a long account of

Below: An extract from Michael Peyron's Lake Warfare book, kept in the school archives.

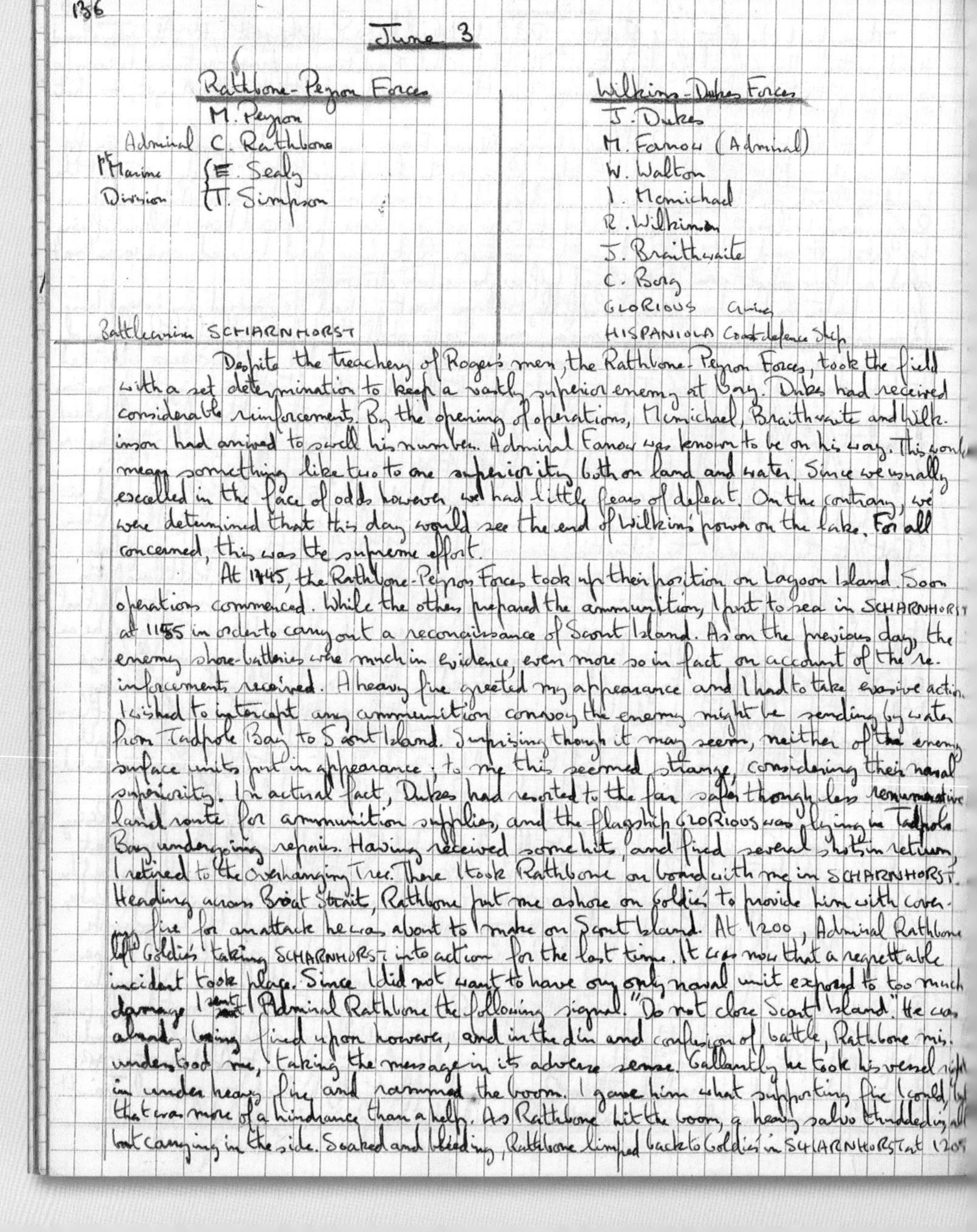

136

June 3

	Rathbone-Peyron Forces	Wilkins-Dukes Forces
	M. Peyron	J. Dukes
Admiral	C. Rathbone	M. Farrow (Admiral)
1st Marine Division	E. Sealy	W. Walton
	T. Simpson	I. Mcmichael
		R. Wilkinson
		J. Braithwaite
		C. Borg
		GLORIOUS [illegible]
Battlecruiser	SCHARNHORST	HISPANIOLA Coast defence Ship

Despite the treachery of Roger's men, the Rathbone-Peyron Forces, took the field with a set determination to keep a vastly superior enemy at bay. Dukes had received considerable reinforcements. By the opening of operations, Mcmichael, Braithwaite and Wilkinson had arrived to swell his numbers. Admiral Farrow was known to be on his way. This would mean something like two to one superiority both on land and water. Since we usually excelled in the face of odds however, we had little fears of defeat. On the contrary, we were determined that this day would see the end of Wilkins' power on the lake. For all concerned, this was the supreme effort.

At 1145, the Rathbone-Peyron Forces took up their position on Lagoon Island. Soon operations commenced. While the others prepared the ammunition, I put to sea in SCHARNHORST at 1155 in order to carry out a reconnaissance of Scout Island. As on the previous day, the enemy shore-batteries were much in evidence, even more so in fact on account of the reinforcements received. A heavy fire greeted my appearance and I had to take evasive action. I wished to intercept any ammunition convoy the enemy might be sending by water from Tadpole Bay to Scout Island. Surprising though it may seem, neither of the enemy surface units put in appearance; to me this seemed strange, considering their naval superiority. In actual fact, Dukes had resorted to the far safer though less remunerative land route for ammunition supplies, and the flagship GLORIOUS was lying in Tadpole Bay undergoing repairs. Having received some hits, and fired several shots in return, I retired to the Overhanging Tree. There I took Rathbone on board with me in SCHARNHORST. Heading across Boat Strait, Rathbone put me ashore on Goldie's to provide him with covering fire for an attack he was about to make on Scout Island. At 1200, Admiral Rathbone left Goldie's taking SCHARNHORST into action for the last time. It was now that a regrettable incident took place. Since I did not want to have our only naval unit exposed to too much damage I sent Admiral Rathbone the following signal: "Do not close Scout Island." He was already being fired upon however, and in the din and confusion of battle, Rathbone misunderstood me, taking the message in its adverse sense. Gallantly he took his vessel right in under heavy fire and rammed the boom. I gave him what supporting fire I could, but that was more of a hindrance than a help. As Rathbone hit the boom, a heavy salvo thudded in, all but caving in the side. Soaked and bleeding, Rathbone limped back to Goldie's in SCHARNHORST at 1205

the battle.] What enemy elements were found at Tadpole Bay seemed indisposed to fighting and, the remainder having dispersed, the arrival of General Dyer was the signal for the cessation of hostilities. In a significant gesture to denote the passing of Lake Warfare, I threw my ammunition container into the lake. Thus had the Rathbonians, it is true in the absence of their C-in-C, been once more worsted and our supremacy on the lake was finally established, having as its symbol the impregnable fortress of Lagoon Island... This proved the last lake battle of my time at Clayesmore...

[There was a sequel: on leaving Clayesmore, Peyron appointed Spittal as Admiral of the Fleet] Now in January 1953 he became Dictator, which rank I had bestowed on him. Spittal was a hardened veteran, well versed in lake matters, and I felt he would uphold my course with loyalty... Following a whim of his, Spittal fired Goldie's Island to celebrate his victory [against the Rathbonians]. All that night the undergrowth and trees burned, together with *Tirpitz*. Next morning only smoke in billowing clouds rose from the lake. It was this sight that met the school's gaze. Many enquiries were made, and the master even spoke of it when giving out notices at lunch. None of the people involved spoke up, however, and a very baffled master had to be satisfied with the explanation that this was either the work of poachers or that Peyron's ghost had come back to the scene of his activities... Thus the last battle of Lake Warfare ended. It had been brutal, thorough and merciless.

Written and illustrated by M Peyron

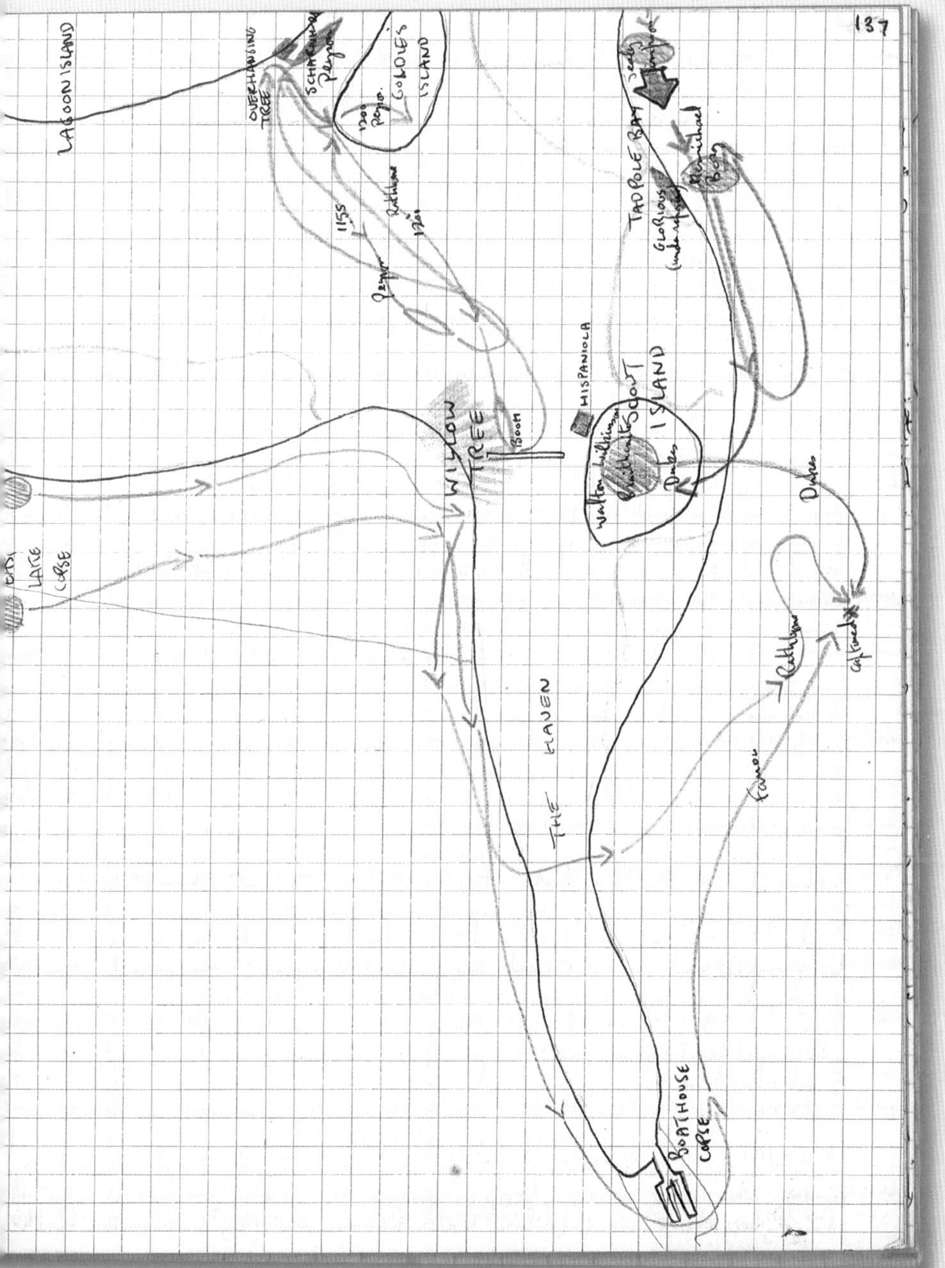

Most Clayesmorian of all, perhaps, was Lake Warfare which, with no masters involved at all, kept 20 or 30 enthusiasts gloriously happy every Sunday evening during the spring, summer and autumn campaigning seasons between 1948 and 1952. Every feature of the lake was named, used and fought over; amphibious and naval operations employed punts, rafts and canoes, with catapults and drainpipe bazookas dispatching mud ball bullets; the winter months were devoted to building larger and more effective craft for the following year; and it was all minutely and conscientiously logged in a detailed account (now in the school archive). Michael Peyron (1948–52) was the presiding genius, James Seddon (1948–54), later to be headmaster of Clayesmore Preparatory School, was one of his loyal lieutenants and his most formidable opponent was Julian Rathbone (1948–53) (*see box on p72*), later to be a prolific writer of fiction within a number of literary genres; two of his novels were shortlisted for the Booker Prize. It was only when this generation left Clayesmore that peace returned once more to the lake.

How Clayesmore helped to make a writer

Clayesmore's presence in what I have written? Most writers deny that they base the characters they invent on real people, not least because of the fear of litigation, but I'll take a risk... The central character of one of my novels is a spy who travels across Turkey in to Russia; well, my best friend at Clayesmore took the Russian option with the Royal Navy for his National Service and then disappeared, only to resurface ten years later as a prep school teacher on the Welsh borders. He later wrote to me: 'I think you've written a book about me...'.

Then there was Humphrey Moore, about whom I had very mixed feelings; he appears twice in one of my books, once as a grossly unlikeable housemaster and once as the eminently likeable teacher who opened up the hero's eyes to the injustices of pre-war society. And my book about Harold, *The Last English King*, includes a housecarl called Walt who was born and brought up in Iwerne and falls in love with a girl from Shroton, having 'dallied' with her on Hambledon Hill.

At the end of the day it is not the particular that counts. Whatever gift I have for writing was stimulated and rewarded at Clayesmore by publication in the *Miscellany* and the *Clayesmorian*, by poetry and story-writing prizes and above all by the teaching and friendship of the man we called Uncle Apples. A love of landscape and a good eye for it came from Scadding and an appreciation that history is made by people from David Spinney – and you'll find a lot of history in my books.

Above all – a love and respect for all humanity, a hatred of anything that stunts and destroys, a cheerful, easy-going hedonism. Some would say too easy-going. When you've been taught to enjoy life you don't go out into the world hungry to make an impression or screw the opposition, and enjoying life is what Clayesmore taught me more than anything else.

Julian Rathbone (1948–53)

Above: Julian Rathbone.

Above left: *The Last English King* by Rathbone, first published in 1997.

Above: The dining room under construction in 1960.

Above: The Memorial Chapel windows.

Above: The chapel dedication service, November 7 1956.

Above right: Chapel service in 2007.

Right: Service sheet from the 1956 dedication.

The chapel, built by staff, pupils and local craftspeople as a memorial to Old Clayesmorians killed in both 20th-century world wars, was dedicated in November 1956 and housed the memorial windows which had been painstakingly moved from Northwood Park, to the Devine Memorial Chapel in the grounds (now demolished) and to their current location.

There was plenty more new building during Burke's headship, including an extension to the stable block, a new dining hall, a boys' house and a more fitting residence for the headmaster, both of the latter completed in 1966. But times were changing, and were about to become challenging to the boarding school tradition. At the time of Burke's retirement at the end of the summer term of 1966, the roll was full; but enrolments for the years ahead were looking disturbingly sparse. A new broom was required.

CLAYESMORE SCHOOL

†

Dedication

of

The Memorial Chapel

by

William, Lord Bishop of Salisbury

WEDNESDAY, 7th NOVEMBER, 1956

Starlings and Humphrey Moore

During my years at Clayesmore I was a natural history enthusiast under the encouragement of Humphrey Moore, the Middles housemaster. We were given a lot of freedom to roam the countryside on our bicycles. Humphrey was renowned for his study of toad migration to spawn in the lake. He would keep a tally of road kill between the Talbot Inn and the watercress beds. He was keen to put together a collection of moths, which he collected in a night light moth trap. Not to be outdone, we boys collected and mounted the district's butterflies.

The biology department was registered to ring birds and I think the rings were supplied by the British Museum. Our main ringing activity centred on starlings in winter. They assembled in vast flocks from all round the district prior to roosting. In order to find the roosting place we would frantically follow small flocks at dusk on our bikes, up the steep hill behind Iwerne Minster and down into Cranborne Chase. The starlings roosted in a dense hazelwood copse, which was a dirty smelly place, as the ground was covered thickly in droppings.

We would raid the football changing room to collect half a dozen long socks that had been left lying about. On a moonlit Saturday night we would set off for the roost armed with these socks, a torch and the rings. There was a constant cacophony of chattering starlings as we waded into the dropping-laden roost. The boughs were bent down with the weight of birds, so it was a simple matter of grabbing birds, shoving them into one of the socks tied round our waists, retreating to the edge of the roost, extracting a starling from the sock and putting a ring on its leg. Back at school we would return the socks to the changing room, a little dirtier and smellier than before if that is possible for boys' footy socks!

David Hammersley (1954–8)

David Spinney, inspirational teacher

A few years ago the BBC asked a number of distinguished people including the then prime minister to name a school teacher who had influenced them in early life. If anyone had asked me I wouldn't have hesitated; I would have named David Spinney.

When I arrived at Clayesmore in the early 1950s the school was a little bit like Hogwarts. It had an academic staff who seemed to have been there forever and to have become part of the fabric of the buildings. In particular there were the three housemasters: John Appleby, the man who taught me the basics of good English writing, Humphrey Moore, inspirational biology teacher and rigid disciplinarian, and senior housemaster David Spinney. I also remember Carl Verrinder, a real-life mad professor, and Norris Scadding, the chaplain and art teacher. But above all there was Spinney. John David Spinney, or JDS, not only taught history, he was a real historian, his speciality the British Royal Navy. It was Spinney who wrote the definitive biography of Admiral Rodney, and of course Clayesmore's official history.

In my earlier years at Clayesmore Spinney was a rather frightening figure. His largely mock rages at the fifth form history classes for forgetting century dates and muddling periods were something to behold. He would lean back in his chair with an exasperated sigh. 'Here am I sweating my guts out…' was the much mimicked beginning of one of his famous tirades. It was only when I reached his sixth form A level group that I began to appreciate, like and revere this man. JDS conducted sixth form history very much as an Oxbridge tutor would. We would gather, just six or seven of us, in his study maybe four times a week with intervening periods of private study and essay writing. It was here that history became exciting and inspiring. I learned a delight for the past that has never left me.

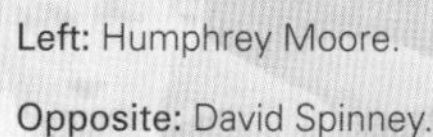

Left: Humphrey Moore.

Opposite: David Spinney.

But it was through the sport of sailing that I really came to know this man. I am proud to this day to have been a member of his 1956 trophy-winning sailing team. Our famous demolition of Canford in the final race was mainly down to the Rogers brothers, but it was a big moment in all our young lives.

One day that I will never forget was the time four of us helped JDS motor his yacht *Seaflower* up the Wareham Channel to a boatyard for some repairs. Halfway there I was the man at the helm and in the winding channel in front of us was a huge, very slow gin palace of a motor yacht. It was clear that we couldn't go any slower and the yacht in front couldn't go any faster. In two minutes we would be overtaking on a blind bend. 'Oh sir, sir, please take the tiller…' I pleaded. My panic was not helped when one of my fellow crew identified the burgee on the yacht in front as the Law Society Yacht Club.

JDS shook his head. He adopted his Hornblower pose as he addressed all of us. 'I am sure,' he said, 'that we all have every confidence in Morley to see us through.' He then turned to me and said something that has remained a sailing rule to me ever since. 'Remember, Morley, it is always better to hit the mud than the other boat.' We safely overtook the super yacht and Spinney gave them a jaunty wave.

There is one famous occasion that I know is fixed in the memory of everyone who was present. One summer evening the Senior House was ordered to a meeting in the common room. We crowded in there, puzzled and slightly worried. JDS entered and fixed us with his maximum scowl. 'This afternoon,' he began, 'I was invited to take tea with the headmistress of Croft House.' He glared again as a titter of nervous laughter spread through the room. 'It is not funny! The lady informed me that two of her girls had been having improper relations with two of my boys.' He glared at us again. 'I told the lady, and may I be forgiven, that nothing untoward could possibly have happened as all my boys are perfect gentlemen. But she told me that she disliked all men and in particular she disliked my boys.'

JDS scowled once more around the room. 'All right, who was it?' Two hearty rugger types sheepishly raised their hands. 'Yes, I thought so,' said Spinney. 'Look here, the world is full of beautiful girls. Now this afternoon's experience was a very harrowing one, so if only for my sake will you please take your base instincts somewhere else.'

Yes, Spinney was irascible but this was I believe largely his trademark. Behind the scowl was a warm personality and a waspish sense of humour. It is significant that, as far as I could tell, almost every boy who was in that room that day was present years later at Spinney's memorial service. It was a tribute to a fine teacher, a motivator and, I believe, a great man.

James (Jim) Morley (1952–6)

In the summer, when all the boys in the Junior House were tucked up in bed and lights were out, it was the custom for my husband David (their housemaster) and me to take a leisurely stroll round the grounds. This perambulation would first of all, surprisingly enough, take us straight to the cricket pitch, so that David, who was in charge of the First XI and fanatical about cricket, could inspect every blade of grass. As this took quite a long time, I would sit under the lime trees and become poetic. I wrote this on one such evening:

Clayesmore: one summer evening
Soft and mysterious evening falls
Owls are hooting their nightly calls
In the distance hills are dim
Swathed in mist, enfolding them
The air is warm with fragrant lime
Life stands still, gone is time.
Down by the lake a moorhen cries
Breaking the stillness, and then dies
Vivid the sky and the setting sun
Telling us that the day is done
The hills throw out a ghostly light
The moon shines bright into the night.

One early morning in the 1960s, as we were lying in bed in the Annexe (as it was then called), we woke to see shadows moving across the curtains and we heard the sound of hoofs. We leaped out of bed and saw a herd of cows passing our house and making for the headmaster's house and, in all probability, the cricket wicket! Fortunately for us, as we were grabbing some walking sticks, we saw Dick Hunt, the farmer, arriving in hot pursuit. A catastrophe was averted.

Alison Watkins

I was at Clayesmore with Tore Jørn Moldung, who was later to become head boy and who is still a close friend. When he came to Clayesmore at the age of 12 or 13 he knew very little English, but within the space of a term became completely fluent and spoke with flawless pronunciation and grammar. When we were in the Upper Vth David Watkins, a new Latin master, arrived. One day during his first few

weeks he was taking us for Caesar's *Gallic Wars* and it was Moldung's turn to read from the Latin text. After he had finished, Mr Watkins noticed Moldung hesitating, and asked him if he found the Latin difficult. 'No,' said Moldung, 'but sometimes I find the English difficult'. 'What do you mean?' said Watkins, who had never guessed that Moldung was not English through and through. 'Well you see, I'm not English, I'm Norwegian.' 'I say,' Watkins replied, 'bad luck!' We have always remembered this and it is usually my first greeting to Tore Jørn when we meet – though of course we immediately knew that it was not being Norwegian that was 'bad luck'.

Bruce Ingham (1956–60)

I was a very new boy in the autumn term of 1952, and early one Sunday morning found myself as a young treble choirboy in the front pew of the choir section of the school chapel, which was full with pupils and teachers. I began to feel horribly faint (I probably hadn't had any breakfast) and groped towards the end of the pew. At that point I put my arms out to steady myself, hit the bible stand, which crashed to the floor, and followed it down as I had completely blacked out. I understand there was a brief silence while I was removed and the stand and bible reinstated before the service continued. I regained consciousness outside in the fresh air, none the worse for the experience. As a new boy I would not have expected to be known by many, but after that performance I was probably known by a few more.

David Clay (1952–6)

Right: Roy McIsaac.

Testing times

There were 20 fewer pupils at the school at the beginning of Roy McIsaac's first autumn term as headmaster than there had been at the end of Peter Burke's headship the term before. Five years later numbers had fallen by nearly 50 more. Stalwarts on the staff were soon to retire or die, and the changing world was to have its effect on the traditions and conduct of the school. Above all, the finances were not in good shape; major economies and cutbacks would be necessary, and if the school was to survive it would need to haul itself into the modern world.

Carl Verrinder (1932–74)

Appointed by Aubrey de Selincourt in 1932 while Clayesmore was still at Northwood Park, Carl Verrinder was one of that breed of public school masters who developed an abiding love of and loyalty to an institution and devoted his whole life to it. The same is true of his wife Eleanor, who filled her roles as headmaster's secretary and lab assistant with admirable ease, and also demonstrated her artistic talents by illustrating some of de Selincourt's children's novels.

Verrinder arrived with dazzling scientific and athletic distinctions from St John's College, Oxford, and could have earned a fortune if he had wanted to lend his talents to industry; but he preferred the challenge of teaching at a forward-looking public school, where he could also indulge his love of the theatre. He was a formidable chemist and physicist, and saw many boys through to medical and scientific careers. And he also stimulated them on the athletic and rugby fields. Not only every boy but also every young member of staff turned out for the Clayesmore cross-country handicap under his influence, and as the coach of the rugby First XV in 1937 he produced the first unbeaten team for ten years. He played too, along with Evelyn King, in fixtures against local clubs, and he formed part of a staff seven which would take on the school. He was a powerful advocate of outdoor activities, such as canoeing, climbing, skiing and youth hostelling, and would take parties of boys abroad to experience the enjoyment of winter sports in more challenging places.

Some years into his retirement, he reflected on these expeditions. 'My heart was in climbing and every chance I got I would take boys up the mountains of Wales or wherever. We were in North Wales on one occasion when a rather large lad approached and asked if he might join our party. I watched him climb for a bit, saw he was a natural and asked him to lead. At the end of the climb he told me his name, which was Chris Bonnington. He went on to do a bit himself. He paid me the compliment of naming me in his book. Another young fellow I took climbing was Stephen Venables, the first man to climb Everest without an oxygen supply apart from what was available in the air.'

He regularly produced the school play, putting on *The Bird in Hand* in 1936 at the Shaftesbury Guildhall before Clayesmore's own theatre was ready, and *Androcles and the Lion* the following year. His 1945 production of *Hamlet*, with John Brooke-Little as the prince, went on tour to Bryanston, Canford, Bishop's Wordsworth and the Pump Room at Bath. An early post-war production was *The Ascent of F6* by WH Auden and Christopher Isherwood, which was vividly remembered, even if not always fully understood, by the boys of the time. In his farewell interview for the school magazine, Verrinder recalled that Auden had offered to write a new ending specifically for the Clayesmore production; he always regretted turning that offer down. In 1966 he revived *HMS Pinafore* for the third time, with Peter Burke as Sir Joseph Porter, in a final tribute to the retiring headmaster, and he was the stage director, alongside Nick Zelle as musical director, of the triumphant 1971 *Figaro*.

When asked in 1974 why he was retiring, he replied 'Old donkeys are put out to grass.' He also recalled teaching several pairs of fathers and sons, and rather regretted that fact that, because he had never taught a third generation family member, he had not been able to say, in a quavery voice, 'I remember your grandfather making the same mistake.'

Clayesmore Dramatic Society

presents

A Dramatised Reading

of

THE WINSLOW BOY

by

Terence Rattigan

Produced by

C. H. P. Verrinder

Right: Carl Verrinder.

The new headmaster proved to be the right man at the right time. An Oxford hockey blue who had finished the war as a lieutenant colonel, he was quite unlike his predecessor, but proved to be equally tactful, knowledgeable, likeable and caring. He began discreetly. Old ways began subtly to change. Long-standing staff provided continuity and tradition, but young new staff offered a fresh approach… and then, momentously, a radical departure: in January 1969 three girls from Croft House, Shillingstone, joined the Clayesmore Lower VI.

The early 1970s saw numbers beginning to rise, but more had to be done, and on Speech Day 1973 John Brooke-Little, chairman of the council, announced that coeducation was to be introduced throughout the school, starting in the autumn term of 1974. The purchase and refurbishment, completed in 1978, of the large vicarage in the village provided a house for senior girls, known as Bower, though they were only to live there until 1980, when they moved back to share the main building with the other girls' house, Wolverton, and boys took it over as Devine House.

Another fundamental change was the relocation of Clayesmore Preparatory School from Charlton Marshall to new buildings at Iwerne Minster; it reopened there in September 1974 (see Part 3). During most of this period of rapid and radical change, Roy McIsaac had acted as his own bursar, a necessary economy that had an effect on his health. At the end of 1975 he was rushed to hospital with a serious heart condition, and Mike Henbest took over as acting

David Spinney (1935–77)

After reading history at Cambridge, David Spinney joined Craigend School in Edinburgh when Evelyn King became its owner and headmaster, and was one of the staff there whom King brought back with him from Scotland when he took over Clayesmore in 1935. Spinney was to spend the rest of his working life at the school, completing an astonishing 99 terms as a housemaster. As he said in his valedictory interview in the *Clayesmorian*, it was easier to list activities in which he had not been involved than those in which he had: 'I have never taught any of the sciences or Latin, but everything else. Never had anything to do with hockey, but every other game, even cricket for a while… I edited the *Clayesmorian*, and did the school timetable for years…' – though he also counted as 'supreme bliss' his managing to persuade the headmaster towards the end of his years at the school that it was someone else's turn to take on that particular task.

The sea was his great love, and naval history his speciality; he was the author of a well-regarded biography of Admiral Lord Rodney, published in 1969. He joined the Royal Navy at the outbreak of the Second World War, and in peacetime was an enthusiastic sailor – many OCs remember learning the rudiments of sailing in JDS's boat in Poole harbour. And his love of all things naval extended to playing an appropriately uniformed Captain Corcoran opposite Peter Burke as Sir Joseph Porter in *HMS Pinafore*.

David Spinney's talents and interests were multifarious. In his younger days he was a speedy wing in the masters' three-quarter line and his elegant skating skills, on view when the lake froze over, allowed him to star in ice hockey teams. He played a fine old viola in the school orchestra but used a cello bow, and his tuning up usually concluded with the cry 'near enough'. He organised dances in the Burney Library, where perspiring boys were inculcated into the mysteries of military two-steps and the Dashing White Sergeant. He kept bees on the roof of the main house, perhaps with the aim of discouraging illegal sunbathing there. And he ran the Archaeological and Antiquarian Society. Above all, he was an inspiring teacher with his own distinctive style, who introduced innumerable boys to a lifetime's enjoyment of history.

He retired to a lovely thatched cottage just outside the school gates, which was the oldest habitation in Iwerne Minster and which he restored himself and loved to show off to visitors. He devoted himself to building up an impressive school archive – many of its holdings exhibit annotations in his small, neat hand – and he researched and wrote his final gift to Clayesmore, his *History*, published in 1987, a year before he died.

Mike Henbest (1957–90)

Mike Henbest's 33-year tenure at Clayesmore spanned four headmasterships and a variety of different roles and challenges, not least of which was the introduction of girls and the arrival of the prep school in Iwerne Minster in the 1970s. Employed as a geography master, he was also severally senior master, houseparent, games coach, musician, not to mention friend to generations of Clayesmorians. Anecdotes about him recall his purposeful striding across the school campus and back again every morning, the faded brown of his duffel coat, the old English rose he favoured in his buttonhole and the talent a man of few words had to say 'Well, my boy' or 'My dear chap' in so many different ways:

Approvingly – 'Well, my boy'
Encouragingly – 'My dear chap'
Questioningly – 'Well, my boy?'
Admonishingly – 'My dear chap' and so on.

Right: Mike Henbest.

Above: Three of the first girls, with a boy.

headmaster, while Colonel Edwards-Stewart, late of the prep school, shouldered the role of bursar until McIsaac returned and a full-time bursar could be appointed.

The 1970s also saw the retirement of the old guard who had been at Clayesmore for decades. Carl Verrinder had joined in the Northwood Park days, and both John Appleby and David Spinney had arrived from Scotland with Evelyn King when he took over in 1935. Verrinder's last hurrah was to produce the school play for the final time in 1975, a year after his official retirement, and Spinney's was to write his magisterial *History* of the school, which was published in 1987.

The school magazines of the period record impressive sports results, wide-ranging literary and artistic endeavours and enthusiastic membership of the CCF and school clubs; but the academic achievements were less notable. Four students gained places at university in the 1973/4 academic year, and five the following year. However, there was major expansion going on, and by 1976 – although the school remained numerically small – both prep and senior schools could report maximum intakes. The editor of the 1975 *Clayesmorian* reported, 'Clayesmore, like the phoenix rising from the fire, is beginning a new lease of life.' Art studios, craft workshops and a new music school had been built, and a new sanatorium was under construction, designed to cater for boys and girls within this newly coeducational institution.

The Claysmore lecture

This was Evelyn King's idea – a public occasion on which an eminent figure would speak to a wide audience on a topic rather different from the usual fare of events such as Speech Day. The first was in March 1969, when CP Snow spoke on 'Kinds of Excellence', followed in February 1970 by Cardinal Heenan on 'The Future of Faith'. The audience on that occasion included the Bishop of Salisbury, the Lord Lieutenant and the High Sheriff of Dorset, the chairman of the County Council and the mayors of Blandford and Shaftesbury, as well as many other local dignitaries. It had not taken long, it appears, for the lecture to have established itself firmly within the local calendar.

The third lecture, given by Enoch Powell on the subject of 'Criticism', was attended in addition by a large contingent of journalists who were hoping for some sort of sensationalism from that most controversial of politicians. But he stuck firmly to the classics, the New Testament and Shakespeare. It was a memorable lecture, but for many this was for the wrong reasons.

The lecture has continued ever since, more or less annually, though with the occasional gap. The most recent, in 2011, was given by General Sir Mike Jackson. Other military figures who have appeared include Field Marshal Lord Carver, Sir Peter de le Billière and Johnson Beharry VC. Lords Denning and Goodman have represented the law, Lord George Brown and Lord Wilson of Rievaulx politics and Sir John Harvey-Jones industry. Lady Archer, along with Richard Holmes and AL Rowse, come from the academic world, Lord Armstrong of Ilminster from Whitehall and Rabbi Julia Neuberger from religion and the House of Lords. Colonel John Blashford-Snell offered tales of exploration and Oscar winner Julian Fellowes insights into the world of Hollywood and television. There have been many others; the roll call of lecturers' names is distinguished and memorable.

Above: General Sir Mike Jackson presented the 35th Clayesmore Lecture in 2011.

Far left: Julian Fellowes gave the Clayesmore Lecture in 2006.

Left: David Beeby, Lady Archer and Roger Kingwill in 1993.

Roy McIsaac's 13 years at the helm oversaw the most dramatic changes in the school's architectural history. The differences between a lesson in the old art room during the 1950s (**above**) when compared to the new Manor House foyer (**right**), opened in 1974, were vast.

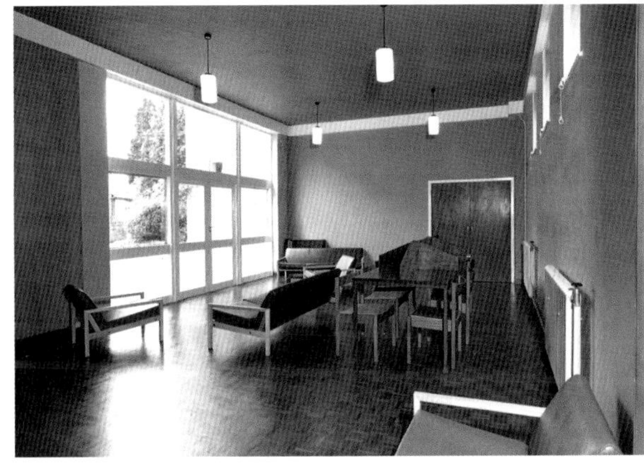

By the beginning of the 1978/9 academic year there were girls in all years of the school, prep and senior, and there were three women on the permanent teaching staff. At the end of that year, in the summer of 1979, Roy McIsaac retired. The 13 years of his headship had been demanding and full of incident, but he left the school in a far stronger and more well-rooted position than he might have thought was possible when he took over in those doubt-ridden mid-1960s.

Roger Kingwill, who was at the school from 1945 to 1950, whose sons attended in the 1970s and who has been closely involved in fundraising and governance since the 1960s, credits Roy McIsaac with saving Clayesmore. When he took over there was no working capital and no financial buffer; there had been no reinvestment and little thought had been given to the future. Peter Burke was perhaps rather of the old school, and the rapidly changing world of the 1960s offered challenges with which he was ill equipped to deal. Kingwill regards McIsaac as a 'real hero', without whom Clayesmore might well have succumbed to the pressures of the times, as many other similar institutions did.

The history of Clayesmore is extremely important to what it has become today, and the direction in which it seems, very successfully, to be going in the future. When my parents chose Clayesmore, they knew they were choosing what was described as 'a minor public school'. It was not Sherborne – and that was what particularly appealed to my mother! She did not want something where tradition was embalmed in stone and where personality played second fiddle to conformity. In Clayesmore and its nearest rival, Bryanston, parents found schools which were both innovative and imaginative, and where you did not necessarily have either to get a first at Oxford or drink yourself under a succession of tables as a 'rugger bugger' to succeed.

Clayesmore has always encouraged the individual. It did that, in its earlier days, through having a succession of headmasters who were innovative and saw the value of experiment; in my day both Evelyn King and Peter Burke did more than toy with politics in the real world, but they also saw that students were schooled to question, long before that became an academic given. Both appointed very imaginative teachers, particularly to head departments and as housemasters, and they saw to it that tradition was created, but also that it was allowed to develop.

Clayesmore always recognised that it needed to be on the cusp of change and imaginative development, and I do not believe the school would have become the success that it is today if it had not had dedicated visionaries working for it in its earlier experimental years. Yes, mistakes were made, and yes it took a while for academic prowess to improve, but improve it did, while at the same time there was an increasing commitment to the 'wholeness' of the individual, which led eventually to the introduction of girls and to a complete revisiting of the house system, and the confident application of new thinking and state of the art technology. What has developed at Clayesmore is in response to what occurred in its infancy and its adolescence; we do not simply write history, we live it.

Jeremy Dowling (1951–6)

Living at Clayesmore

For many parents considering Clayesmore for their children, there are two major selling points. One is that they can be educated on the same site from the age of two-and-a-half in the nursery up to the sixth form, and can live on site as boarders from the age of seven. The school offers 'childhood and education' combined and in that order, without a selection process, and as a result the intake is unusual both in range of ability and range of social background. The second is that the school is well known for its supportive family environment; its approach is to develop every child as a natural, happy learner, achieving

Some things never change – boarding play during the 1990s (**top**) and the 1950s (**above**).

Right: Pupils relax in the grounds.

Above: The school's youngest pupils enjoy a walk in the grounds.

Top right: The sixth form in their common room, 'The Capital'.

Above right: Modern boarding.

success without pressure and being offered the opportunity and support that will allow them to work to their optimum ability. Clayesmore pupils know that they will be known and noticed. The aim is to boost self-esteem and make every child feel confident, valued and needed.

The children of armed forces families are well represented, partly because of the many service bases in the neighbourhood but mainly because the school has a reputation for understanding the difference military service makes to the lives of its personnel and the specific needs of their children. In addition, Clayesmore at all ages is a local school, catering for the community; year 7 sees a large influx of local children who attend as day pupils. The atmosphere is friendly and warm, and the good relationship between staff and pupils is palpable. As one inspector commented in recent years, all the young people she met showed 'natural good manners'. The message that greets any newcomer to the school is that it is a happy place. Vera Peevor, who is part of the learning support team, says that it is the best school she has ever worked in, and that staff are valued and supported.

The unusual house system at Clayesmore during its earlier history – where the boys were grouped

chronologically as Juniors, Middles and Seniors, rather than being assigned to houses and housemasters at the start of their school career and staying in the same house throughout – prevailed until the late 1970s, when the more common system was adopted. There are now five houses in the senior school: Wolverton and King's for girls and Gate, Manor and Devine for boys, the latter the old rectory in the village. Day pupils, who make up roughly 40 percent of the numbers, are also allocated to houses so that they have a base to retreat to during the school day and a focus for loyalty and friendship.

Anne Jancis, who has been at Clayesmore since 1992 and is now head of biology, was housemistress of Wolverton for nine years, living there with her husband Alan, also part of the science department at the school, and their two children. She remembers with fondness the break-up lunch at the end of every term, when the whole senior school would be seated in their tutor groups and houses in the dining room, along with all the staff, and certificates and games colours would be handed out and achievements praised. The dining room is now too small to take the whole school together so the event has lapsed; but she vividly recalls the bonhomie, the family feel and the sense of unity and purpose that suffused the atmosphere. She is another who would not choose to work anywhere else.

Each house has a housemaster or housemistress and a resident tutor who live on site, along with visiting tutors and non-resident matrons.

The food is excellent, under the superintendence of Andrew Croft who took over as catering manager in 2011 from Neil D'Allen, both having been involved for years with Clayesmore. The meals the catering staff offer – around 1,000 lunches every day – are varied, well cooked and cater for all tastes and dietary needs. Choices of hot dishes and salads are prepared fresh daily by the 30 cooks and servers, and the meals are designed to suit everyone from a small child to busy members of staff and hard-working maintenance men. The day starts early with breakfast for the boarders and ends late after their supper. There are also match teas to prepare – and on top of the work for the school there are around 150 external functions a year, ranging from weddings using the beautiful buildings and grounds, language courses, high level sports courses and religious retreats.

Top: All appetites are fed by the school's in-house catering team.

Above: Prep boarders enjoy reading before bedtime.

Like all the support staff, those working in the kitchen and dining room get to know the children, often by name, and enjoy seeing them grow up over their years at Clayesmore. The same is true of Moe Mitchell, the household manager, and her staff of 42, who cover all the laundry and cleaning work for both prep and senior schools. Moe has been at Clayesmore for 24 years, six of them in her current role following many years in Devine House, and several of her staff have notched up over 30 years' service.

Ray Norris, the head groundsman, is another who has been at the school for over 30 years, having joined in 1979. When he started he lived in the lodge at the entrance, where he had a dog and kept chickens, turkeys and ducks; 'happy days', as he recalls. With his staff of six, including a gardener, he has a large estate to look after: 62 acres with seven cricket squares, ten rugby and football pitches, four grass hockey pitches as well as Astroturf pitches. There is also the lake: fed by a spring, the water level can be hard to maintain, but it is used for fishing and some boating, and the semi-wild area around it provides a welcome contrast to the more managed estate around the school buildings. Ray is another who cannot praise more highly what he calls 'the lovely family ethos' of the school. He sees his job, at its root, as 'selling the school' – ensuring that first impressions count and that the striped lawns, the beautifully kept flower beds and the splendid games pitches bear full witness to the pleasures of living and being educated here.

Bill Willetts lives in the lodge now and says 'when I go it will be in a box', although he knows well that there is a queue forming up behind him for his coveted house. He has been at Clayesmore for 24 years, and along with his colleague Win Walmsley (31 years) plus seven others, he attends to all the regular maintenance work that needs doing around the place. Major electrical and plumbing jobs are now undertaken by contractors, but there is a great deal to be done to keep the school running smoothly. As they both say, 'everyone mucks in', particularly for occasions such as open days; Win adds to his role by regularly umpiring cricket matches, and it is Bill's job to ensure that everything is locked up and secure at night.

Below: Relaxing in the grounds.

Learning Support

Clayesmore does not operate a selection policy and as a result, the school incorporates a broad spectrum of academic ability and offers a wide range of both academic and non-academic subjects. Parents tend to choose Clayesmore for their children because they feel that they will be happy there and will get the teaching and support that they need, whatever their specific needs or talents.

A particular strength is the Learning Support Centre, which serves both schools and is very well resourced and staffed by dedicated teachers. Clayesmore was a pioneer in offering this facility, which started life in the senior school in 1987 as the Language Development Unit, headed by Susan Billington. She went on to become assistant head in 1996 and then head of the renamed Learning Support Centre in 1997. Maria Pond started the Prep School learning support unit in 1989, and her motto 'if pupils don't learn the way we teach, we must teach the way they learn' remains a central tenet of the department's philosophy today. These departments not only provide help with specific subjects, but also with particular difficulties like handwriting, essay writing techniques and exam stress. Pupils come for one-on-one sessions at regular times in the week, and there are also group sessions for particular skills. The LSC allows Clayesmore to offer a niche for children with difficulties such as dyslexia, where they can receive individual help and advice within a warm and caring environment.

Left: Maria Pond – 'If pupils don't learn the way we teach, we must teach the way they learn.'

The buildings have improved greatly in recent years, and were considerably enhanced through the energetic efforts of Richard Tremellen and David Little, estate manager and bursar respectively, who arrived in the late 1990s. Today's estate manager, Jonathan Handley, along with Valerie McKinlay, buildings and estates coordinator, continue to make improvements in all areas of the School.

When Lex Devine founded Clayesmore it was as an Anglican institution, and daily worship was de rigueur for its first century of existence. Daily chapel is no longer compulsory, but the school aims to support Christian values and there is a weekly service on Friday afternoon which everyone is expected to attend unless there is a good reason. This includes those who follow other faiths, but their separate religious needs are also part of school life, with their major festivals celebrated in assembly.

Sandra Tew, whose husband, Tony, was the lay chaplain from 1993–8 and whose three children all attended the school, joined the prep in September 1990 to

cover a term's maternity leave and is still at Clayesmore. She has played a variety of roles in both prep and senior schools, teaching religious studies, English, Latin and PSE, and since 2003 being part of the Learning Support Centre. Sandra marvels at what she calls Clayesmore's 'magnetic quality', which draws people in and welcomes them back. There is a great deal of mutual support at all levels, and there are no stereotypes; staff and pupils are allowed to be themselves and accepted for their differences and their idiosyncrasies as well as for the varied talents and gifts they can bring to the community. As she and so many others say, Clayesmore uses the advantage of being a school small in numbers to encourage achievement and allow individuals to shine.

Tiara
Club
Jessica

PART 3:
Clayesmore Preparatory School

The link between Clayesmore and its preparatory school was first forged in 1936, when Evelyn King opened discussions with Dick Everett, the founder and headmaster of a flourishing prep school at Charlton Marshall, some eight miles from Iwerne Minster. Founded in 1929 as Charlton Marshall House Preparatory School in Everett's own beautiful 18th-century house set in 45 acres – 'ideal for every sort of small boy activity' – it was modelled on the principles of AS Neill of Summerhill. Charlton Marshall was more than holding its own during those depressed times under his enlightened and happy rule, but it seemed to both headmasters that some form of collaboration would be mutually beneficial. Clayesmore had always taken in a few boys of preparatory age, and the transfer of these to Charlton Marshall would augment numbers there while making room for some of those on the rapidly growing waiting list for the senior school at Iwerne. Moreover, the link between the two schools would help to ensure a ready flow of promotions from prep school to senior school in the future. The autumn term of 1936 saw both schools squashed into Iwerne Minster while conversion work was carried out at Charlton Marshall, until in January 1937 Everett and his school moved back home under the new name of Clayesmore Preparatory School. The preparatory age juniors at Iwerne seem to have accepted the move with equanimity – with one exception. Eleven-year-old Nigel Sampson defiantly refused to move, and was allowed to stay on at the big school as its youngest pupil for a few more terms.

Everett saw his school through the war years, contributing to the war effort not only by carrying on his vocation of educating the young but also by donating his sailing boat, the *Blue Moon*, to the government for use during the evacuation of Dunkirk. Nigel Bill, who was at the prep from 1953 to 1958, remembers the splendid buildings and grounds: 'Clayesmore Prep School was in a large area of beautiful countryside, with the main building (the original house) near the front. New Wing was built onto it housing the classrooms, some dormitories and the headmaster's study. At the front of the main house was a very nicely laid out garden (incidentally, still there).

Below: The prep school at Charlton Marshall, 1952.

At many times during my life I have thought back to my years at Clayesmore, both prep and senior schools, and feel very honoured to have been a part of an institution that is still alive and buoyant today. May 1 1953, my eighth birthday, was my first day. My older brother Michael was in his last term at the prep school before going up to the 'big school' at Iwerne Minster. I remember being excited and not at all homesick. On arrival we new boys were introduced to Mr Everett, the headmaster. He was a total disciplinarian, but at the same time a very fair man. He demanded and received the respect of all the boys.

The next thing was being shown to my dormitory and finding the bed and wooden cupboard allotted to me. Miss Stubbs and two under-matrons supervised us. Miss Stubbs always wore a green hospital uniform and a white hat and was quite definitely 'one of the old school' when it came to young boys; one did not argue with her! She would come round making sure we had cleaned our teeth and washed with pink carbolic soap. Bed was at 6.30, lights went out at 7 and there was no talking. The rising bell went at 7.10 in the morning, when everyone's temperature was taken by one of the matrons.

Every boy was allocated a place in one of the house teams, named Huntley's, Truelove's, Hopgood's and White's, I assume after previous masters. I was in Huntley's. We were given weekly plus or minus marks for good or bad behaviour; if your total for the week was more than minus 11 you were put into detention, with an extra 20 minutes for every minus over 11. But the worst punishment by far was to be sent to bed for the day. One had to lie in bed with the shutters drawn and appear at mealtimes in your dressing gown in front of all the other boys. An accumulation of pluses was rewarded with the 'star' holiday at the end of term – a day out on a beach or in town. And every year on Whit Monday there was a day out at Studland Bay, which was the highlight of the year.

Nigel Bill (1953–8 prep school; 1958–61 senior school)

Bottom: Aerial view of Charlton House, now demolished. The site is still readily identifiable by the remaining layout of the formal garden.

Right: Rugby in the early days at Charlton Marshall.

At the rear was a large space containing the school pond and orchard and also a walled kitchen garden; most of the vegetables and fruit for the school were grown here. Then there was a huge grassy field used as the cricket pitch, rugby pitch and athletics track in the summer, and leading off it an extensive meadow with a wooded area at the side. Further on was a generous wooded region known as the Beech Walk.

'Running straight through the school grounds alongside the playing fields was the main Somerset and Dorset railway line, raised up on a bank. In the corner

Sport, pastimes and fun at Charlton Marshall

I was very grateful to have the opportunity to compete in a number of sports, and to be helped by a number of excellent sportsmen on the staff. Mr Everett and Mr Glazebrook were both outstanding cricketers who gave a great deal of encouragement and knowledge to their pupils. Cricket was our summer term game, and various members of the staff supervised the younger boys. If it was thought you showed promise you could progress into training for the Under 11 team, and then perhaps on to the Second XI and finally the First XI. We really had to work hard to make that team. I finally made it by hitting a six through the potting shed window much to the chagrin of Frank, the head gardener.

One of the highlights of the summer term was the staff cricket match when members of the staff, including the assistant matrons, were coerced into playing a match against the First XI – always a big occasion, watched by the whole school. Although the match was keenly contested, the bowlers did always bowl gently for the ladies. However, where the likes of Dick Everett and Hugh Glazebrook were concerned, they met the bowlers' full force. I remember Hugh Glazebrook knocking a six over the train embankment, which was always a challenge.

During the winter and spring terms we played rugby; football was never an option. I loved the game and, being tall, was always in the scrum. In my final year (1957) we had a very successful season, beating many schools; Sherborne was always the main challenge. In the spring term we also took part in cross-country runs, some of them paper chases when a few boys set off scattering pieces of paper behind them and the rest of the pack would set off a little later to catch them.

Sports day was on a Saturday in early July, featuring the finals of various events after heats in the previous weeks. This was also half term weekend, when we could see our parents and stay out until Monday evening. Therefore on the day most parents arrived during the morning, and lunch was a picnic around the field. Apart from the main races there was an obstacle race, and fathers also had their own race as well as a three-legged race with their sons. Later on there was a musical play on the side lawn, and then we left with our parents for the remainder of the weekend.

The big thrill in the summer term was swimming when the weather was hot. Since there was no school swimming pool the River Stour was the official venue. The part of the river where we swam was ideal: non-swimmers could paddle around in a shallow part, which gradually became deeper towards the middle, and finally at the top end there was a bend on the river and a large overhanging tree, where good swimmers could dive off the bank into deep water.

Cycling was very popular as the grounds were extensive and offered some great tracks. A favourite was to tear down the Beech Walk and come out in an area we called 'the switchbacks' where races were held. Towards the end of my time we could also get permission to cycle out of the school grounds; a good ride was to Badbury Rings, an old Roman fort about ten miles away.

We loved climbing trees; one particular tree named 'pepper heights' by the railway line had grown at an angle, so we could climb up and swing down on a branch of a neighbouring tree. We also made dens, looked after our garden patches and – a great favourite – get permission to have a fire and cook anything we could get our hands on.

Above: Canoeing on the River Stour.

Below: The modelling club, 1950s.

Right: Waiting for the train at Charlton Halt.

A great place for this was in a hollow in the Beech Walk area, in the much loved 'doughnut dugout'; this hollow still exists, although it is a shadow of its former self.

Situated behind Orchard House were the bicycle shed and pet club. A few boys would bring an animal to school, such as a guinea pig, and keep it in a cage here. We also regularly rescued young rooks and jackdaws which had fallen out of their nests, and encouraged them back to health. Many of them became quite tame. I remember a particular jackdaw who would fly down and sit on an arm or shoulder if he was called, all the better if you were offering him something to eat.

Membership of the Modelling Club was prestigious, as intricate work was carried out – mainly the building of balsawood model planes which would be flown from the top of the steps leading up to the club room. The more ambitious boys made larger models and fitted little diesel engines into them. Some were attached to two long wires controlled by the owner, which flew round in a large arc; others were larger and could be launched into free flight, though they had to be tracked so that they could be found when they eventually landed. There was also something called a 'Jet-Ex' motor – an oval canister into which was put 'jet' pellet with a small fuse protruding from a small hole at the back. When the fuse was lit and the flame hit the pellet, a satisfyingly powerful jet was created which propelled whatever the unit was fixed to. It was ideal for balsawood boats in the school pond, model planes and 'rocket cars'.

Nigel Bill (1953–8)

at the top end of the Beech Walk was Charlton Marshall Halt where local trains occasionally stopped and also deposited boys travelling from London. Train enthusiasts could always see an interesting range of British Rail traffic, including the famous "Pines Express" which came through twice a day in opposite directions. From the middle of the playing fields there was an entrance through a tunnel under the railway line to another extensive area called "the park", where there were two rugby pitches used for the more junior games; I remember cowpats and thistles.'

Everett was ahead of his time in believing in a degree of democracy. Every term an assembly was held at which pupils were allowed to put forward their ideas or grievances for debate. They were discussed, a vote was taken and if the ideas were reasonable they were passed and came into force. The head boy had considerable authority and even attended certain staff meetings. The prep school equivalent of prefects were called 'leaders' and 'seconds', with the power

Above: The Pines Express.

Dick 'Hefty' Everett (1901–96)

With feelings mixed with regret, admiration and gratitude we have to record the retirement of Mr Everett – 'Hefty' – the founder and headmaster of Clayesmore Preparatory School.

Many Old Clayesmorians started their school life at Charlton Marshall, and many others have wished that they too could have enjoyed that experience. The word 'headmaster' is in Mr Everett's case a misnomer; it connotes mastery, pomposity, 'red tape', 'order inordinate', 'he goeth', 'he cometh', and to Hefty all of what these terms stand for was anathema. As an educationist he was an idealist, and during his early days and prime he was well ahead of his times. In those days he undoubtedly suffered financially for his nonconformity – neither preparatory schools nor their patrons, the parents, were very enlightened in those pre-war years. He knew what he wanted for his boys – freedom of thought, speech and action with simultaneous training and guidance to avoid their abuse. In 1946 he instituted the school assembly – a prep schoolboy's parliament; this proved a great success. His own tolerance and humility in the assembly converted many a stiff-necked assistant, who had a diehard attitude towards this type of experiment. From first to last he strove to create and preserve a happy atmosphere, not only among the boys themselves and the staff themselves, but also between the boys and the staff. And in normal times, excluding war years, he did not hesitate to replace staff, however efficient their teaching, if they did not measure up to his requirements in this respect. Conversely, on occasions one or two poor teachers were retained longer than they should have been if he deemed that the school profited from their kindly dispositions and tolerance.

Good teacher as he was, he was always most anxious that scholarship and games prowess should not be the main arbiters of the school's endeavours. No, firstly, boys were to be happy during their formative years, they were to develop self-discipline, imposed from within freely and sincerely and guided by example, and both public and private advice and help. He did not aim to produce a Balliol scholar, a Cambridge blue, but good citizens who could think for themselves. His curriculum was liberal – a great deal of time was given up to cultural pursuits – and there were many activities other than rugger and cricket.

Old Clayesmorian, *October 1963*

to maintain discipline and give out plus or minus points. There were also 'freemen', boys in their final term who were allowed certain privileges denied to others.

Dick Everett was described by those who knew and worked for him as a quiet, charming, unassuming man who was never heard to raise his voice. He was much missed when he retired in 1963, as the tribute to him in the *Old Clayesmorian* records; radical for the period in refusing to sacrifice happiness and a well-rounded personality to academic or sporting achievement, he was an admirable partner within the Clayesmore enterprise and yet another of that long tradition of masters in both schools who promulgated, developed and carried on the genuinely progressive educational principles of men like AS Neill and JH Badley of Bedales – and also, of course, of Alexander Devine.

His successor as owner and headmaster of Clayesmore Prep was Lieutenant Colonel Ivor Edwards-Stewart,

Right: James Seddon.

Far right: Lieutenant Colonel Ivor Edwards-Stewart.

who ran it until 1973, when James Seddon, the Old Clayesmorian who had been a stalwart of Lake Warfare, took over as headmaster in preparation for the imminent move to Iwerne Minster. A property company had made Edwards-Stewart an offer for the estate which was too good to refuse, though it sadly involved the demolition of the beautiful old Georgian house which had been the heart of the prep school. The sale funded new school buildings on the Iwerne Minster estate, which took over the old kitchen gardens and the games pitches to the north of the main school. The prep reopened there in September 1974, and it was at that point too that, along with the senior school, coeducation expanded. There had been a few girls during the final years at Charlton Marshall, but both prep and senior school now took girls all the way through. And at both sites there had always been a pre-prep department for five-year-olds up to age seven; the provision was to grow even further in the mid-1990s, when a new nursery department started to take very small children, two-and-a-half years old up to five. Clayesmore Prep was unusual in Seddon's time both for enjoying custom-made school buildings and for being fully coeducational; it is unusual today in occupying the same site as its senior school, enabling children of all ages to be educated together.

Below: The prep school reopening at the main Clayesmore site, September 1974 – (from l–r) Sir Douglas Bader, Roy McIsaac, Col. Edwards-Stewart, JP Brooke-Little and James Seddon.

The school continued to flourish under James Seddon, who was a great sportsman and a very experienced teacher. He was a traditionalist in many ways, firm but fair, and very supportive of his staff and pupils. When he arrived at Iwerne the grounds were a sea of mud crossed by planks as walkways, and the gym was about to be delivered on the back of a lorry. But as he recalled on the prep's 75th anniversary in 2004, 'We were all so delighted with our brand new school, there was a wonderful feel-good factor throughout and such happy and productive times followed.' He very quickly initiated good contacts with the many armed forces bases around the area, spearheading a major initiative aimed at building up boarding. He and his wife Anne, along with the matrons, took full, hands-on care of the boarders, and made them feel as if they were home from home; during his tenure the school was always full both of day pupils and boarders.

Seddon was headmaster until 1983, when he was succeeded by Mark Ross, a Dubliner who taught history and loved hockey. With the support of his wife Anthea, known as Andy, who taught French, he considerably enhanced the academic standing of the prep school and was known for the rigour of his approach to preparing pupils for scholarships. He regarded himself as privileged to have been able to build on the legacy left by James Seddon, and remembered 'fantastic children, fantastic staff, a brilliant prep school'. Under his leadership, art, music and sport continued to flourish and became real strengths of the education on offer; art, under the tutelage of Mike Geary, 'ventured out of the

The Gent family memories

Early contact with Clayesmore Prep came in matches played against them when we were at Forres and then Chafyn Grove, and as a result our eldest daughter, Alison, joined in 1975 soon after the school had moved to Iwerne Minster. She went on into the senior school.

Twelve years later, in October 1987, we were about to leave Chafyn Grove and have a two-term sabbatical when Roger Kingwill telephoned to ask us whether we'd be prepared to run Clayesmore Prep for two terms. So it was that we started there in January 1988. As we had animals at our house near Bishops Caundle, David lived in what was in effect an unfurnished flat, while Sally commuted daily.

The school was in good heart and flourishing both academically (especially a brilliant learning support department) and on the games field, but was out of touch on the domestic front. With the support of David Watson, who had been appointed to the headship from the following September, we set about redesigning the layout of the dormitories, doing away with most of the double bunks by putting partitions between beds and therefore providing some privacy. We had a great deal of help in doing this from a responsive matrons' department and an equally supportive bursary. The dining room too came under scrutiny when we discovered the mini pre-prep children carrying trays; it was back to family feeding for them. And we made better provision for the cleaning ladies when we realised they had to have their break in the passage since there was nowhere else for them to sit.

The children were happy, pleasant and well mannered, and we made, and have retained, many friends. We much appreciate the warm welcome we still receive at both schools and are delighted to have been made OCs.

David and Sally Gent

Having spent two years at Clayesmore Prep from 1975 to 1977, our year group in the senior school was only the second proper year of girls. We lived in the downstairs wing of the prep, which was not the best, but we all had fun with two dorms of our year and two of the year above. Sarah Samuels, Jackie Allwright, Harriet Brockhurst, Sarah Townsend, Caron Jones and myself were good friends. The sixth form direct entry girls lived at that time in the annex of the main house, and we later spent one or two years in that house before moving to the Old Vicarage in the village, which was fantastic. We had breakfast there, cooked on an Aga that no one could use except me as we had one at home, and we used to have huge fry-ups on a Sunday. During O levels it was bliss lying in the garden revising or playing tennis on our grass court. I remember the holidays when the old classroom block burnt down and everything smelt for ages after – I still have some textbooks that smell of burning. The new classroom block was fantastic and a huge step into the 20th century. The summers stand out the most in my memory, with lessons outside, lots of tennis and swimming in the old outside pool – it was an idyllic school life. I have many very happy memories from school, and good friends that I still have to this day. There are millions of little things that stick in my mind – along with some things we did which can't be repeated!

Alison Parnell (née Gent, 1975–80)

Above: Previous prep headmasters and their wives gather in the drawing room during the 75th anniversary celebrations.

Above: Mark Ross.

Above right: David Watson.

Below right: Dartmoor Adventure Camp, gorge walking.

Below: Prep school camp, *c*2001.

classroom and occupied our walls', as Ross later recalled, and trophy cabinets were full of silver. Outdoor pursuits also became more of a focus, with children going camping and on field trips and being taken on visits to outside attractions. The introduction of a post-Common Entrance holiday in the form of a camping expedition to Dartmoor Country Park was initiated by Trevor Cooke, prep deputy head. The report of the camp in the *Junior Clayesmorian* of 1984–5 records that 'The rain never once relented and after only two days, replacement tents were summoned from HQ. The children remained amazingly buoyant, despite the incessant rain and the mud underfoot.' The notion that education and self-reliance outside the school classroom were an important and integral part of the education of young people was the driving force behind this move towards education outside the classroom. Prep pupils over the age of ten also enjoyed a diversion known as the 'senior beech walk', when they would be given sausages, baked beans, a tin opener, matches and a pan and would be allowed to cook their own supper in the open air – a tradition that survived until recently, when health and safety considerations forced its abandonment.

Mark Ross left in 1988, and was temporarily replaced by Patrick Gent, who had had a daughter at the school, so knew it well and was admirably suited to hold the reins until the new headmaster, David Watson, could start. Watson was both a renaissance man and a hands-on tackler of everything that needed doing. A former professional singer, an organist and a painter, he particularly encouraged drama – the Cecil B de Watty productions, which he produced and directed as well as painting the sets. The combination of a testing financial climate and better public transport contributed to a decline in boarding at this time, but the academic reputation of the prep remained high. David Watson and his wife Gwyneth left in 1994 when he wished to retire, and Martin Cooke arrived.

Extracts from 'the diary' – an account of the year in the *Junior Claysmorian*:

- Mrs Milton gives 'Joanne Woodward' +3 for good grades. It is the first time a film star has been so honoured. (Joanne Waters is actually taking the credit.)
- Star Holiday at the ice rink. Mrs Geary: 'Walk over my front, not over my behind.' We think she was guiding children over the road.
- We break up. First time ever on a Tuesday. Mr Geary can't understand it.
- Mrs Geary and her drama group locked in lecture room by Mr Cooke. Phylip Scott climbs through window to raise the alarm.
- Girls' bathroom flooded. Warminster did not arrive for their matches. Alterations and extensions to the camera position. A blackbird has claimed nesting rights up there. Four eggs.
- Common Entrance etc day two. Mr Cooke and Mr Barron can't even make out what a geography question means, let alone answer it.
- Pre-prep sports. Publicans' and staff children do suspiciously well. Dope tests?
- Beautiful day for Open Day. Mrs Longdon wears a hat, to the disgust of the Longdon brothers.
- Senior fires. Breadmore finds Nesquik is inflammable.
- No forks for breakfast. Knives and spoons attack sausages.
- In the continuing saga of Cerys Jenkins and the carpentry shop she saws all the way through a shelf instead of half way. Her bird table is more successful – it's only blown down once.
- Cerys is given a free transfer from woodwork to drama.
- On the way to woodwork Robert Thomas tries to dropkick his scarf and instead kicks his shoe onto the carpentry shop roof.
- Jonathan Scott asks how to spell 'hollow ear'; he means 'alleluia'.
- The first XV challenge the U13 girls to a netball match. Mrs Parfitt gives them an hour's coaching but although they do quite well the girls win.
- Paul Thompson says that he can't read his letter because his mother writes too fast.

November 23rd
Cheese and Wine Party in the Sports Hall, given by the Parents' Association.
November 26th
Everybody plays Millfield — Rugby.
November 27th
1st and 2nd year Parents' Evening. Lecture on the International Boys' Trust.
November 28th
5B and 5R boarders to Milton Abbey — 'The Boyfriend'.
November 29th
1st and 2nd XV v Hazlegrove. U10 play Chafyn and Girls hockey v Port Regis.
November 30th
Last leave out. 3rd year Parents' Evening.
December 1st
U10 v Port Regis
December 2nd
Reports go to form teachers. Team photos.
December 3rd
2nd XV and U10 travel to Swanage to play Malthouse.
December 4th
Hockey coaching video.
December 5th
Pre-Prep play.
December 6th
Prior Park games. Girls play Croft House at hockey.
December 7th
Carol Service — well attended.
December 8th
Star Holiday — Ice Skating.
December 9th
Staff soccer match. Christmas dinner and fancy dress disco.
December 10th
The Choir sings at Dorchester.
December 11th
Tidying up. Final Carol Service and off home.

EASTER TERM 1987

January 12th
Term begins. Skiers return from France. New tutor system.
January 15th
Joseph rehearsals begin.
January 17th
Hazlegrove VI's Tournament. OCs' Dinner — Clayesmore Prep School well represented.
January 18th
Orienteering — Bristol.
January 19th
Common Entrance trials and 4th year exams. No time to draw breath!
January 20th
Exams continue. The worst nearly over.
January 21st
Exams over. Just when we were getting used to it. Now for the marking.
January 24th
Hockey and netball as well as an U10 Rugby match.
January 25th
More orienteering, more good results.
January 28th
Busy day: Netball; Hockey; Swimming, as well as a lecture on Antarctica.
January 29th
More 'Joseph', as well as 'My Fair Lady' at the Senior School for 4th and 5th years.
January 30th
5R and 5B go to the Tate Gallery in London.
1st, 2nd and 3rd year go to 'My Fair Lady', which leaves the School pleasantly peaceful.
January 31st
Grades. The staff prepare for 5th year parents, while the netballers go to Bryanston (U13 and U12 North Dorset) and Millfield (U11).
February 1st
Orienteering in the Forest of Dean. A different kind of exercise for 5th year Parents' Evening.
February 4th
U10 Rugby. U11 Netball. North Dorset Swimming Heats for girls.
February 5th
1st and 2nd XI Hockey at Bryanston. No 'Joseph' rehearsal.
February 6th
5A and 5S go to the Tate Gallery. PC Knight comes to the Pre-Prep.
January 7th
Netball at Leweston and U11 at Walhampton Tournament. 1st XV at Sherborne, mini-Rugby v Chafyn Grove.
February 8th
Orienteering at Puddletown. Indoor Hockey Tournament at Bruton.

Like David Watson, Martin Cooke was a musician and an organist and came to Clayesmore after 15 years at Bembridge School on the Isle of Wight, where he had been director of music, and for ten years deputy head. A former chorister of St Paul's Cathedral and organ scholar of Bishop Otter College, Chichester, he was a graduate of the University of Sussex. Throughout his career he had taught the whole school age range from nursery to sixth form, so taking on the headship of a prep school attached to a senior school could not have been a more natural move for him. He remembers his first evening: 'While Eleanor tucked up the younger boarders, my office was invaded by a great bunch of super-confident children, all checking out their new headmaster. "This is going to be brilliant," I remember thinking.'

The early 1990s were not prosperous times in independent schools, and Clayesmore had taken its share of the pain. The 'new' 1970s prep school main building was looking down at heel both inside and out. Winning the confidence of staff, parents and governors, and, importantly, the bursar of the day, Commander David Isard, the Cookes set about making the very best of everything. After befriending the clerk of works Alan Newman and his team, things started to happen. Redecoration was the key – new exciting and contrasting colours, carpets and lighting and little by little, more and more prospective parents came to see the school and registered their children. Each year, for six years, there were more children in the school. And so, larger projects began to happen: a new library, a new ICT room. Then in 1997 the first new building at the prep school for many years appeared in the shape of a wonderful double classroom for year 4 on the site of the old swimming pool. This allowed much development elsewhere – an extra science lab – more space for the nursery and pre-prep. The Cookes always worked as a team – and still do – and while Martin was always interested in every detail, it was Eleanor whose imagination and eye for colour were responsible for much of the new feeling at Clayesmore Prep. She also took a great deal of interest in the pupils and the staff, and there were not many bedtimes when she was not to be found sitting on a bed chatting to the boys and girls, or helping one of the matrons.

The model whereby the headmaster of the prep school was also largely in charge of the boarders was not something that could be maintained, given the continuing success and growth in the school. So that married resident houseparents could be appointed, a new home was built for the head's family in 1997 on the site of the old rifle range. This beautiful building was designed by Philip Proctor and was to herald very considerable involvement by Philip in the school's future.

Other key figures in the prep school at this time were Trevor Cooke, the deputy head and his wife Margaret, who ran the pre-prep, and Debbie Geary, who was senior mistress. Trevor and Margaret retired after 21 years in 1995 and at a dinner held to mark the occasion, all the heads under whom they had served attended. Upon Trevor's retirement, Graham Moxham – another long-serving teacher – was promoted deputy head and Graham Jones became director of studies. With Debbie, this was

Above: Martin and Eleanor Cooke and their children soon after his arrival.

Bottom right: The retirement dinner of Trevor and Margaret Cooke in 1995 – (from l–r) Mark Ross, James Seddon, Martin Cooke, Margaret Cooke, Trevor Cooke and David Watson.

Below: The IT department in its early days.

Art, music, drama and sport at Clayesmore Prep

Art, music, drama and sport have always been a way of life in the prep school, and remain so to this day. In the art room and pottery pupils have always been encouraged to experiment and to find the medium that suits them. The department under Mike Geary produced such talents as sculptor Giles Penny, contemporary artists Anna McNeil and Andrew Curtis and winner of the first prestigious Jerwood Art Commission, figurative painter and head of art at the prep school, Harriet Barber.

Every child in the prep is involved in the various dramatic performances that are staged throughout the year. There are old favourites such as *Oliver* and *The Wind in the Willows*, which have been reprised over the years, as well as more modern musical theatre pieces such as *Camp Rock* and the traditional nursery and pre-prep nativity plays. As in the senior school, dramatic productions also call on the talents of other departments such as music and design technology.

Clayesmore's chapel choir's appearance in the 1994 film adaptation of Terence Rattigan's play *The Browning Version* was one highlight of a particularly busy period in its history, which included two performances for the Pope (in 1982 and 1990) and tours to West Germany, Washington, Italy and Spain, along with many concerts and appearances in and around Clayesmore. Writing in the *Junior Clayesmorian* in 1990 about their trip to Rome and audience with His Holiness Pope John Paul II, choir member Richard Williams recalls, 'We stood up and began to sing. The hall became very quiet and one was conscious of being the focus of attention for 12,000 people and several video cameras. At the conclusion of the piece there was warm applause and it was noticeable that the choir received the most sustained and animated acknowledging wave from the Pope of any group present. As hoped, Ridout's motet had made its mark.' (The school had commissioned a piece from Alan Ridout of Canterbury who produced a short four-part motet, 'Christus Factus Est' for the occasion.) He went on, 'The audience lasted a little over an hour and a half and concluded with the Apostolic Blessing of all those present. There then followed a quite unexpected bonus. The choristers were invited onto the stage steps to be presented to the Pope, who spoke to them for several minutes.'

There has always been a strong tradition of music-making at the prep school, with a high percentage of

Above left: Mike Geary.

Below: Performances of *Wind in the Willows* from 1949 (left) and 2000 (right).

Bottom left: Members of the choir meet Pope John Paul II in Rome, 1990.

Bottom: The Arts Week orchestra, 1990s.

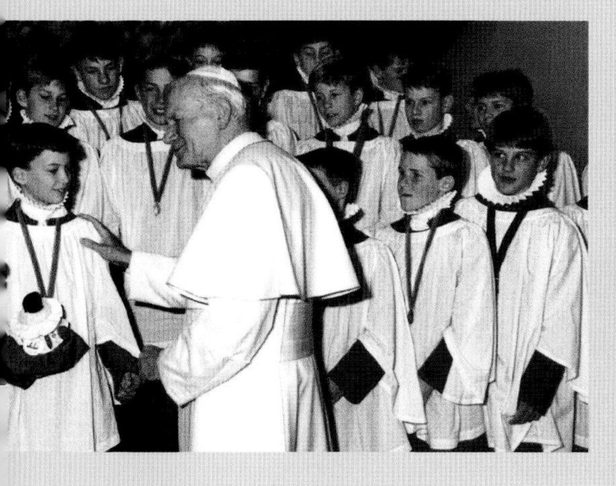

pupils taking individual lessons in addition to class music, sitting examinations and often passing grade 6 or higher and taking part in one or more of the many groups and ensembles. Some of them go on to perform at regional and national level in orchestras and choirs.

In years 3 and 4, the children learn the recorder at no additional cost. There are regular concerts, and at any time there are a considerable number of ensembles in rehearsal, so that as many children as possible gain pleasure from the experience of shared music-making. We are able to field an orchestra of very considerable size and quality.

Tuition is available on all orchestral instruments, singing, piano, electric guitar, bass guitar, classical guitar and percussion. There is no reason why a tall enough pianist of some ability should not also learn the organ – we have a magnificent three-manual pipe organ in the school chapel!

Altogether, it is difficult to imagine that a school could offer more breadth of opportunity for individual or group music-making and, certainly, our prime objective is to help young people to enjoy music to the full.

Arts Week was initiated during Martin Cooke's tenure at the prep school. Billed as a 'Festival of the Arts', the inaugural theme was 'Water', and a week's activity in the summer term was dedicated to poetry, drama, music and art, as well as geography and science with a watery theme. A lasting memory of the week was created by pupils with artist in residence John Hinchcliffe, who created a tile panel seascape which was mounted in the prep hall as a lasting memory of the week. Subsequent themes have included 'Fire', 'Earth', 'Journeys' and 'Japan', and Arts Week currently alternates with Science Week each year, giving pupils the opportunity to dedicate a whole week to exploring a new cultural dimension across their subjects of study.

The Clayesmore Prep sporting mantra is 'sport for all', with major sports each term for boys and girls, fixtures against local rival schools and tournaments held at the school to which other schools are invited. Among those who excelled at sport in the prep school have been Rob Hill (England and Great Britain hockey international) and Aadel Kardooni (Leicester and England rugby), both of whom returned to present the prizes at the July 1993 sports day.

The walls of the prep school pavilion are adorned with images of successful teams and the sporting achievements of pupils, and cricket features strongly here: Darren Stones who took 10 wickets for 33 in May 1985 against Perrott Hill and Ben McHardie-Jones who took 9 for 2 against All Hallows in May 1998.

Just as in the senior school, orienteering has been a hugely successful sport in the prep. It was started by the head of science Dick Keighley in 1980 (who had himself represented Great Britain in the sport and been a member of the world cup winning team in Japan), who encouraged and trained the squad and individual pupils to national victories. Included among these were Charlotte Frankiss and Daniel Maughan, who won their classes at the 1996 British Schools Championships, and Julia Blomquist who, after several successful seasons at the prep school, competes internationally, coming 14th at the Junior World Orienteering Championships in 2011.

Top right: Rob Hill and Aadel Kardooni present the sports day prizes, July 1993.

Charlotte Frankiss (**right**) and Daniel Maughan (**far right**) won the orienteering British Schools Championships in 1996.

a strong team and between them all, they brought wise leadership to bear upon the prep school. Meanwhile, in the matrons' department, the school enjoyed great fortune in their choice first of all of Mrs Diana Hamer and then of Mrs Catherine Mawhinney, both of whom were a most reassuring and loving presence for the boys and girls.

During the beginning-of-term staff meeting in April 2000, there was a surprise for all the staff when the Chairman of Council, Ron Spinney, arrived accompanied by David Little, the bursar. Lovely though it was to welcome the chairman to a staff meeting, nobody had foreseen what news he bore! Having dropped the bombshell that the Cookes would be leaving the prep school to take over at the senior school the following September, Ron Spinney departed and Martin carried on with the meeting.

And so, in September 2000, a new period in Clayesmore's history began. Martin and Eleanor Cooke were always going to be a hard act to follow, but Andrew Roberts-Wray made a considerable mark on the school with some stimulating ideas and considerable energy. He was a hockey player and his wife Charlotte was a musician, so both sport and music, particularly choral, thrived. A major initiative during his headship, which was championed and seen through by deputy heads Deborah Geary and Graham Moxham, was the beefing up of the tutorial system with tutor meeting tutees every day, so that help and support were always on hand. This system was held up as exemplary by social services inspectors at the time.

The present prep school head, Richard Geffen, joined in September 2006. He took over a flourishing school, its boarders living contentedly in their family-like house and with happy staff and a very good relationship with the senior school. Times were changing again and the school had to adapt and re-establish itself in response to local changes to the state schooling which saw a move away from the middle school system and a resultant increased intake at y ear 7. Relationships have been fostered with local primary schools. Music, drama, art and sport form the basis of much of this cooperation, with Clayesmore organising choral days, putting on plays with other schools, running art competitions and holding cross-country and other sporting tournaments. For the youngest members of the school, local nurseries are invited to a carnival or circus day each June.

In recent years the nursery has received excellent Ofsted reports, with language, literacy, mathematics and physical, emotional and creative development all awarded the highest grades. The pre-prep too has expanded, with French on offer from the reception class onwards, and a vibrant activities programme including gym, pottery and photography as well as sports, art, music and drama. A new nursery and pre-prep building opened in 2007, offering purpose-built accommodation and an exciting new playground, and that year also saw foundations laid for new science laboratories and classrooms for geography and years 3 and 4. This building was named for Richard Everett, and provided much needed new space – and also allowed the demolition of the rather scruffy huts which had previously housed some of the classrooms.

The tradition for outward bounds continues, with annual residential trips for years 3 to 8 each year, and a joint ski trip with the senior school. A major initiative under Richard Geffen's headship is the development of an international programme within the curriculum. This has the aim of broadening the horizons of pupils and staff and so far has included e-twinning with a school in Italy, a pen pal project in Kenya and a link with a school in Bangladesh. The scheme has been awarded the British Council's International School Award in consecutive years. Boarding has also grown in recent years, under the caring management of current houseparents Dan and Isobel Browse. As with all boarding schools, there is total commitment by the staff and in many cases their families. Ann Geffen teaches some PE and dance, but does much more: lending a hand in the boarding house and the administrative offices, always there to help with events and special occasions and – in the words of a visiting inspector – being 'the glue that holds everything together.'

Both senior and prep schools now regard themselves as 'two schools, but one', an improvement on the sometimes strained relations in the past, when the separation between senior and prep was rather more marked. Differences remain. Though both schools share the Clayesmore identity, the prep school has always maintained its own traditions and systems. The prep uniform differs from that

Above: Andrew Roberts-Wray.

worn by the seniors, the prep has its own houses named for previous headmasters (Everetts, Edwards-Stuarts, Seddons and Rosses) and, through a tradition whose origins are lost in the mists of time, afternoon break in the prep school is known as 'muck'.

The vast majority of prep school pupils go on to the senior school – the percentage in the last ten years has varied between 85 and 90 per cent. About one-third of the prep pupils board, starting in year 3 at the age of seven; the proportion of boy boarders to girls is around 60:40. Staff tend to stay many years at the school, often in a variety of roles, and to send their children there. Barbara Barnes, who retired in 2011 as deputy head of the prep, started 22 years previously as a part-time teacher when her children were young, went on to the Learning Support Unit and then became head of history in the prep before appointment as deputy to Richard Geffen. She, like so many of the other long-standing staff at senior and prep schools, talks enthusiastically about the friendliness and warmth of the school at all levels.

Mike and Deborah Geary agree. Both taught at the prep school for many years – Mike joined when the school was still at Charlton Marshall. All three of their children went there, grandchildren are now at the school and Deborah is a governor of Clayesmore School and a member of the prep school committee within the governing body. Mike was head of art and second master, while Deborah taught year 4 and was assistant head. Both now retired from teaching, they maintain their links with the school, and Deborah, of course, is closely involved with its governance.

Right: Barbara Barnes worked at the prep school for 22 years before retiring in 2011.

Below: Richard and Anne Geffen with pupils.

The Prep School Prospectus

An early prep school prospectus: 'Clayesmore is a school with the object of enabling the master and every member of staff to know each child as an individual.'

Today's mission is to 'Discover and develop the unique gifts of every girl and boy within a happy and relaxed environment where every individual is valued.'

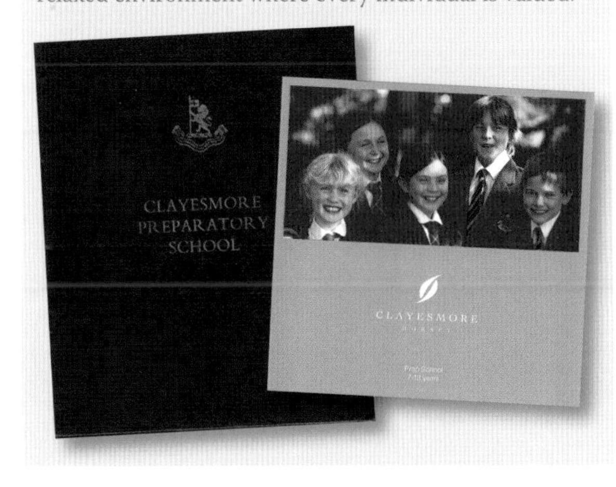

Art, Music and Drama

Art

Clayesmore has produced several well known and highly regarded artists, the first of whom was Edward Ardizzone, who was at the school from 1912 until 1918, and was encouraged in his artistic ambitions by the visiting art teacher, Miss Hazledene. He wrote and illustrated his own children's books, notably the 'Tim' series, and also illustrated the works of other writers. Briefly at the school in the 1930s was John Craxton, later to be a leading light of the 1940s 'Neo-Romantic' movement and a prolific artist; although he was at the school for only one term in 1937, while he was there he painted an oil of the view over the pond and playing fields which is still locally owned. A prominent artistic Clayesmorian of the 1940s was Robyn Denny (1945–8), who was later part of a transformational group of artists who dominated the late 1950s and 1960s and moved British art into the international mainstream; another was John Eveleigh (1940–4), a figurative artist who exhibits to this day; yet another was David Maude-Roxby-Montalto di Fragnito (1949–51) who became a highly successful glass sculptor,

Above: Robyn Denny.

Norris Scadding (1940–62)

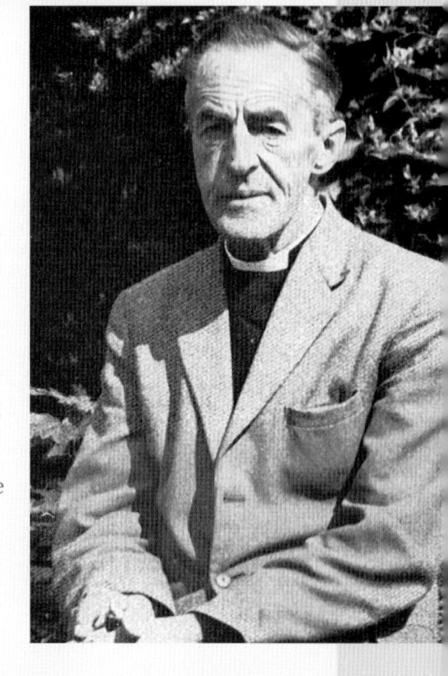

Chaplain and art master, the Reverend NA Scadding was an institution, and one of the many members of staff who served the school for his whole working life and remained nearby until his death. His 'Romish' ways worried the Nonconformist Harold Bellman when chairman of the council, but he was determined to ensure that every school service should be as perfect and as well presented as possible. By contrast, away from the chapel, he was urbanely good humoured, greeting unruly behaviour with a weary lift of the eyebrow, and somehow infecting his charges in the art room with the principles of fine art through doing his own work and expecting them to acquire the necessary skills by osmosis. He produced remarkable results. During the war he started keeping bees, and was always afterwards to be found among the hives when he was not needed elsewhere, or when he was not abroad, during the holidays, painting. He retired to East Kennett parish near Marlborough, where he was vicar before his death in 1969. In 2011 an OC, Barry Stevenson (1952–6), visited the churchyard where he is buried and, finding his grave in a sadly neglected state, organised funds to restore it to a more fitting condition. As he says, 'Scad now rests in an English graveyard looking spruce and upright – just as a gentleman should.'

In September 1912 when I was rising 12 I left home for the first time for boarding school. A horse-drawn fly took me up the hill from the station to the school on the heights above the River Thames at Pangbourne. It was a large, handsome, Victorian building approached by a long drive through woods, and it was with some trepidation that I entered a rather grand front door to find myself in a milling crowd of boys.

Our headmaster was an unusual man as headmasters go. He was short and stout and of a dark complexion. When on his rounds he invariably smoked a large cigar and was preceded by his black cocker spaniel. The smell of cigar smoke and the advent of the dog would give us warning of his arrival and enough time to be on our best behaviour – though there was one time when he dispensed with both and ran straight into a booby trap we had set for another boy. The suspense in the dormitory was awful when we saw the door opening and a number of our night bags come tumbling down, not on the head of the intended victim but on Lex himself. However, he took it in good part and though he was usually free with the cane, none of us was punished.

By the time the Great War had started Clayesmore had moved to the village of Sparsholt. It was a delightful place, except that the lavatories were appalling – a row of holes in a wooden seat over a long shallow pan which was cleared I know not how often, but certainly not often enough. The result was that I was permanently constipated and would hold all until I could get to some pretty woodland dell and there relieve myself in comfort.

An oddity was our new French master, the Conte di Balme, known always simply as the Count. What a name! It demanded a rag. A small boy stepped out in front of his desk and asked the Count 'Are you barmy, sir?' The Count descended from the dais and hit the boy a resounding blow which felled him, as if dead, to the ground. A ghastly silence followed. The blow must have sounded worse than it was, as the boy, though suffering from a sort of shocked surprise, was totally uninjured. As for the Count, at that moment he gained an ascendancy over and a respect from the boys which spread to the whole school. He became a loved and venerated master and a legendary figure in the annals of Clayesmore.

Our regime in those war years was a spartan one. The dormitories were large and in the winter the water in the tin basins beside our beds was sometimes frozen. In the winter, on getting up, we had to take a cold shower and in the summer bathe; a swarm of naked boys would hurl themselves downstairs and along the passages to the swimming bath, hurried on by prefects with knotted towels. Always before breakfast there was the morning run, a barbarous habit which I am glad has now been largely abandoned.

Disaster came when Lex appointed me a prefect, a position which I soon found I could not hold down. I simply couldn't bring myself to exercise authority. I was ragged by the boys and hadn't quick wits enough to deal with the cheeky. Small boys had a horrid way of chanting behind my back 'Ardizzone, fat and bony'. Finally I went to Lex and resigned my prefecture before the sacking I felt was inevitable. He accepted my resignation kindly, knowing, I suppose, how wretched I felt. But my last term at school passed pleasantly enough. I was made a prefect again but took my duties lightly. The weather was fine; I was excused cricket so spent many happy hours idling or doodling in my sketch books. At the end I left with no regrets and with a great sense of relief that my school days were over.

Edward Ardizzone (1912–18)

Edward
Ardizzone
INDIAN DIARY
1952–53
Introduction by
Malcolm Muggeridge
THE BODLEY HEAD
LONDON SYDNEY
TORONTO

STIG OF THE DUMP
by
Clive King
Illustrated by Edward Ardizzone
A Puffin Original

I remember Mr Burke, the headmaster, giving me six of the best, as they say, because I forged a letter from my mother asking if I could leave early for half term as I wanted to go on a very early train to London with a friend of mine who had legitimate permission. I don't think the cane had an adverse effect on me at all in the short or long term. Mr Appleby, my housemaster, said I would never get English O level if I read the *Daily Express*, which I used to do. Being an English scholar he hated it. In fact I did get my O levels in English language and English literature and am a published author.

I am a creative person, so Clayesmore was perfect for me. Pottery classes in my time were in the 'pottery shack' just past the sanatorium, if I remember rightly. We had a well-known pottery teacher called Bettina Garcia, who came once a week on the bus from Bournemouth. She was young and quite bohemian, with masses of back-combed black hair, make-up and trendy clothes, and she always wore a black leather coat. She was a bit ahead of her time and very knowledgeable, and discussed the texture, shape and image of pottery and china in great detail (which was all a bit over everyone's head at the time), as well as being very experienced in colours and the firing effects of different clays. I think she was a bit dismayed when some boys only wanted to make a bowl or an ashtray, while her imagination envisaged something like a rough-edged, moon-shaped piece of art or a tall, spiral-moulded pot as a centrepiece. I made some beautiful pieces with her help and still have one or two of them.

One Saturday a friend of mine, David Lancefield, and I visited her in Bournemouth where she ran an arty cafe which, when we arrived, was full of art students and Bohemian-type

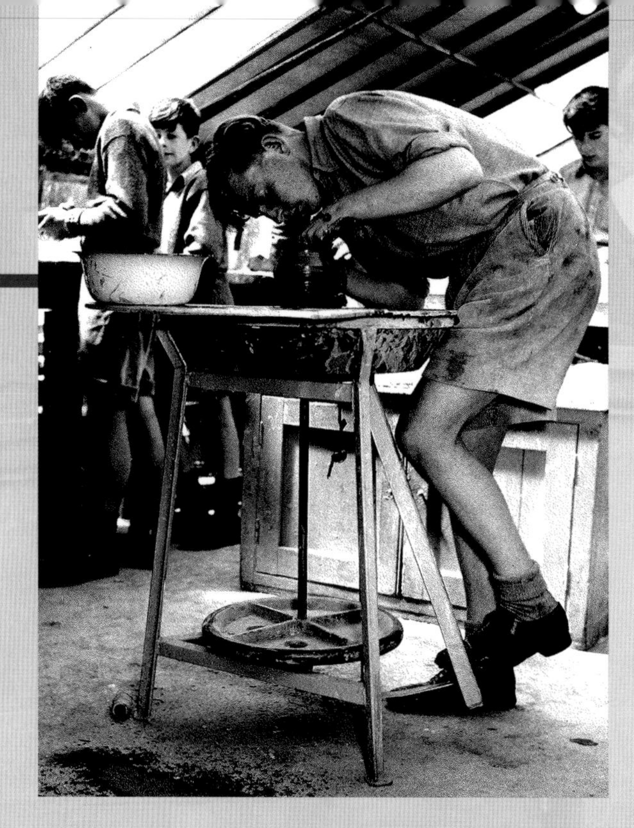

characters (known then as beatniks). We must have stood out in our shorts and Clayesmore uniforms, but she greeted us warmly and served us coffee and sandwiches on pottery that she had made herself. I think she left Clayesmore after about a year as not enough pupils wanted to do pottery, but she was a great influence on me and a nice person.

We used to take the bus to Bournemouth to see pop concerts at the Winter Gardens and I remember seeing at the stage door such up and coming artists as the Rolling Stones, the Isley Brothers, Dionne Warwick, Jet Harris, John Leyton and Billie Davis. One night we missed the last bus, and I have no memory of how we got back. I was very happy at Clayesmore generally. As my father was a diplomat overseas, I didn't see my parents that often, but I always felt that it was a second home.

George Banks (1963–6)

engraver and jeweller. Michael Gaskin (1948–52) would go on to spend his whole career running the family Art Bronze Foundry just off the Fulham end of the Kings Road. Henry Moore, Elizabeth Frink, Epstein, Chadwick, Hepworth and Ayrton all demanded that their sculptures be made and cast at his foundry which employs fellow OC Paul Van Veen (1988–91). And there was also Tony Hart (*see p108*).

That generation of artists at Clayesmore was truly remarkable. Their success and their prowess can perhaps be attributed to the arrival in 1940 of Norris Scadding as both chaplain and art master – though he refused actually to teach the subject in an academic sense. Neville Jacobson (now Jason) and Douglas Heap (both 1946–52) were keen artists but in order to do School Certificate they had to enter themselves for the course and follow the curriculum on their own without any input from Scadding; both did this, and passed. His teaching method was hands-off in the extreme; he would be present in the art room doing his own work, and would raise a weary eyebrow if asked for advice or help. But he would then proffer closely observed and constructive criticism, would suggest changes and improvements and would encourage his budding artists to recognise their own talents, experiment with new approaches and media and spread their artistic wings. There is now an Old Clayesmorian prize named for Norris Scadding and awarded every year to 'a pupil showing artistic flair and excellence'.

The closure of the village school in Iwerne Minster in the early 1980s provided the School Council with the opportunity to create a new art facility, in which it operates today. Martin Roots was head of art for ten years and during this time, Tom Denny, nephew of Robyn Denny, painter and stained-glass designer of note, developed it into a department which the *Clayesmorian* of 1994–5 records as 'a facility envied by other schools'. The art department became something of a haven from the hustle and bustle of the main school campus, belying the energy of the enterprise within.

1996 saw a major renovation and refurbishment which created much needed additional work space, such was the popularity of the subject. This 'new' art school was formally opened in 1997 by John Booth, head of art at Eton, who praised the vision and commitment of governors and staff in providing facilities of such a high standard. He was particularly impressed with the 'friendliness' of the architecture, with spacious studios full of light and a fully equipped pottery. It also has a gallery, a study area, an extensive library and slide and video collections. John Booth advised prospective parents to judge a school from its art department: 'It is here that pupils are inspired and can express their individuality, and that will tell you a lot about a school.'

Martin Roots' retirement in 1995 was followed by the appointment of Alan Peters, whose tenure in the art department lasted until his retirement in July 2010. No sooner had he arrived than his presence was felt around the school, encouraging every pupil to stretch their imaginations and leading by example by creating some of the most remarkable set designs Clayesmore has ever seen. Work produced by the department was soon on display right

Brian Epstein

Ruth Dear always had paintings on her walls, some by Norris Scadding and others by the boys. John Appleby was another member of staff who supported the endeavours of Scadding and his art classes. He would often wander over to the art room, and when he saw a picture he liked, he would offer to buy it for £1. These pictures would be changed every week in his sitting room, and there was eventually a large portfolio of work stretching back over a number of years. After Appleby retired, Ruth salvaged his collection, and later showed it to Nick Zelle, who helped her to list all the pictures and, where possible, attribute them to the artists. The list was published in the OC *Newsletter* and the artists were invited to claim them back. Unclaimed ones, including one by Brian Epstein (*below*), are now in the school archive. Douglas Heap (1946–52), a talented artist, remembers being incensed that Appleby had chosen Epstein's painting before buying one of his, and so decided the next week to paint a subject that would appeal to him – his own sitting room. The painting was duly bought, but it rankled for a while that Epstein had got there first.

around the school – even down to the year 9 sculptures along the length of the underground.

The school carol services of December 1995 witnessed another art department first – the unveiling of the first chapel hanging or altar piece by students. The inaugural hanging featured the nativity and was painted by A level pupils. The concept has evolved over the years and at the time of writing hangings are now produced by year 9 pupils in their first term at the school, with themes and artistic styles ranging from Chagall to Klimt. The 2011 frontal took the theme of 'I saw three ships'.

Art at Clayesmore is as strong as ever. Exhibitions of pupils' work have been held in recent years at the school and in London and Salisbury, and visitors are inevitably amazed at the diversity of media and work on display. Many pupils each

Chapel art hangings.

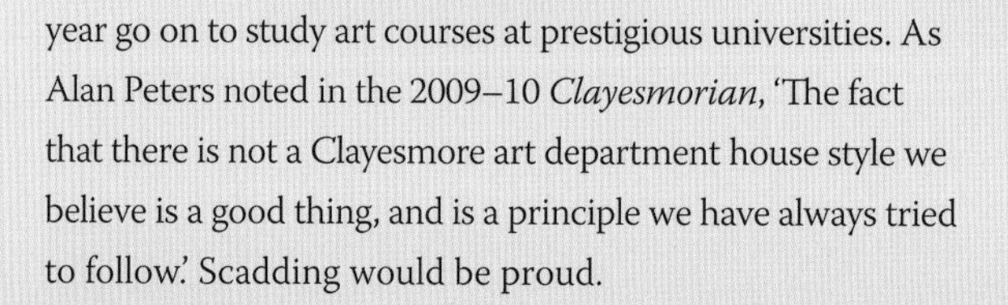

year go on to study art courses at prestigious universities. As Alan Peters noted in the 2009–10 *Clayesmorian*, 'The fact that there is not a Clayesmore art department house style we believe is a good thing, and is a principle we have always tried to follow.' Scadding would be proud.

Tony Hart (1925–2009)

Creator of Morph and much-loved children's television presenter from the 1950s to the 1990s, Tony Hart found Clayesmore the ideal school within which he could expect his artistic talents to be nurtured. He arrived, aged 15, in 1940, having won a scholarship, and was very quickly taken under Norris Scadding's wing. But Clayesmore also offered him more than enlightened art teaching. He joined the JTC and discovered a talent for map reading and shooting, becoming an excellent marksman and winning several competitions. He also took part in school plays, memorably playing Cecily in *The Importance of Being Earnest*.

As his daughter Carolyn Ross notes in her biography of her father, 'the waspish but witty' Scadding was the first real artistic influence in Tony's life. He noticed that his pupil was concentrating almost solely on linear drawing, so introduced him to the subtleties of colour and the varying effects of using different brushes, and provided helpful and constructive criticism of his work. As his daughter says, 'For my father, this tutelage in his favourite subject, combined with the beauty and grandeur of Clayesmore, was indeed heaven.'

Tony Hart always acknowledged his indebtedness to Scadding and Clayesmore, and returned several times after leaving. On one occasion he encountered a very elderly retired teacher having tea on the lawn. Recognising his former pupil, the old man asked after Tony's brother, Michael, who was at the time acting in a West End play. 'He's in *The Pyjama Game*, sir' was the reply. 'Hmm, oh dear, is he? Still, I suppose somebody has to make them.'

Music

Part of Alexander Devine's radical educational philosophy was the belief that 'the higher enjoyment of literature, music and the arts' was crucial as part of the rounded education he wanted for his boys. He himself could not read music – though he was remembered as being able to reproduce a piece of music on the piano after a single hearing – and music teaching in the early decades appears to have been reliant on casual members of staff who came in occasionally. His successor, Aubrey de Selincourt, was an accomplished cellist and formed part of the small, only five strong, school orchestra which performed in the early 1930s. Reggie Sessions, who joined Clayesmore at that period and was there until the mid-1950s, instilled his own deep love of music into his pupils, and would invite them to his rooms in the evening to listen to classical music on his ancient gramophone, which had fibre needles that needed trimming whenever the record was turned over. As boys of the time recall, since each side of a record in those days lasted only about five minutes, listening to a whole symphony required true dedication.

Music became an increasingly important component of school life during Peter Burke's headship; indeed, his final appointment in 1965 was of OC Nick Zelle as director of music, a post he was to hold until 1981. Roy McIsaac continued to champion both academic and recreational musical activities. David Spinney records a memorable school concert in March 1978, when the orchestra performing Mozart's double concerto in E flat for violin and viola included three of the distinguished and musical OC Koster family: Martin Koster, who was at the school from 1942 to 1945, who had gone on to the London Philharmonic and was the viola soloist; his brother Raymond (1944–5), double bass player with the Academy of St Martin in the Fields; and Martin's son Richard (1974–7), who was the violin soloist. Headmasters ever since have regarded music as at the core of Clayesmore's life, and today the teaching and performing of music at all levels of the school is an inescapable fact of everyday life.

A choir trip to Malta in 1980 was followed by visits to Jersey in 1986 and Budapest in 1987 under the baton of Chris Mahon, with concerts and recitals given by pupils both at the school and in the local community. Writing of his tenure in the 1992 *Clayesmorian*, a colleague commented 'that he put his pupils first was endlessly evident. His choirs sang musically, not loudly.'

Below: String ensemble.

Below right: James Tew.

During my time at Clayesmore, we spent hours listening to our wireless sets (crystal) or transistor radios if you were lucky. We usually listened to Radio Luxembourg and the top 100 hits of the day. Then it was bands like the Shadows, Dave Clark Five and of course Elvis and Cliff. The Beatles and Rolling Stones came in during my time. Election nights were always popular listening, for some reason.

Needless to say, being somewhat old fashioned in my music tastes, I found pop music no more than amusing. On my first morning we all went to morning service in the rather smart, newish chapel, and afterwards I was immediately set on by Ronald Smith, director of music, who asked me to join the choir. Someone must have told him! As I was able to read music I was asked to sing alto, along with Kemp, I recall. From that day onwards at Clayesmore, I sang at every service, as well as being taught the organ by Smith, an accomplished player and teacher. Sadly he left shortly after my arrival, and was replaced as director of music by a young Geoffrey Keating and later by Nick Zelle. Both were excellent choral trainers and organ tutors. During my time at Clayesmore, the school choir enjoyed two fabulous tours of Norway and Holland. I also remember attending the first performance of Britten's War Requiem at Coventry Cathedral with Humphrey Moore and Ronald Smith and a few other boys. That was a memorable occasion. I have since sung the work, and in Coventry, and can vouch for its greatness. We often sang in concerts in Salisbury Cathedral, including Bach's B Minor Mass.

I played a lot of sport, but for me music was the most important activity of them all. The beautiful chapel was where you would find me a lot of the time, practising Bach and Mendelssohn on the lovely, newly enlarged pipe organ. It was a lonely existence, but one I was used to. I guess all that time paid off, as I am still playing the organ today at my local church, and I also grew to love church music, which no doubt helped me spiritually.

Music for me extended beyond the chapel. I was grafted into the school orchestra as a cellist and used to play alongside Mike Henbest (viola) as a member of the Clayesmore String Quartet. We used to give recitals in music clubs in Shaftesbury and Blandford. We were the first school quartet to tackle Tippett's demanding Second Quartet and we relished its challenge. I was also given a few tutorials in music theory by Harrison Birtwistle, then a peripatetic member of staff.

Douglas Reed (1961–5)

I've always been a 'Jack of all trades and master of none' kind of musician. But it was my particular good fortune and privilege to be at Clayesmore at the same time as a number of people who were to exercise a vital formative influence on my musical development. They included both pupils and teachers of astonishing calibre, foremost among them Nick Zelle, director of music (1962–81), with his cheerful ambition and irrepressible enthusiasm, and Ian Crabbe (1967–72), with his towering genius and dazzling ability. Ian gave many memorable performances, including

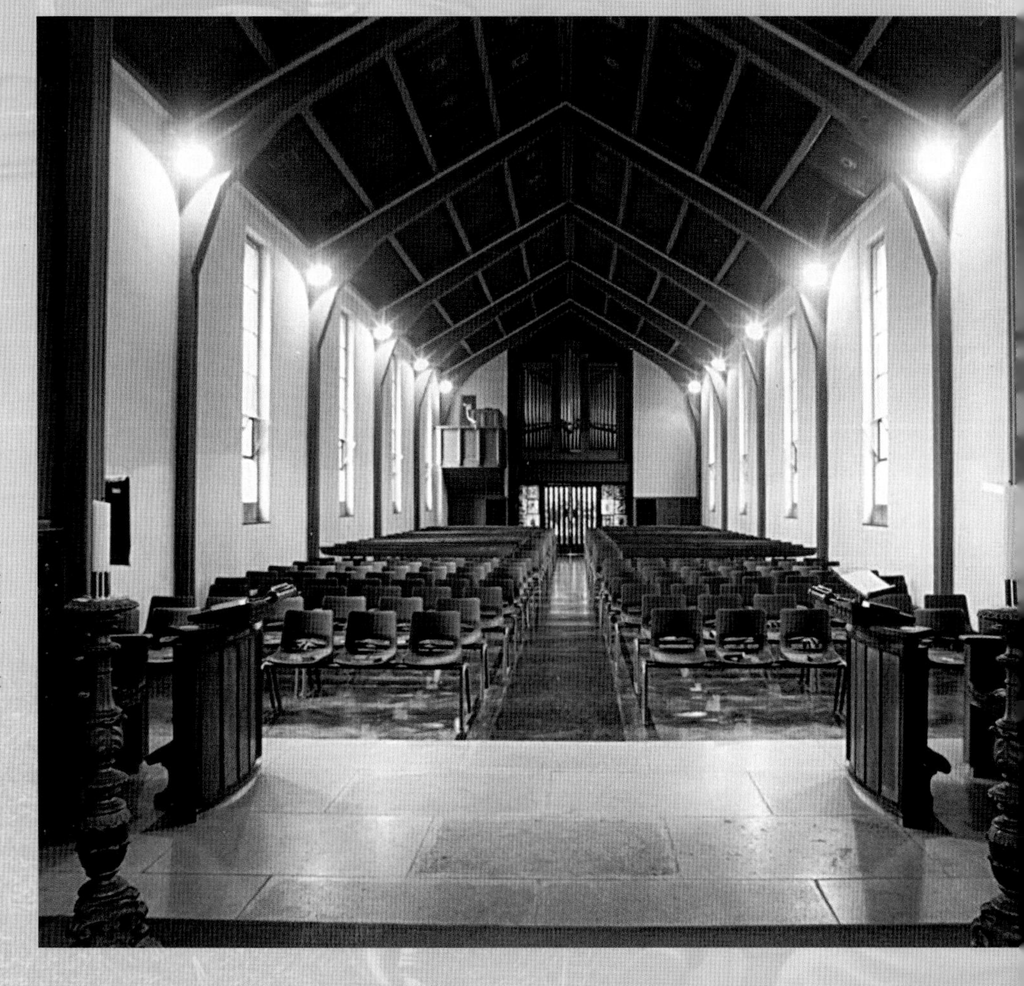

Beethoven's 'Emperor' Concerto and Poulenc's organ concerto. Having achieved his ARCO at 15, he got his ARCM at 16 and the coveted FRCO at 18.

In his history of the school David Spinney wrote: 'Young Andrew Shaw's voice was still unbroken when Carl Verrinder and Nick Zelle made the most daring decision in the long history of the Clayesmore theatre. With only eight and a half weeks to prepare, but with just sufficient musical and dramatic talent to cast it, they would attempt Mozart's *Marriage of Figaro*. During the Lent term of 1971 there was hardly a moment, day or night, when somewhere in the school *Figaro* was not being hammered out on a piano or played on a gramophone. As probably the best, as well as the most ambitious of any Clayesmore production ever, here is what one of the critics had to say: "The impudence of youth! To beat the professionals at their own game and carry off the whole of *Figaro* with such sparkling enjoyment as to make this reviewer quite sure it was the happiest performance he had ever seen; and most of the audience too, if rapt silences and delirious applause are anything to go by."'

Andrew Shaw continues: *Figaro* played twice in London with Ian Crabbe dressed as the young Mozart at the piano at the Duthy Hall, three times in the school theatre with orchestra, and was recorded on LPs. This was an immensely ambitious project which still brings back wonderful memories. As Susanna I had some taxing tunes, but can still recall much of other people's parts as well, such was the impact of the experience.

Another significant project was the performance of the musical Godspell produced entirely by the boys, plus four girls from Croft House. This was an enterprise which achieved remarkable success against the odds and exercised a considerable influence on all of us who took part. However, there seemed to be a general sniff of disapproval among the staff at this particular venture. The exception was Carl Verrinder, who gave us a glowing report in the Clayesmorian. For me, the opportunity to direct the music was pivotal, and credit must be given to Tony Coe (1971–4), whose inspiration and perseverance were key to the musical's success.

Andrew Shaw (1969–74)

Louise Salmond-Smith (née Thompson, 1989–94) writes: 'Clayesmore's music experienced great change in January 1992 with the arrival of a new director of music, Robert Fitzgerald. Fitz had been teaching in Germany, and had accepted "the first job I applied for when I stepped off the boat". To many he may have appeared aloof, but his tutees and pupils were permitted to glimpse his intelligent wit and the mischievous rebel within. He did not say anything without meaning it, so if a compliment was casually lobbed in your direction, you knew you it was well deserved – although the opposite was equally true!

'Fitz possessed the elusive talent of making the mundane interesting. In our A level music lessons, Joe Lovelock and I must have spent hour upon hour investigating the finer points of a Neapolitan VIth, or the aural atrocities of parallel Vths. Fitz made it fun. Every lesson was full of lively banter between the three of us, so much so that we often failed to notice how much we had learnt. Joe and I were complete opposites in our musical styles and tastes, and cannot have been the easiest combination of pupils to teach but, rather than allow that to frustrate him, Fitz very cleverly engineered a healthy rivalry between us which was, I am sure, the largest contributing factor in the music department's exceptionally

Robert Fitzgerald.

high A level results. I still have all the handwritten revision notes he made for us – which must have taken him hours – and they are still frequently referred to. If we worked particularly hard, he would sneak to the staff room to get us coffee, biscuits or cake. Many of Fitz's protégés have gone on to successful careers in music, and must count themselves very lucky to have been so inspired and supported during their time at Clayesmore.

'There was a strong team of peripatetic staff surrounding Fitz, helpfully bolstering the orchestra as and when required. Tony Waller was head of instrumental studies and founding director of Clayesmore Concert Band, which was atypical of many school concert bands in that it included pupils from both prep and senior schools. Tony was responsible for CCB's first ever tour abroad, to the Netherlands. Wearing our striking red and turquoise sweatshirts, I think it is true to say we dazzled audiences wherever we performed. There were many other notable characters buzzing around the department but none more astonishing than one of the piano teachers, Ian Purseglove, frequently seen walking up the path to the music department on his crutches. In spite of a shopping list of medical ailments, he was one of the jolliest characters the department has seen.'

Other highlights of the 1990s include the awarding of the ABRSM Sheila Mossman prize to Andrew Dollerson for gaining the highest marks in the country for his Grade VII piano exam, scoring 141, and the official opening of the Simon May Room in March 1993, creating an ensemble room for the various musical groups to rehearse in.

Music continues to play a very full part in the life of the school and, since 1998, the senior school director of music has been Keith Pigot. There are many highlights during the course of the year, none more popular with the pupils than the annual House Music Competition held in October. Occasional celebrity concerts and recitals are held: Evelyn Glennie, the Swingle Singers, Carlo Curley and the international baritone, Stephen Varcoe, number themselves among distinguished musicians who have visited in recent years. Choir, Concert Band, Orchestra and a large range of other instrumental and choral groups perform at concerts both formal and informal, and thanks to the expertise and enthusiasm of peripatetic singing teacher, Leslie Thompson, pupils have also staged performances of *Dido and Aeneas*, *Amahl and the Night Visitors* and *The Marriage of Figaro*. It has become the custom to undertake biennial overseas tours, the most recent of which was to Venice where the choir sang at Mass in St Mark's, while instrumentalists had the opportunity to perform in other venues. In the last three years, 27 pupils have taken Grade VIII in singing or on their instrument with no fewer than 11 gaining the much-prized Distinction.

Above: Concert Band, early 1990s.

Below left: Simon May at the opening of the ensemble room, March 1993.

Above: A production of *The Marriage of Figaro*, 2009.

Right: Choir and Concert Band trip to Venice, 2011.

Some musical curios

From time to time the school has commissioned works for performance at special events. In the 1980s Dr Francis Jackson, prolific composer and organist of York Minster, wrote a setting of the Magnificat and Nunc Dimittis for the prep school choir. For the centenary service in Salisbury in 1996, Richard Lloyd wrote a new anthem (*below*).

In 2006, thanks to the help and generosity of the Old Clayesmorian Society, and to mark the 50th anniversary of the dedication of the chapel, the school embarked on the production of a school hymn book, *With cheerful voice*. This is noteworthy for a number of musical curios: a beautiful descant to the advent hymn, 'O come, O come, Emmanuel', by one-time director of music, Christopher Mahon; a noble tune called 'Devine' by Keith Pigot; and some words by Archdeacon David Walser, OC – 'Lord God of Hosts, let warring factions cease'. Pride of place, however, goes to the splendid hymn tune 'Clayesmore', which was especially commissioned from Malcolm Archer, organist of St Paul's Cathedral at the time, and written for words by Bishop Timothy Dudley-Smith: 'O God, whose throne eternal stands'. The thought had been to bring the name of Clayesmore School to a wider audience – a rather specialist one at that – in the same way as the name of Repton School is linked to the famous tune by Hubert Parry for 'Dear Lord and Father of mankind'. Finally, the new book includes the Clayesmore School Hymn with words written by the Reverend Michael Arnold, a former chaplain, which is set to the tune of the 'Dambusters' March' by Eric Coates.

Other musical relics include a number of Christmas carols specially composed for us; notable among these is 'The Clayesmore Carol' by Christopher Tambling which has recently been published. In 2008 the well-known composer and arranger, Simon Lole, responded to a commission from the headmaster and wrote an arrangement of the end of term hymn, 'God be with you til we meet again' for the Valedictory Service. This incorporates references to Frank Sinatra's 'My Way' and also – hauntingly – 'The Last Post', but ends in a triumphant final verse with descant, trumpet and timpani all lending weight to the mighty organ accompaniment.

Drama

It is clear from the memories of Clayesmorians, right from the early days, that drama was a regular part of school activities, and that the pupils usually put on at least one play a year. But it was with the arrival of Carl Verrinder in 1932 that drama took a step upwards, further enhanced in 1936 when Peter Burke, another keen thespian, joined the school. In addition to teaching science and coaching a variety of sports, Verrinder was passionate about the theatre, and was the force behind major productions during the whole of his career at Clayesmore; he even returned a year after retirement, in 1975, to produce the school play. Ruth Dear was a formidable wardrobe mistress and make-up artist, and there were always large numbers of members of the school eager to be cast – including Peter Burke himself, perhaps most memorable as regularly playing Sir Joseph Porter in *HMS Pinafore*, though also taking a hand at producing; David Spinney particularly remembered his *Noah* in 1938 and *The Rose and Glove* (1939), both with Frank Whitbourn.

A gymnasium with a stage at the end, part of the flurry of building during Evelyn King's early headmastership in the 1930s, almost immediately became a full-time theatre and cinema, though plays were also put on at the Shaftesbury Guildhall before the building was ready. The school theatre carried on its useful life until it was demolished in 1984, prior to the construction of a brand new, purpose-built theatre, named after Peter Burke, which opened in 1988.

Today, drama is central to the school, both academically and recreationally. It is a part of the curriculum from year 9, a popular choice for GCSE and A level and often beyond to university courses covering the technical and design elements of the

Right: Ruth Dear applies make-up in a 1960s production of *HMS Pinafore*.

Right: *The Boyfriend*, 2010.

Carl Verrinder was an angular man. Pipe smoke and a whiff of chemicals hung around his tweed jacket and diffidence clothed him. To a 13-year-old who had decided, on impulse, to go to a play reading in his first term, CHPV possessed a kind of laid-back authority which I had not met before. He seemed loosely in command of a strange mixture of young men – no girls at Clayesmore in the 1950s, of course – who seemed to be taking a very relaxed attitude to the play they were reading, which was Shaw's *St Joan*. I knew next to nothing about George Bernard Shaw, and even less about the medieval peasant girl who had caught the imagination of the French nation. As the youngest there, I was told I could read several minor parts, page boys and the like, I think.

There were natural actors there; even I, who had never acted on a stage in my life, could see that. Neville Jacobson, handsome, aquiline, polished, with perfect enunciation of every word, and the headmaster, DHP Burke, Bunter to all and sundry, who read with bluster and bombast. I do not remember, 60 years later, who was reading Joan when we started, but I do know that it was halting and uncertain and critical looks were exchanged. Three quarters of an hour in, when I seem to remember that I had read around three lines, Mr Verrinder said he would like to swap some of the parts around, which was apparently the norm for a play reading. 'You,' said CHPV, 'what's your name? Dowling? You read Joan for a bit, if you will.'

I can still see the Penguin edition from which we were reading; post-war paper, with page after page on which Joan seemed endlessly involved. I had never read the play before, but it flowed effortlessly, I remember, and the pages began to move on at a rapid rate. I was enjoying the part, wondering what each new page might bring. Another half an hour, CHPV changed parts again, and I wondered whose role would now become mine. But that was not to be. 'Dowling, stay with Joan, if you will.' And I did. I had always enjoyed reading, but to read a play like this and see it jumping to life off the page was something entirely new. And it was certainly fun; I got the impression we were all enjoying it as much as I was.

End of play reading. 'Well, I think that's what we'll do, then,' said Carl. 'Shaw's *St Joan*. Lots of work involved. Meet again next Thursday in the theatre. I'll give out parts then.' He lit his pipe thoughtfully. 'Dowling: can you learn lines easily?' I supposed so. 'Ever acted before? You do surprise me. Well, we'll see you back here on Thursday, and I promise you, you will be in this play.' He disappeared in a haze of pipe smoke.

Carl Verrinder enjoyed the drama of giving out parts. The stage of the squat little theatre behind the art studio was where he allocated the cast of *St Joan*, giving out a couple of lengthy roles, then two or three minor ones, then more plum parts. I ticked off various possibilities and began to think he had forgotten about me. Boys who now knew they had a role to play were looking, for the most part, pleased. 'Which leaves us with Joan,' said Carl. 'Dowling, do you think you can do it?' I am not sure now what I said or indeed if I said anything, but I know there followed a quite intensive list of rehearsal times and dates by which things must be learnt. I do not believe now that the fact really sank in that night – though it certainly did in the following days.

John Appleby, who was the housemaster of the Juniors, sent for me. He purred from behind a light directed at the armchair in which I sat. Little wreaths of smoke escaped from his thin cigarette holder as he gently lectured me on the dangers of the stage, the pitfalls of popularity and the

Above: A production of *Murder at the Cathedral.*

Opposite: *A Twelfth Night* production from 1951.

fear that I might be lured to 'shallow pleasures'. I was not entirely sure what he was talking about, but he meant well, and sent for me on several subsequent occasions to see that I was not being lured into undesirable liaisons – an exciting possibility if I had had the faintest idea what he was talking about.

'The stage' at Clayesmore in those days was fun – but it certainly wasn't the primrose path to perdition. On the whole there was too much work to be done, and it would be fair to say that all of those in Carl Verrinder's productions became properly involved, whether in painting or making scenery, scrounging props from Blandford or Shaftesbury antique shops or getting gently merry after long, long rehearsals which sometimes ended in tears. I learnt words with surprising speed, which stood me in good stead with CHPV, who was exasperated by those who flannelled rather than learning their parts. I also learnt, for the first time in my life, how to use the voice to convey emotion. Where it came from, I do not know, though I have always enjoyed watching people's mannerisms and listening to the cadence of accent, hesitation, fear and enthusiasm. I enjoyed, as I still do now, the business of being.

One of the things about the Clayesmore plays in the 1950s was that the Dramatic Society always took them to London, to a theatre in the East End called Toynbee Hall. Its capacity was four or five times that of Clayesmore's narrow stage and tunnelled auditorium. A voice had to carry at Toynbee Hall, or the play would curl up and die. So we did *St Joan* to capacity houses in Iwerne Minster and then headed for London, which was scary for a 13-year-old boy, and one who had been feted by the Bournemouth *Daily Echo* as 'on stage for nearly every minute of this challenging production'. Yet, once the play began in Toynbee Hall, the magic of the words took over, and there were no limitations of time or place. It was, I am told, one of the best productions that Carl Verrinder had ever mounted. I have never since experienced such total immersion in any part; I knew I could convey emotion, be credible as someone entirely other than myself.

A few moments in time held in the memory for 60 years. I do not remember it all, of course, but I do remember the triumph of being part of a group of people with one purpose in mind – to bring Joan the Maid and the corruption and intrigue of her time effectively to life. Carl Verrinder is now long gone, but he awoke in me, and in countless others, the possibility of escaping out of oneself and inhabiting another world where anything can be achieved through imagination, enthusiasm and observation. In succeeding years I enjoyed *The Dark is Light Enough, Le Bourgeois Gentilhomme, Hamlet, Salad Days,* not to mention several sorties with Bunter and Spinney into Gilbert and Sullivan, but it was *St Joan* that I will always remember and the confidence that Carl Verrinder was prepared to place in a very green 13-year-old boy.

Clayesmore in those days was full of benign inspirers: Humphrey Moore, David Spinney, Norris Scadding, John Appleby, Carl Verrinder. Eccentric? Sometimes a little benignly so; but they opened the windows of possibility for us, and they are not forgotten, for in large measure they made us what we are.

Jeremy Dowling (1951–6)

We arrived at the school at the same time, in 1946, and both went on to careers in the theatre, Neville as an actor and Douglas as a set designer. The school certainly nurtured our budding talents; indeed, Douglas's parents chose Clayesmore because it had a reputation for its art teaching – though Norris Scadding's method lay less in direct interaction with his pupils and more in persuading them, through his constructive criticism, on to better things.

We were very isolated in those days before television, mobiles and the internet, when phoning home was a rare event only to be undertaken in an emergency. When we arrived at Iwerne at the start of term, our world was focused entirely and solely on the school; we were on our own there until it was time to go home again. We had to make our own entertainment – and much of it revolved around the Dramatic Society and the theatre. We were fortunate in that both Carl Verrinder and Peter Burke were passionate about the theatre and not only encouraged us but were very active in putting on productions – both of them as producers and directors, and Burke also as actor and singer. We also had Ruth Dear's considerable talents as costume designer and seamstress; many an announcement at lunch, while a play was in rehearsal, involved boys being summoned for costume fittings.

We did a lot of Gilbert and Sullivan – *HMS Pinafore* and *The Mikado* were particularly memorable – as well as *The Importance of Being Earnest*, *The Government Inspector*, *She Stoops to Conquer* and *St Joan*; Neville remembers appearing in Henry V with Brian Epstein, who was only at the school for two terms, and who played the French Ambassador. This play was unusual in being staged without scenery in the Middles courtyard in front of the double arch that led to Verrinder's chemistry lab. Douglas was Brian Epstein's page in that production, but that was almost the limit of his acting ambition; as he says, 'my forte even then was set design'. We also put on evenings of short plays, dramatised readings and shows where we mimed to singers such as Bing Crosby and the Andrews Sisters. Such events played a huge part in school life outside lessons and sport.

We were a threesome with Stephen Maer, now sadly deceased, who passed his driving test while we were at Clayesmore and regularly used to ask Peter Burke whether he could borrow his car for our expeditions out of school when we were Seniors and prefects. Whether we drove or walked, outings to tea on Saturdays were a great pleasure; we would walk across the countryside for tea at Lilac Cottage, the Anvil at Pimperne or Mary's in Blandford, and sometimes when we had the car we would break the rules and go to a pub, sufficiently far away from Iwerne that we would be unlikely to be found out. Our use of the car was so regular that Burke was heard sometimes to ask, jokingly, 'I suppose it's all right to have my car tonight, Maer?' Although Clayesmore maintained many of the usual trappings of public schools of the time – beatings, fagging and the like – it was in many ways forward-thinking, and even in our time there were questions raised about the propriety of such conventions.

Clayesmore has produced a remarkable – for a small school – number of boys who went on to artistic or theatrical careers. Neville went from the school to RADA and a successful acting career, Douglas to art school and then on to theatrical set design and others included Michael and Tony Hart, Michael Anderson, who later became Neville's agent, Michael Balfour, actor and impresario, and Howard Panter of the Ambassador Theatre Group. The school nurtured originality and self-expression; apart from our dramatic efforts, our generation also saw such eccentric exploits as Lake Warfare. The masters seemed to take a benign attitude towards whatever we wanted to do, within limits, and we were remarkably free to pursue our own interests and passions.

Neville Jason (formerly Jacobson mi, 1946–52)

Douglas Heap (1946–52)

Above: Michael Balfour in the film *Albert RN*, 1953.

Below: Howard Panter.

Bottom: Neville Jason.

Right: *My Fair Lady*, 1987.

Below right: *The Winslow Boy*, 1997.

Drama also flourished in the 1980s and 1990s. In the days before modular exams and examined Drama it was easier to persuade the Lower VIth to take part in productions. With nowhere else to perform these took place in the dining hall and I remember Birnham Wood marching across the (again piled up) dining room tables. I think the last production there was *My Fair Lady* with Jeni Toksvig (**above**) as Elisa and staff participation in the form of a memorable Doolittle, David Isard (the bursar) and David Patrick (an Australian more British than the British) as Higgins. The first production in the new theatre, and the first Chew production, was *A Penny for a Song* (**left**) in December 1988 (and the first word spoken on the stage was 'Humpage!'; Humpage, alias Graeme Owton, became head boy and is now a headmaster. I have a picture of him sitting on top of a high stool wearing a colander on his head (and am bribing him not to hand it over to his staff). Another memorable production was *Royal Hunt of the Sun*, with remarkable performances by a young Duncan Todd as Pizarro and Duncan Olby as Atahualpa. We bought the costumes from the original National Theatre production at Chichester for £100 and occasionally they still turn up in productions (though I have not seen the llama headdress recently).

Tony Chew

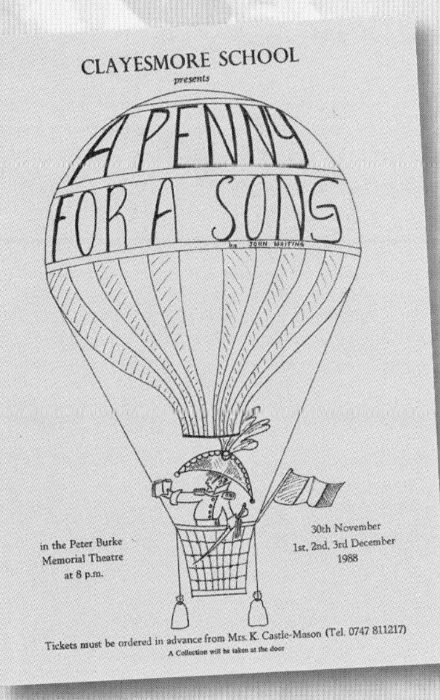
CLAYESMORE SCHOOL
presents
A PENNY FOR A SONG
in the Peter Burke Memorial Theatre at 8 p.m.
30th November 1st, 2nd, 3rd December 1988
Tickets must be ordered in advance from Mrs. K. Castle-Mason (Tel. 0747 811217)

subject as well as performing. There are regular slots each term for a play or performance, and there are three or four major productions a year including a summer play for years 9 and 10; but all other productions are open to everyone in the school who wishes to take part, whether on stage or behind the scenes. There is usually a musical every two or three years, similarly a Shakespeare play, and otherwise the range of plays which the drama department chooses to put on is wide and often challenging: Lorca's *Blood Wedding* was done in December 2011. Dance too is a strong element in drama at the school, with pupils choreographing and performing their own dances and often writing the music as well; a recent example of a contemporary dance production was *Forty Tales of the Afterlife*.

George Devine

George Devine (1910–66), Lex's nephew, when he was president of OUDS in his last year at Oxford, invited John Gielgud to direct the society's production of *Romeo and Juliet*, with himself as Mercutio alongside Christopher Hassall as Romeo, Peggy Ashcroft as Juliet and Edith Evans as the nurse. This gave him an entree into the professional theatre, and he spent the rest of his life working to encourage new talent, changing traditional approaches to training for the stage and creating theatrical environments where all the disciplines – performing, writing, directing, designing and the technical underpinnings – were given equal respect.

In the 1930s Devine set up the London Theatre Studio with Michel Saint-Denis, and was reunited with him after the war, along with Glen Byam Shaw, in the Old Vic Centre, which included a Young Vic touring company which Devine directed. The group was the nursery for scores of young theatrical talents, but eventually fell out with the management and was closed in 1952. Devine went on to be part of the English Stage Company at the Royal Court Theatre in London, which devoted itself to putting on plays by new writers including, to phenomenal success, John Osborne's *Look Back in Anger* in 1956. Devine was awarded the CBE in 1958 for services to drama.

Stephen Joseph

Stephen Joseph (1921–67) was the son of Hermione Gingold and the publisher Michael Joseph. He left Clayesmore at the age of 16 to attend the Central School of Speech and Drama, and then served in the Royal Navy during the war and was awarded the Distinguished Service Cross. After the war ended he went to Cambridge, where he was a member of Footlights, and then joined the Lowestoft repertory theatre as a director. Although he did sometimes perform, he was later to be called, by Alan Ayckbourn, 'the worst actor in the world'. He moved on to manage the summer season at Frinton, and it was while he was there that he saw a play performed in the round which, in his own words, 'set a bee beginning to buzz at the back of my mind'.

He became determined to establish a permanent theatre in the round, which he finally achieved in Scarborough, using a room on the first floor of the public library. This was the first theatre in the round in Great Britain and it has continued to flourish ever since, though in different venues. Joseph left Scarborough for Stoke-on-Trent, where he took over an old cinema and established the Victoria Theatre in 1962. He died in 1967 aged 46, but his name lives on in the Stephen Joseph Theatre in Scarborough, which found a permanent home in an old Odeon cinema and reopened in 1996 under its long-standing artistic director, Alan Ayckbourn, to whom Joseph had been a mentor and an inspiration. All but four of Ayckbourn's plays have seen their first performances there.

Kenneth Mackintosh

Kenneth Mackintosh (1919–2006) was 15 when he joined Clayesmore in September 1935, one of the Craigenders who had ventured south with Evelyn King. Shot down in 1941 whilst serving in the RAF, he was imprisoned in Stalag Luft III where he and a group of prisoners built a theatre in which they performed *Macbeth*. Returning to England

Above: Stephen Joseph.

Far left: George Devine is seen here, seated, to right of Lex.

Above: *A Midsummer Night's Dream*, 1991.

Opposite: *Red Hanrahan*, 2002.

Above: The Stephen Joseph Theatre in Scarborough.

he was asked by the Air Council to stage a musical revue *Back Home* in aid of the Red Cross, directing a cast that included Rupert Davies, Peter Butterworth, George Cole and Alec Lewis. Seasons with the Bristol Old Vic and Birmingham Rep and a friendship with Albert Finney followed, and he went on to maintain a continuous working relationship with the National Theatre from its inception in the 1960s until his death in 2006, as actor, director, senior staff director and latterly consultant staff director. Described by Lady Olivier (Joan Plowright) as 'an absolute backbone' to the company, he attended most first nights at the National Theatre until his death.

The head of drama, Mark Fraser, works with three other teachers, a technical tutor and a costume tutor, both teaching drama and its related subjects throughout the school and managing and producing the performances. There is a great deal of inter-departmental cooperation in a dramatic production. Drama at Clayesmore has benefited hugely from Alan Peters' innovative and ingenious approach to set design, using perspective trickery and manipulating and raking the stage to produce amazingly sophisticated effects.

An innovation was the *Clayesmore Mystery Cycle*, which involved the whole school from the nursery to the sixth form coming together to tell the Bible stories in the medieval tradition. The performance in 2006 had the nursery and pre-prep doing the Nativity, the prep school telling the stories of the Fall of Man and the Plagues, and each senior school house taking on episodes such as the Resurrection of Lazarus and the Flood. Every part of the cycle was in the control of the students, from the music to the direction, which resulted in a stimulating mix of styles and pace.

Perhaps one of the most resounding recent dramatic successes has been the puppetry production *Red Hanrahan*, adapted by Mark Fraser from stories by Yeats of Irish folklore, with puppets designed by Alan Peters and made by him and other art department staff and pupils. The life-size puppets are manipulated by four cast members – one each for the legs, one for the left hand and head and one for the right hand and rear – who also speak the lines. There is awesome, and hard-won, skill involved in manipulating the puppets so that they move convincingly, develop characteristics and convey emotion; they can even be made to shuffle a pack of cards although the two hands doing the shuffling are operated by two different people. The show was put on at the school in 2000 and was performed at the Medieval Hall in Salisbury in 2002.

Many pupils who first trod the boards at Clayesmore have gone on to careers in stage and screen. Behind the scenes these include film producer Hugh Stewart, controller of Granada Television Mike Scott, musical theatre bookwriter Jenifer Toksvig and West End theatre impresario Howard Panter. Several OCs are now employed in the West End theatre, and others have gone on through costume design to careers in the fashion industry.

PART 4:

The Modern Era

Roy McIsaac's successor as headmaster, Michael Hawkins, a philosophy graduate of Melbourne University, arrived for the autumn term of 1979 at a school firmly on its feet. Numbers in the senior school had reached 244, the first girls' house was full, the prep was flourishing and the balance sheet was healthy. His background at Bedales, Dover College and a new boarding school in Portugal for expatriate children made him ideally suited to carry on McIsaac's work in developing coeducation further and expanding Clayesmore's overall educational offer. During the months before he took office he was closely involved with the departing headmaster and the School Council in the detailed plans for change and development. Such was his vision that Clayesmorians returning to school at the start of the autumn 1979 term found it markedly different from the school they had left just a few months before.

Perhaps the most shocking change was unplanned; a fire had devastated the classrooms within days of Hawkins' arrival and less than a month before the start of term. Temporary classrooms filled the void, and the insurance payout resulted in the building of new permanent facilities rather earlier than could have been hoped. But there were other differences too, perhaps most notably a change to the house system. Hawkins was strongly in favour of the more usual 'vertical' pattern, with pupils aged 13 to 18 in each house, rather than the type that had endured at Clayesmore for several decades, where pupils started as members of the

Junior House and moved on to become Middles and then Seniors. His preference was mainly for pastoral reasons, and he met some opposition among traditionalists, but his view prevailed and was quickly put in place.

He also recognised that more accommodation for girls was a priority, and that changes to the house system could go happily hand in hand with moving the girls into the main house, where Wolverton joined Bower as a second girls' house, and distributing the boys between Gate, Manor and the vicarage in the village, now renamed Devine. As numbers increased, more building became essential: the new King's House for girls, a remodelled dining hall and, later in his tenure, the magnificent new Sports Centre. More pupils allowed for more staff and a wider range of subjects – and inevitably resulted in improvements in academic standards. More and more students in the larger, stronger sixth form went on to universities, colleges and vocational training.

SarahJane Newland (née Kennard) recalls that the school seemed full to bursting at this time, with more and more girls and more and more day pupils changing the balance and nature of the house structure within the school. She also remembers the capes which formed part of the girls uniform – bright blue with red hoods.

The magazines of the early 1980s reflect changes beyond the school gates. The first computer was puchased in 1981 and a Computer Club made its appearance, games of Dungeons and Dragons were played, table tennis gave way to darts, snooker and pool, and badminton and squash were on the rise. Young Enterprise schemes, mentored by local businessmen and women, offered the opportunity to learn about forming companies, manufacturing useful products, running budgets and meeting deadlines. Sports results continued to be impressive, and academic achievements were visibly on the rise.

Editor of the *Clayesmorian* at this time was John Skinner, who transformed the magazine in the 23 years he was responsible for it from the blue-covered booklet to a larger, more lively and engaging format. Along with his wife Joy, John was houseparent of first the Middles house and then the newly vertically arranged Gate, from where Mike Henbest recalls him 'gazing down benevolently on the kaleidoscopic panorama of legal (and illegal) activities taking place beneath the windows of his flat'.

Above: Michael Hawkins.

Below left: Building King's House.

Bottom left: Sports Centre under construction.

Below: Science room.

An initiative in 1983 was the inception of a Pupils' Council to provide a forum for discussion on all aspects of life at Clayesmore. Membership consisted of the head boy and head girl together with three representatives from each year group – a boy boarder, a girl boarder and a day pupil. There was some apprehension among the staff that complaints and trivia might take up the bulk of the meetings, but this quickly proved not to be the case. The headmaster and bursar were impressed by the quality of the proposals and requests resulting from the discussions, some sensible suggestions were implemented and ideas for charity fundraising came thick and fast; moreover, the representatives showed themselves admirable delegates for the ideas of their year groups and the meetings and the voting were managed efficiently.

John Brooke-Little (1927–2006)

Prize Day in 1983 saw John Brooke-Little (*left*) give his valedictory address as chairman of the School Council, a post he had held for 12 years. As he pointed out, when he was first in office Clayesmore was the smallest public school in the country with only about 160 pupils; it had now become a coeducational institution with 550, and educated children aged from five to 19. He himself had a distinguished career at the school (1941–6), sent his sons there and served it for many years after leaving.

His interest in heraldry started while he was at Clayesmore. He founded the Society of Heraldic Antiquaries at the school, and when he went on to read history at Oxford, he used the same title for the society he set up there; it later became the Heraldry Society, which flourishes to this day and with which Brooke-Little was involved for the whole of his life.

His entire career was spent in heraldry. He held a variety of offices within the College of Arms, ending up as Clarenceux King of Arms, second only to Garter. He served on the planning committees for HM Queen Elizabeth II's coronation and Prince Charles's investiture as Prince of Wales. He wrote many books on the subject and remained devoted to the heraldic community until his death.

Below: *The Clayesmorian* magazine transformed under the editorship of John Skinner.

It was a scary experience arriving at Clayesmore at the end of 1981 and boarding for the first time in a dorm with about ten strangers. I was in Gate, and the first night we arrived and were tucked up in bed we were woken by the traditional 'welcome' from the next year up (the Removes), who came in with pillowcases full of shoes, clothes, anything that was lying about and proceeded to attack all the newbies in their beds. This lasted about 20 seconds and afterwards all was quiet apart from sniffles from homesick 13-year-olds. God, I thought, is this is what it is going to be like? I want to go home!

Things settled down after that, and we soon learned the rules. Prefects were God as far as we were concerned and, if asked, you were expected to 'fag' for them – everything from making tea to making their beds, cleaning their rooms and running errands. They were also responsible for the other onerous activity at the time, known as 'specials', which was a punishment dished out for unruly behaviour and involved being woken up early on a Saturday morning, when everyone else had a lie-in, changing into games gear and heading downstairs. The next hour was hellish, and could be anything from crawling around a frost-bitten field on your belly to press-ups in the lake (not nice in midwinter) or a cross-country run. Once you had finished you were greeted with a 30-second freezing cold bath or shower. Although I was quite a cheeky youngster, I think I deserved only a handful of the specials that I ended up doing; I don't remember many lie-ins during my early years.

Our next year was 'Remove' year, and as was traditional we were packed off to an Outward Bound course in Wales – a week of camping, climbing, hiking and all manner of activities. My group seemed to include all the 'toughies' and pretty much everyone who either ruled the roost or was the coolest, a fact that scared me rigid; but after a week of bonding we all ended up firm friends. The next year was the next big turning point for most Clayesmorians, as hormones began to rage and girls started to become interesting instead of just annoying. This of course led to all sorts of dubious night-time treks across the grounds to meet with whomever it was you were 'going out' with. I never really understood the term 'going out' as I remember finally plucking up the courage to ask a girl called Angie Blaber out while watching a film in the old, rickety cinema, and when she said yes I was completely flummoxed as to 'where' we were supposed to 'go out'. I remember, to great amusement from the rows behind, gradually sliding my arm around her shoulders, her going stiff as a board and then walking out... I didn't see her for a term and a half.

I had entered Clayesmore as a music scholar and a flautist, and the choir under Chris Mahon became a large part of my life – hours of flute practice in the new music block and then choir practice and of course Sunday service. One young boy in the choir would always have a big broad smile on his face, and loved the music, but was completely tone deaf. He made up in enthusiasm what he lacked in musical skills and would 'rap' the hymns in his own style, leaving the choirmaster desperately trying to work out where this underlying monotone was coming from.

Top: A lazy sunny afternoon in Gate Tower, 1984.

Above left: The Outward Bound course in Wales, 1983.

Above: Kevin Jones, left, and Phillip Mott, right, enjoy the aftermath of a shaving foam 'battle', 1984.

Of course in all schools there are the naughty kids, and I am happy to say that I was one of them. Giving the teachers a hard time and getting away with murder was all part of the fun, as long as the work was done for the reports. It is difficult to remember all that we got up to as there were so many things, and of course every generation thinks that they invented how to misbehave.

An Old Clayesmorian who had been at the school during the Second World War came once to give a talk at Sunday chapel, and told us about a German bomber that had been shot down a few miles away over Hambledon Hill. Of course, we were all banned from going there on threat of expulsion, and the excitement gradually passed... but about a month later there was a random locker check and one teacher was shocked to find a German machine gun complete with ammunition among the games kit in one boy's locker. He was hauled in front of the headmaster who demanded to know what he was playing at; 'I just thought it would be a great souvenir to take home, sir' was the answer.

It has to be said that I had gone from being homesick to not wanting to leave. Clayesmore became my life and world, and all the important changes that happen when you are an adolescent happened in those grounds and became forever etched in my memory. The teenage years are shaping years, and important ones, and while we would bend the rules, it was all in good fun. Did we invent new tricks and new jaunts? Not really. Every year has new characters and new stories, and creates new memories. Happy days.

Kevin Jones (1981–5)

A muddy afternoon of football... (from l–r) Charles Schofield, Matthew Beynon, Kevin Jones and Jonathan Weatherall.

A number of long-standing members of staff retired towards the end of Hawkins' tenure. Among them were John Skinner (23 years), Jim Tilden (22 years) and John Macdonald (24 years). Each of these had continued the Clayesmore tradition established by the previous generation of masters and contributed to all areas of the school's life, in the classroom, the boarding houses, on the games pitches and, perhaps most importantly, as a friend to their charges at the school throughout the significant upheavals they encountered with the introduction and establishment of girls.

The Remembrance Service in November 1985 celebrating 40 years since the end of the Second World War saw the headmaster joined at Clayesmore by his four predecessors: Evelyn King (1935–40 and 1942–5), John Appleby (1940–2), who had retired from the teaching staff only three years previously, Peter Burke (1945–66) and Roy McIsaac (1966–79). This was to be Michael Hawkins' final academic year at Clayesmore. He and his wife Angela were an extremely effective and popular team, and a great deal was achieved during their time at the school – much building work, the full development of coeducation and the full integration of prep and senior schools. But they wanted to move on, and an opportunity came up for a different kind of headship in 1986; they left at the end of the summer term of that year.

OCs and headmasters gather at the November 1985 Remembrance Service.

Clayesmore when I arrived in January 1985, as housemaster of Devine and head of history, struck me as a curious school. I had come from a reasonably disciplined all boys' school in Scotland and found the whole atmosphere of the place distinctly casual.

- No school uniform in the sixth form, which meant that they were the scruffiest members of the school, wearing trainers and a surprisingly uniform colour of grey or blue. Ties and jackets were not worn by a number of the male staff.
- No bells (and still none) meant that lessons came together in an arbitrary fashion (still no change?). At least students (three in the sixth form) turned up for my lessons. One of my colleagues sat in his classroom in solitary splendour, unperturbed by the lack of pupils.
- Assembly on Mondays was in the dining hall. Everything was swiftly whisked away after breakfast and the school piled in. The younger pupils sat on chairs while the sixth form lounged around at the back or perched on the tables piled up at the sides. The staff huddled in the passage beyond.

Other things struck me as odd:

- The strategic siting of the chemistry labs under a boarding house.
- I was a housemaster to 50 boys but I was tutor to boys who were not in my house.
- One of the most successful societies in the school was the Paranormal Society.

Despite the apparently chaotic nature of the place, it did seem to work. Very early on in my time here I was sent to a local prep school to 'sell' Clayesmore and found myself on a platform with housemasters from Marlborough, Winchester, Sherborne and others. I remember that, unable to be particularly boastful about either exam results or facilities, which the others focused on, I said to the assembled parents that they needed to come and see Clayesmore and that what had struck me about it was the warm and friendly atmosphere of the school, where pupils respected each other and where there was an easy relationship with the staff. That has certainly remained true, perhaps achieving Lex's 'liberal democratic state', while both the exam results and facilities have steadily improved.

Communication of what was happening or might happen was pretty arbitrary, and in the days before registration or risk assessments anything went and usually did. (One of the items printed by the print shop was a chit 'This entitles the bearer to do anything they want'.) There were advantages in being able to do one's own thing (and this was another great advantage of being in Devine), but it did make for considerable confusion and sometimes mild (and not so mild) disagreements. The school seemed to be run by three formidable women: Jill Knight, the headmaster's secretary, Vendela Elverson, the director of studies, and Di Foot, the housemistress of Wolverton. Jill had her finger on the pulse and if nobody else (including the headmaster) knew the answer to a question she always did. Vendela, in the days before computers, produced the timetable from an office of apparently complete chaos. Not much was on paper but she had everything clear in her mind. Di Foot was the senior member of the house staff in the days when house staff meetings were the nearest thing to SLT. We always knew when she was going to disagree with the headmaster as she would begin 'Quite honestly Michael…'. She had high standards and kept the house staff in line.

Vendela Elverson was the pioneer for girls' and women teachers' rights at Clayesmore. The first housemistress of the single girls' house, she fought every inch of the way to make the girls an integral and equal part of the school with the boys. With the transfer of the girls to the main house from the former vicarage, she decided to retire to her own house in Sutton Waldron, but her commitment to the school was not lessened with her appointment as director of studies. To construct a timetable either requires the mind of a Short or a Kasparov, or it requires a computer. In the days before the latter hit Clayesmore, Vendela grappled with the timetable and fitted in an amazing number of demands, requests and quirks.

I was very impressed by the music, which seemed to be an area in which we really did excel and where we were lucky to have some very talented young musicians. Concerts abounded and there were also more informal bands. Who can forget (well most of us can easily!) Brazen Hussy?

I have to admit that the house music competition was never my favourite Clayesmore occasion, mainly because it was difficult for three Devine boys armed with triangles (I exaggerate but not much) to defeat the Wolverton violin quintet. I actually thought I had managed to destroy the competition by encouraging the house to dress up as smurfs and sing 'Here we go, Here we go, Here we go again/ to sing along a boring song to drive you round the bend', but fortunately the competition has proved resilient.

Tony Chew

Left: Chapel service, 1985.

Below: Damage caused by the hurricane in 1987.

His successor was David Beeby, historian and keen sportsman, who arrived with his wife, Anne, from Gresham's in autumn 1986. The building of the new Peter Burke Theatre began during his first year. It opened in 1988, and was immediately appreciated for the fact that more time could now be given to producing drama rather than also having to set up stage, sets and lighting systems in the dining hall. That year also saw the opening of the new Social Centre, incorporating a tuck shop, a clothing shop and a sixth form common room. Much of the work on both these new buildings was carried out by the school's own maintenance staff under the direction of Alan Newman, clerk of works. But these years also saw much destruction at the school as the result of the hurricane of 1987 and the huge storms that followed it in later years. A chilling indication of the power of the wind was the discovery after one storm of a slate blown through a classroom window and embedded in the whiteboard on the opposite side of the room. During the storm that occurred on Christmas Day 1990 the bursar, walking his dog round the lake, saw a magnificent tree planted a century before by Lord Wolverton gently heel over onto the sunken tennis court, followed by several others. Two of the mature beech trees by the A350 were blown onto the road, but were cleared away in time for Christmas morning church services in the village by head groundsman Ray Norris and his chainsaw. Mercifully, no one at the school was injured in any of those great storms.

Clayesmore continued to offer more and more to its pupils. There were increasing numbers of trips both home and abroad, to ever more far-flung places and with both educational and adventurous aims. The magazines were full of clubs and activities, sporting achievements and musical and dramatic events. The Duke of Edinburgh Award Scheme, which had started rather tentatively in the term before David Beeby arrived, had grown two years later to such an extent that over half of those involved had already gained their bronze or silver awards and were motoring on towards the gold. The first to reach that goal was Freya Miller-McCall, head girl in 1990/1.

September 1992 was the first Clayesmore Expedition Day, when deputy head Roger Denning wrote 'Don't come to Clayesmore today! Clayesmore is coming to you', describing the event in the next *Clayesmorian*. For one day – thus minimising disruption to the general teaching curriculum – every pupil would go on an educational trip. These excursions initially focused on local attractions – perhaps to Lulworth, or to Jane Austen's Bath, but they also took in London museums and theatres, golf, dry slope skiing, and even day trips to Calais.

Academic results continued to improve, and the curriculum expanded to include new subjects such as computer studies, originally introduced in the early 1980s as a peripheral activity, and now part of the mainstream curriculum, with increasing numbers of pupils opting to study it at both GCSE and A level. Maintenance and building work improved dormitory

Above: The Beebys with prefects, 1998.

Right: School trips in the 1980s and 1990s.

accommodation in the houses and transformed the dark basement corridor in the main house into a tube station tunnel with brightly coloured pipes and suitable signage. And 1996 saw Clayesmore celebrating its centenary.

As Alan Gilmour – OC 1943–6 and chairman of the centenary appeal committee – wrote in the *Clayesmorian* for 1994/5, 'There is one thing we can all be certain of – this is the only centenary any of us will see at Clayesmore in our lifetimes, so we'd better make the most of it.' As Tony Chew also wrote, 'Reading the early history of Clayesmore, one suspects that few would have laid bets on it reaching this milestone'; it was poignant that Evelyn King, without whom the school would certainly not have survived beyond the 1930s, had died only the year before. But there was a strong feeling that 100 years of history must be not only celebrated but also marked in a suitably permanent fashion, and the decision was taken that efforts should be put into fundraising for an all-weather pitch for hockey in winter and tennis in summer.

This decision came about partly because the Foundation for Sport and the Arts had offered a staggering £100,000 for the project – provided the work could be

completed in 1995. Dorset County Council also put in £20,000, but the total needed was £300,000 for the pitch, lighting and a pavilion, leaving the school to raise £180,000. Energetic efforts to conjure up donations and covenants were supplemented by fundraising activities, including dividing the 6,000 square yards of the pitch into individual squares worth £50 each. At the centenary Speech Day of 1996 it was possible to announce that the fund had raised £215,000, and the all-weather pitch was already in use, having been opened by former prep school pupil and Great Britain Olympic hockey player, Rob Hill. As David Beeby said in his address, 'Given that the alumni of the school include two fellows of the Royal Society and, in Sir Rodney Sweetnam, the current president of the Royal College of Surgeons, and given the calibre of this year's school leavers, I think Lex would be full of approval, and approval too of the way in which Clayesmore had celebrated its first 100 years.' That memorable Speech Day was attended by many long-standing stalwarts of the school, including 83-year-old George Dobie, Evelyn King's chauffeur, who had come with him from Scotland and stayed at Clayesmore for his entire working life, along with his wife Ivy. He retired in 1985, having spent his final years at the school as the general handyman in Devine House, and continued to live in Iwerne Minster. He died in 1997, remembered for his long service and faithfulness to the school and, as Tony Chew recorded in the *Clayesmorian*, as 'a man of modesty, loyalty and exceptional courtesy'.

Centenary celebrations

The centrepiece of centenary celebrations was the special service held at a packed Salisbury Cathedral on March 2, the nearest available date to that of the school's founding in February 1896. Pupils from both prep and senior schools, alumni, parents, governors and friends heard the Bishop of Salisbury's address and music provided by the school choir and orchestra, including two specially commissioned pieces.

Most moving was the rededication, when pupils from countries all over the world lit a candle, repeated the prayer each in his or her own language and took their lights to the far corners of the cathedral. Finally, in order to honour Clayesmore's centenary of existence, the oldest Clayesmorians present were each given a copy of David Spinney's *History*; the oldest there was 91-year-old Richard Clarkson.

Top left: Rob Hill at the opening of the Centenary Pitch.

Above: The Centenary Fair.

Right: David Beeby, John Elderkin, Alan Gilmour and Tony Hart at the Centenary Fair.

Below right: Old Clayesmorians, headmasters, pupils and the Bishop of Salisbury at the Centenary service.

The Centenary Ball was bedevilled by extremely rainy weather, which looked likely to put a damper on the activities that were planned for the lawn; nevertheless, over 300 guests came to enjoy the dancing, the excellent food and the chance to meet up with old friends. The Centenary Fair, held on June 23, was much luckier with the weather and the event was a great success, in terms both of money raised and the enjoyment had by all. The school houses each had their own activities to promote to the willing punters, external attractions set up their stalls and tents, there were hot air balloons, a bouncy castle, a dog show and a vintage car display, and the Sports Hall hosted a collectors' fair. Musical events took place in the chapel, there was an inter-village cricket match going on and there were artistic exhibitions and gymnastic displays. And of course there were endless cream teas being served – to the extent that one of the pupils helping in the tea tent stated afterwards that she had decided never to be a waitress, and another that she 'wouldn't really mind never having to see a cup of tea or a scone again.'

A highlight was the presence of Tony Hart, who was part of the opening ceremonial and who did a series of drawings of the event which were later auctioned off. It was quite clear that he was delighted to be back at his old school and to be adding his considerable weight to the fundraising activities.

After the fair officially ended the school carried on enjoying the hired attractions and a disco. The beer tent on the lawn was where the staff were to be found enjoying a few well-earned drinks and a buffet supper. The finale was the cutting of the centenary cake, a toast to the school and fireworks in front of the main house.

Other events taking place to celebrate included receptions and dinners at Lord's and Blandford Camp, a fashion show, a celebrity organ recital given by Carlo Curley. Lastly, in September, the whole senior school spent Expedition Day walking in house groups from a point near Salisbury back to the school in a scene reminiscent from the school's earliest history and last enacted as a fund-raising exercise by Michael Hawkins in 1985 to raise funds for the building of a cricket pavilion.

David and Anne Beeby left Clayesmore at the end of the summer term of 2000, having spent 14 years at the school and taken it into the new millennium. As a housemaster at his previous school, Beeby was all too conscious of the need to make a boarding house a home from home, and under his guidance pastoral care and the tutorial system flourished and strengthened. His love of all things sporting led to increased emphasis in that area, and as he was proud to claim, 'the strength of games at Clayesmore is remarkable for a small school'. He left Clayesmore thoroughly fit for modern educational purpose while also true to tradition and history. His wife Anne too was a huge asset to the school. She built up the Friends of Clayesmore, she taught in the Learning Support Centre, concentrating on pupils with dyslexia, she turned her hand to anything that needed doing and, as the *Clayesmorian* reported, she was 'generous with her time, her house and above all her emotional energy'.

Above: Martin and Eleanor Cooke with their first group of prefects in 2000.

Below left: King's girls take a rest on the whole-school walk, Expeditions Day 1996.

The new century

The new headmaster and his wife, Martin and Eleanor Cooke, did not have far to travel when he took office in the autumn term of 2000, as he was already head of the prep. His mission right from the start, as the *Clayesmorian* reported, was that 'Clayesmore will be one of the most exciting, stimulating, vibrant and innovative schools in the south of England... building on all that David and Anne Beeby have achieved in their 14 years of service'. He recognised that there were some issues that needed to be addressed and some changes that had to be made, and he came into the job brimful of ideas and energy and with the huge advantage that he already knew the school and a great many of its staff and pupils.

His first term was frantic, as the new head of the prep school was unable to start until January 2001, so Martin had to combine both roles for an exhausting few months. But this did not stop him embarking on major new building projects and considerable improvements in the boarding houses. The 'Bricks and Mortar' feature in the *Clayesmorian* for 2001/2 had a great deal to report. Even the magazine itself was bigger and better, with much more colour photography – and

Left: The Jubilee Building.

Below: The Spinney Centre.

four years later it developed further into an even more glossy new format. And there was yet more building to come: in 2004 the Spinney Centre for the humanities opened, named for Ron Spinney, an Old Clayesmorian.

In October 2007 the school was subject to an ISI inspection which, as the chairman of the council was able to report at the following year's Speech Day, was 'without a doubt the most impressive inspection report that the

Robert Mash

July 1999 saw the retirement of Robert Mash, who is perhaps unique in the annals of Clayesmore in that he was at the school man and boy; his association spanned almost his entire life. He joined the prep school, then at Charlton Marshall, in 1946 and moved on to the senior school at Iwerne in 1952 as the winner of an academic scholarship. His life at the school was very full: he played first team rugby and cricket, was a regular member of John Appleby's Arts Society, both listened to and played music (the horn was his instrument) and was both a prefect and, in his final year, head boy. He was a keen naturalist and biologist, under Humphrey Moore's tutelage, and left Clayesmore in 1958 for Balliol College, Oxford, where he had won a scholarship to study biology.

He returned to the school in 1969 after Humphrey Moore's death, when he was appointed by Roy McIsaac as head of biology. He was to stay at Clayesmore for the rest of his working life. Among his first tasks was the design and organisation of the new biology laboratory, which was named for his old teacher, Humphrey Moore. And on top of his duties as an excellent head of the biology department, he continued as teacher to embrace the wide range of activities and interests that had marked his time as pupil. He played a central role in music at the school, took a hand in sports coaching and ran the Burney Library for a while. He was instrumental in reviving the fortunes of the Old Clayesmorians, for whom he acted as secretary for several years as well as editing the newsletter. And beyond his life at the school he played the horn in the Dorset County Orchestra, enjoyed driving rather outré cars, had a passion for fine wine and wrote the definitive book on *How to Keep Dinosaurs*. His retirement in 1999 marked the end of an era, and was celebrated in the *OC Newsletter* by a long appreciation of his remarkable contribution to Clayesmore and a page of photographs of him at various stages of his school career.

school has ever had'. As he went on to say, 'We seem to have a magical mix of staff and pupils who believe in each other, and who are deeply loyal to the tremendously strong family ethos that we all recognise pervades the school.'

Martin and Eleanor Cooke made a massive impression on the prep, and continue to do so at the senior school; everyone who works or is educated at the school acknowledges the huge difference they have made and the stimulating, supportive and vibrant environment they have created. Clayesmore and Clayesmore Prep continue to offer their pupils an extraordinary environment within which to grow up, live and be educated. While the Learning Support Centre is an invaluable asset, the academic teaching is of a very high standard, and the consistently excellent exam results demonstrate the huge strides that have been made in the last decade. The range of sport on offer is wide, the

Ron Spinney (1941–2008)

While he was at Clayesmore, between 1954 and 1958, Ron Spinney – David Spinney's nephew – was academically bright, a good all-round sportsman, a prefect and full of enthusiasm for school life. He was, however, no stranger to misbehaviour – in his later years as a governor, he relished spending time in the headmaster's office where he had been beaten many times so many years before. What was clear was that he loved his old school, and when he was able to, decades later, he was all too willing to give a great deal back.

His first involvement, during the 1990s when he was chairman of Hammerson plc, a building development company, was as chairman of the Old Clayesmorian Society, a duty he carried out for two or three years and which, as a moderniser, he may have found more than a little frustrating; alumni associations are after all notoriously resistant to change.

He then joined the School Council on which he served from 1997 to 2004, most of the time as chairman. His tenure saw momentous changes, perhaps the most important being the appointment to the headmastership of the senior school of Martin Cooke, then head of the prep. His work set the school up for HMC status, and in his time both the Jubilee Building and the Spinney Centre were notable additions to the campus – the latter named for him. His professional expertise ensured that both these buildings were delivered on time and within budget.

He had a close eye for detail and was an excellent communicator, making his views on what was most important very clear, and he possessed, above all, the ability to cut through the chaff and concentrate on what really mattered – exhibiting great leadership combined with patience and charm. He was a shrewd judge of character, but was also very easy to work with because of his enjoyment of life and sense of fun. He believed strongly in support for the young and was immensely generous with his time when he believed the cause to be worthwhile. His untimely death at the age of 67 in 2008 was a great blow – but as Stephen Levinson said in his address at the memorial service (from which this account of Spinney's involvement with Clayesmore is taken), 'Clayesmore should be very proud of what it produced in Ron Spinney and very grateful for all that he gave back'.

Above: Ron Spinney.

drama is frighteningly good, the art and music stimulate and nurture the talented as well as those who are less so – and all this within fine buildings, splendid grounds and the beautiful Dorset countryside. It is undoubtedly true to imagine that, although Alexander Devine would find many of the norms of modern education surprising, he would recognise in today's Clayesmore the ethos he sought to create and the high-quality education he wanted for his charges.

The winter of 2009/10 brought some of the heaviest snow falls in recent years. Shaftesbury has a micro-climate; the town is often shrouded in mist and always a little cooler than the surrounding area. Because of the height of the hills at Win Green (1,200ft and nothing higher looking east until Russia), the weather can move in quickly, is often wet and on this occasion particularly snowy.

Many pupils rely on the school bus service to get to and from Clayesmore; a twice-daily stream of navy blue winding through the villages of Wiltshire and Dorset. But what if the buses could not run – almost unthinkable? The decision on whether 'to run' fell to the headmaster. George, my son, said the way to check was to look at the school website, early. How early? Very early, as it turned out. Posted on the website at 6.30am, it became essential reading. Somehow, mention of his own attire began to filter into the weather observations. 'Pyjamas'. 'What sort?' came a parent enquiry. 'Striped' was the reply. And so the headmaster's pyjama weather commentary became an integral part of our lives during those days of 'no school' and 'buses cancelled'. For some of us who lived nearby, the prospect of driving on fresh powdery snow with little or no traffic was irresistible, and so George and I managed to get to school most days. On the first day, we arrived a respectable ten minutes late. George jumped from the car and was gone. I glanced to my right and there, on the paths leading to the DT block, was the headmaster – no longer in pyjamas, but now resplendent in tweed cap, wellingtons and sensible wool overcoat topped off with day-glo vest and whistle. The whistle was in full use, as were the arms, slowing down excited and speeding children coming from all directions. My memory of that sighting will remain always as a reminder of the wonderful dress style and commitment of the headmaster.

Lynn Button, mother of George Button (2003–10)

Outdoors

Above: The 1913 football team.

Sport – and 'manual'

One of Lex's more unusual educational convictions was his belief in the power of manual labour in educating and shaping his boys, rather than sports and games (*see box below* for his tract on 'manual', one of a series written while the school was at Pangbourne). Clayesmore always played sports as well – cricket in summer and football in winter, limited tennis and boxing when the school had an ex-army drill sergeant, as Graham Mervyn recorded – but manual work was in Lex's time an integral part of physical education and one that he certainly regarded as preferable to team games.

Lex himself would turn out occasionally on the football field where, as David Spinney wrote, 'there were two opinions of his prowess – his own and that of everyone else'. Football was Clayesmore's winter game, until the 1916/17 season when Lex suddenly decided that he wanted the school to change to rugby. Unusually, he was outmanoeuvred by George Vaizey, the football captain, who had no wish to see his final season spoilt, and went ahead with planning football fixtures for the following term in the teeth of Lex's displeasure. However, he eventually got his way and rugby was officially adopted. Statistics for the 1920s show that the school was conspicuously successful at the sport – and the same was true for cricket too; significant victories in both sports were won against formidable teams. There were some barren years – once when mumps ruined half

Off to work.

A practical lesson in lumbering.

AT SCHOOL IN THE FIELDS.

An article of special interest to the youthful readers of the "London Magazine."

By Herbert Heward.

THE old-fashioned notion that a gentleman is one whose hands have never been soiled by manual labour, receives a sound shock when one lights upon a community of sons of peers and other youthful members of the aristocracy, stripped to their skins and hard at work road-making, just like any ordinary gang of "navvies."

Such is the sight that may often be witnessed on a summer's day, within ten miles of London, at Clayesmore School—one of the youngest and most promising of our English educational establishments.

A boy is, in a sense, born a gentleman: it is the aim at Clayesmore to make a man of him! After all, the son of wealthy parents comes into the world very considerably handicapped for his life's work. He is provided with everything necessary, and a good deal that is not necessary as well; he has servants to relieve him of every arduous or irksome task; he is kept quite apart from the classes that he is taught to regard as below him; and generally he acquires an altogether unreal and distorted view of life.

To a certain extent the life of an ordinary public school meets the case of such a lad. Whatever may be said against the system of fagging, it must be admitted that it knocks some of the nonsense out of a pampered boy, and that it helps to establish a healthy relation between seniors and juniors. Still, public school boys are to a considerable extent a race apart, and the very "tone" that is so highly prized is little more than a well-bred aloofness. It is also a matter of common criticism that our great public schools are hampered by traditions of the past which prevent them from adopting really efficient and up-to-date methods, and in many cases they fail to give an all-round education. Thus one occasionally meets with a boy who can write capital Greek verse, but is unable to spell his own language correctly.

Clayesmore was founded by its present head-master to combine the best qualities of the old public schools with all that is up-to-date, and with certain features that are altogether novel, and perhaps a little surprising as well. The school does not seek publicity, nor does it feel any need of advertisement, for it is already overcrowded, and at the beginning of a recent term it was necessary to refuse applications amounting to £750 per term! But the school possesses so many novel features that the

An open-air natural history class.

(171)

Manual training as an element in a liberal education

Our English schools have for long done full justice to the cultivation of athletic sports… Wherever two or three Englishmen are gathered together, there you will find the insignia of their race – goal posts and cricket stumps. Your public school boy, whatever he does not know, at least may boast of perfect familiarity with 22 yards of cricket pitch. With the exception of that modest strip of ground, he may not know as much of the earth he walks on as a fly does of its window pane... What then is the remedy for excessive athleticism? If we want to make our boys men, as well as scholars and gentlemen, we must put them in touch with the simplest conditions of life. Not the least important element in a liberal education is a practical acquaintance with manual work… It is your street-bred manikin who has never handled axe or spade that does no credit to his country. The man who cannot dig is very often the one who is not ashamed to beg… Of course, manual training at school has well-defined limits. The idea is not so much to turn out skilled craftsmen, as to give boys some insight into practical craftsmanship. The work done is not an object in itself; the value lies in the doing of it… Far be it from us to belittle the value of games. The boy who has 'no play' in him, besides being a 'dull boy' is in nine cases out of ten a wicked one; but surely Jack need not devote all his spare time to chasing balls of leather and india-rubber over level playing fields. The toil that has some useful end in view is not less noble. The lily-handed youngster who thinks it beneath him to handle a pickaxe is qualifying for the ranks of the brainless 'gilded youth'.

The School beagles, October 1939.

the season – but there were glories too, and throughout the school's history a number of Clayesmorians have gone on to perform on the university, national and international sporting stage in a variety of sports.

At Northwood Park Desmond Coke's generosity allowed the laying out of lawn tennis courts, and both at Pangbourne and at Northwood Park the school had a nine-hole golf course where, in 1923, Lex and a staff team were soundly beaten by the boys. And of course manual produced swimming pools at all three 20th-century school sites, the one at Iwerne Minster an ambitious enterprise that remained in use until the 1980s. The pre-prep building now sits on its site and the swimming pool is in the new Sports Centre.

The splendid sporting country around Iwerne allowed the boys to follow the hounds, go beagling and even keep their own horses at school. In 1937 the school had its own stable of six horses, which cost 4s an hour to ride, and boys who brought their own paid a pound a term plus the cost of feed. Riding at Clayesmore came to an end after the Second World War, when the cost of corn made keeping horses at school prohibitive.

Cross-country was promoted by Carl Verrinder, with every boy and many of the younger masters regularly turning out. Rugby and cricket continued to be played enthusiastically and successfully in the 1930s, with Evelyn King and Carl Verrinder reinforcing the First XV for features against local clubs – though both were remembered with some bitterness for their reluctance to pass the ball out to their wings. Staff and boys took each other on in rugby sevens, and in 1937 the school's First XV was unbeaten all season – though it is sad to record that four of that team did not survive the war.

The Iwerne estate offered ideal facilities for rugby, cricket and swimming, as well as athletics, and could also be adapted for girls' sports when the school went coeducational; the arrival of the prep school in the 1970s of course required further changes to accommodate sports needs there too. The influx of girls in the late 1970s and early 1980s and their impact on school sport is reported

Hambledon Harriers

While I was at Clayesmore, during the war years, I developed a considerable interest in cross-country running. During winter months we used to sometimes turn out, as a house, for a pre-breakfast run, usually to Fontmell Magna and back – a distance of about three miles. There was an acknowledged school cross-country course which involved running across fields on the school estate and up a rather narrow track towards a major feature of the area, Hambledon Hill – a long hill with rows of ditches dating from the Iron Age and Roman periods. The course took one up to the top of the hill and along the ditches and finally down through Shroton village and back to school. It was about six and a half miles in length, but for some reason – probably because it was considered too tough – competition had been abandoned. Dudley Clark and I, with others, decided to form a club and organise cross-country matches against other schools. We started training, using the Hambledon course.

It was a fellow prefect, RA Kirkby, who suggested that we call ourselves the Hambledon Harriers, and the name stuck. We had several matches against other schools, the most memorable of which was a three-way (six runners on each team) encounter between Kelly College, Clifton College and ourselves. The venue was at Tavistock, where Kelly was based, and the rigours of train travel in wartime meant that we had to change trains twice and arrived only shortly before the race was due to start. It was a very tough course over a small part of Dartmoor, involving rugged stone walls with long drops and plenty of mud. The organisation and stewarding by Kelly were excellent; they used their cadet corps and short-wave radio to keep the spectators near the school well informed of progress. Clifton – at that time evacuated to Bude in Cornwall – had a formidable cross-country reputation and two of their runners were first and second home. We achieved third and fifth, but actually won the match because the rest of our runners were well packed together.

We were a weary but triumphant team that eventually arrived back at Semley railway station, near Shaftesbury, to be met by the headmaster, Evelyn King. I remember so well how thrilled he was that we had won. Somehow we all managed to cram into his small car, and we all hoped that it would manage to climb that long hill to Shaftesbury. King gave the whole school a day's holiday to celebrate, and we were all awarded our cross-country colours. It was a heady period.

One year most of our Hambledon Harriers team entered the national juniors southern counties' cross-country match, held on Wimbledon Common. Several hundred runners took part and there were some very strong competitors. Dudley Clark achieved a magnificent third place and I was very pleased to come in 37th.

Alec McCallum (1939–44)

Above: Ingram, Dadson, Jell and Price on the 800 yards starting line, 1961.

Below left: Jell about to move from third to first and win the mile, 1961.

Clayesmore in the 1950s and 1960s was a small school with only 216 boys in residence – too small in many ways to support the number of sports and activities undertaken and to be competitive with other much larger schools. Smallness had its advantages too in that coaching staff had more time to spend on fewer sports participants. Those participants also tended to play most of the sports – if you had any ability you were unlikely to be neglected! Just thinking back to those 'good old days' I seem to remember consistently outstanding squash teams able to take on any of the really big schools and usually win, national schoolboy boxing champions, hockey teams who won most of their matches, including wins over the likes of Millfield, Canford and Bryanston 1st XIs and even a win over the full Dorset county team, great athletics performances and cricket teams that were always likely to pull off surprising results. In rugby terms, we always seemed to be short of choice for bulky forwards but often had plenty of speedy players outside the pack.

Clive Wilkinson (1955–61)

Now 78, I look back on my days at Clayesmore as some of the happiest of my life. Reading David Spinney's *History* brings back so many memories. I get a mention for being the All England Schoolboy boxing champion for my weight in 1951 – a tribute to Bill Aldworth, our PE instructor at the time. I also get a mention in Flora Scott's book *And One Ran Away*, written when she was matron at Clayesmore Prep in Charlton Marshall.

I was at Clayesmore from the age of seven in 1939, at the outbreak of war, until 1952, when I left to go to Guys. Having moved to the senior school in Iweme Minster, I was inspired by several of the masters: David Spinney, the historian, whose house I was in, John Appleby, lover of literature, Peter Burke, headmaster, Carl Verrinder, physicist and athletics coach, Humphrey Moore, biologist, Reggie Sessions, musician, Norris Scadding, priest and art teacher.

Carl Verrinder and Humphrey Moore probably had more influence on me than anyone, and it was because of them that I took up medicine. I had already been a sports enthusiast at prep school, including rugby, athletics and boxing, and this continued at Iwerne Minster. Carl Verrinder was our athletics coach and he organised numerous outings for us. I remember going with him to watch the athletics at the first post-war Olympics in London in 1948, when Fanny Blankers-Koen won four gold medals, and again in 1952, when a few of us from school went with him by sea on a cargo ship to Finland and watched the Olympics in Helsinki. We saw Emil Zatopek win his three gold medals, in the marathon, the 10,000 metres and the 5,000 metres.

Carl also took some of us on a cross-country skiing trip to the Austrian Alps, climbing on skins and then skiing down. We stayed in mountain huts. There was never a dull moment with Carl, and how fortunate we were to have known and been inspired by him. In the 1951–2 season, we had an unbeaten rugby First XV side and in 1952 an unbeaten athletic team. What a way to finish! My pleasure and enjoyment in being a family GP, now happily retired, are only matched by the memorable 12 years spent at Clayesmore.

Richard Hawley
(1939–46 prep school; 1946–52 senior school)

in various Clayesmorian magazines with successes and failure against local school teams. There was also a squad of synchronised swimmers and a gymnastics team comprised entirely of girls. Following completion of the Sports Centre, the land behind was developed, and in July 1987 the cricket pavilion was formally opened by Lieutenant Colonel John Stephenson, secretary of the MCC, and named for Old Clayesmorian cricketer JWA Stephenson. 1994 saw the inaugural running of the school 10-Mile Cup competition, a fiercely contested inter-

house relay race around the school grounds, now firmly established in the school sporting calendar and run at the end of the spring term each year.

Orienteering was introduced as a senior school sport in 1993, and the team has been one of the school's most successful since then, winning the national small schools title a total of 14 times to date. Several team members have gone on to compete individually on the national and international stage.

The opening of the Centenary Astroturf in 1996 coincided with the U18 team winning the county championships for the first time. The then head of senior girls games, Sarah Brown, commented, 'At last we have the facilities to help us reach our true potential.' The late 1990s saw much county and national and even some international level representation in all manner of different sports. Sports teams took Clayesmore's name to a global stage. Among the highlights were cricket teams taking part in the Jersey Cricket Festival in 1997 and the prestigious Garfield Sobers Cricket Festival in Barbados in 1998, a netball tour to Malta in 1998 and hockey tours to Holland in 1987 and South Africa in 2001. More recently readers of the 2007 edition of Wisden would have seen Clayesmore listed among its 'outstanding schools', with a separate mention of pupil Matthew Geffen for his bowling averages of O 107, M 32, R 260, W 26, Best 4–14 and an average of 10. In 2009 the school won the prestigious Forty Club Trophy (the Henry Grierson Cup) judged on the side's sportsmanship, captaincy, turnout, skills and behaviour.

Sport naturally played a huge part in my life – well, except for one term in January 1963 when I spent the whole term with my leg in plaster having broken it just after Christmas. I was a useful rugby second-row forward through being 6ft 4in tall, and a handy catcher in the lineout. Mac was a great coach and encouraged us hugely. We never in my time beat Bryanston First XV but managed some great wins against Kings Bruton, Milton Abbey, Shaftesbury Grammar, Downside, Millfield and Canford, to name a few. Cycling was a big activity, mainly at weekends. A group of us regularly cycled as far at Sherborne, Yeovil and Bournemouth for the day along virtually empty lanes and roads, carrying our packed lunches and portable burners to cook our baked beans and sausages. It was a chance to get away and see a bit beyond Iwerne Minster.

Mike Henbest was a great tennis partner. We were the doubles champions one year, though as Mike was 6ft 5in tall our opponents hardly stood a chance against two giants. Squash under Captain Aldworth's eye was ever popular, though swimming was restricted to a few dips in a usually freezing and filthy pool where you were more than likely to pick up some ghastly infection of one kind or another.

Douglas Reed (1961–5)

Right: Shannon Falcone.

Far right: Anthony Allen.

Top right: The Garfield Sobers Cricket Festival in Barbados, 1998.

Old Clayesmorian sailors have excelled over the years and include Jeremy Rogers, the designer and builder of racing yachts Contessa 26 and Contessa 32 and England representative in the Admiral's Cup, Great Britain Dinghy sailor Paul Clements, John Burnie who enjoys frequent sailing success in the Caribbean, Shannon Falcone who was part of the victorious America's Cup team in 2010 and Tom Tait, who at 90 was the oldest competitor at Cowes Week in 2011.

Throughout the school's history, a number of Clayesmorians have gone on to perform on the university, national and international sporting stage in a variety of sports. Among the most notable of these are John Stephenson (first class cricketer in England and India), Anthony Allen (rugby for England and Leicester Tigers) and Eric Fernihough (former holder of the motorcycle world speed record). There are a number of OC 'Blues' including Tom Hicks, who won four Oxford Blues for cricket, captaining them for the varsity match at Lord's.

Today's director of sport is Chris Humpage, assisted by Richard Miller as head of boys' sport and Tracy Cook for the girls. Competitive sport sees a major sport being played each term – for the boys rugby in the autumn, hockey in the spring and cricket in the summer; for the girls hockey, netball and tennis or athletics – augmented by other options such as football, cross-country, riding, squash, swimming and sailing, with PE and fitness in addition. As well as competitive fixtures against other local schools, teams and individuals enter national competitions and there are inter-house competitions, swimming galas, relay races round the campus and an annual Sports Day for the whole school. A focus for the sports department is a scientific approach to physical exercise; and pupils who show talent are encouraged not just to try for the school teams but to go on to area, county and national level events and championships and attend professional sports training camps at Club La Santa in Lanzarote.

The Duke of Edinburgh Award Scheme had been started in the mid 1980s and for a time was run as part of the Cadet Force programme. Now it is a popular part of the School activitiy programme with up to 40 per cent of each lower-sixth cohort working towards their Gold award.

Combined Cadet Force

John Jevons, who was at Clayesmore from 1917 to 1921, remembers the rudimentary Cadet Corps of his day: 'The war was on, so of course we had a Cadet Corps, led by Mr Stephenson, but we were not an HMC school, we were not an OTC, so we only had wooden imitations of rifles, which was disappointing. We did, however, have an occasional route march, and I have a memory of one when we passed beside a field where three army horses were apparently convalescing. On hearing our drums and bugles they

God, today's been a smashing day, I was detailed off to report to the armoury at 13.40 hours. I turned up prompt on time and I was bundled into an army lorry with a lot of Seniors, be hanged if I knew where we were going. There was me squashed in the back of an army lorry surrounded by millions of Seniors. Our average speed was about 70mph. Well, after being bumped about like hell for about 25 minutes we started slowing down to a mere 50mph. I was able to make myself heard and asked where the _____ hell we were going. Well, I won't tell you what they said but apparently we were going to a rifle range at Okeford Fitzpaine to fire rifles.

MY job, mind you MY job, was to stand at the side of the targets, and every time someone hit the target I'd got to wave a flag – huh! Well we speeded up again then suddenly the driver jammed on his brakes and Charlie (Regimental Sergeant Major Banfield to you) got out of the front and came round to us, he said 'Have we brought them _____ rifles?'

We discovered we hadn't, so Charlie said 'Well, me sons, there's only one damn thing we can do, that's go to a pub and have a drink.' Phew! Was I amazed, anyhow we stopped at the next pub we came to and we all got out and went into the taproom. We all had a pint of cider except Charlie and the driver, they had beer. God – was that cider powerful.

Then Charlie said 'Now, me lads, mum's the word.' Then we got in the lorry and came back to school. We had been away for about two hours when we got back, Charlie said to us 'Well, me sons, as that was such fine shooting you can break off now,' and I was free for the rest of that afternoon. All this may sound impossible but I swear it's the truth.

Another thing, I've started my dancing lessons. I can now practically waltz and quick-step. Miss Hunt teaches us and we dance with her and Mrs King. It's wizard dancing with Mrs King.

Peter Wightman (1944–8)

lined up eagerly, dressed to the right, their ears pricked up as they watched us, and as we proceeded they wheeled, keeping their formation, and galloped to a new position to take up their disciplined rank to review us before we marched away from them. Just horses, but homesick for the life for which they had been trained.'

During the Second World War there was a Junior Training Corps, three members of which famously joined in the Victory Day parade in London, claiming that their JTC shoulder flashes stood for 'Jungle Training Corps' and that they represented the small country of Clayesmoria (*see p63*). Wartime JTC training was in many ways in deadly earnest, and not just because the boys and masters took on certain observational roles: in the early days of the war a German invasion was a distinct possibility, and on several occasions they had to cope with real air warfare taking place over their heads. Sir Rodney Sweetnam (*see p58*) remembers the real fear he felt when a downed aircraft near the school spewed out fierce-looking, armed soldiers talking in what sounded like a foreign language; he was very relieved when they turned out to be broad-brogued Scotsmen.

The cadet corps has continued at Clayesmore, alternating between a voluntary and compulsory basis since the 1940s. Reports in the *Clayesmorian*s of the 1950s, 1960s and 1970s show a force focused on proficiency tests, with regular camps both locally (at Lulworth and Bovington in particular) and further afield nationally (Longmoor and in the Brecon Beacons) and internationally (to Osnabruck and Malta). Gliding had been introduced in the late 1930s and continued to be a popular activity, with the addition of canoeing in 1968. Jim Tilden led an intrepid party of cadets in a canoeing expedition on the River Wye in 1970 and another group along the full length of the Thames in 1971. Highlights for

the CCF during the 1980s were the opening of an indoor rifle range in 1983 and the entire contingent's appearance as extras in a BBC1 drama based on the Gor saga by Maureen Duffy and starring Charles Dance as Dr Forrester.

CCF was made compulsory for all fourth and fifth formers from September 1989, and an RAF squadron was formed to accommodate the extra numbers involved. As Captain George Scott recorded in the 1989 *Clayesmorian*, 'We have now had a number of cadets performing aerobatics over the school on a Thursday afternoon in an attempt to distract the cricketers.'

Today membership of the Combined Cadet Force is voluntary and the six sections are formed out of around 80 participants. Sixth formers act as NCOs and instructors. The squads drill, learn map reading and camping skills, including cooking, and are instructed in handling rifles.

The current commander is Sqn Ldr Mark Newland, who teaches history and lives in Wolverton House, where his wife SarahJane is housemistress, and its administrator and instructor is Warrant Officer Colin Evans, who came to Clayesmore 19 years ago after 23 years in the Royal Army Physical Training Corps. He looks after the weapons and the uniforms as well as organising activities both at the school and away from home at camps.

There is an annual camp, usually in the last week of the summer term, when the students put into practice what they have learned on site, and also take part in sporting activities; the summer 2011 camp at Longmore near Aldershot allowed them to enjoy sailing, kayaking and wind-surfing.

A Memorable Day: CCF Formal Inspection, March 2007

'The cadets will make you very welcome but what they would really like is a helicopter.' Such was the advice I was given by a friend who had recently inspected a school cadet contingent. Having been honoured with an invitation to conduct the biennial inspection, in March 2007, of the Clayesmore Combined Cadet Force – whose ranks then included my eldest son Rory, a cadet sergeant – this seemed to me a challenge which simply had to be met. On the day, a benevolent local headquarters, favourable weather and a very accommodating pilot combined to bring me by Gazelle helicopter to Clayesmore. The inspection was a great success. The cadets made a fuss of the brigadier and put on a brilliant show; Rory coped admirably with the discomfort of having his squad inspected by his father; and, of course, the cadets went flying. My friend's advice was sound: they really liked the helicopter. It was, above all things, a memorable Clayesmore day.

The strong affinity between Clayesmore and HM Forces, reflected and sustained by the many service families who belong to the Clayesmore family, helps the CCF contingent to thrive. So too does an enlightened and supportive headmaster, splendidly found in Martin Cooke. That memorable day celebrated the success of the CCF as a modern movement for active young citizens preparing to take their places in an uncertain world. It celebrated Clayesmore too. The contingent then was hallmarked by the dedicated leadership of Major Stephen Smith, Flight Lieutenant Robert Farley and WO1 Colin Evans. Under their guidance and encouragement, the cadets learned the practicalities and inestimable value of disciplined and selfless teamwork. These lessons, not taught in words but by example, are the legacy of many generations of Clayesmore officers and instructors. They have woven the CCF contingent into the fabric of Clayesmore life. Long may it be so – Lex Devine would have approved.

Inspecting Officer,
Brigadier Stephen Andrews

Above: 'The Clayesmore Conquistadors' visit Machu Picchu in Peru, 2002.

Right: Morocco, 2007.

Below: Everest Base Camp, 2008.

Expeditions

Colin Evans spends half his time running the CCF and the other half organising expeditions abroad, which usually take place during the Easter half term. Norway is to be the venue in 2012, where they will enjoy husky sledging, ice fishing, snow-holing and spider crab fishing, and will hope to see the Northern Lights as they will spend the entire time above the Arctic Circle.

Colin was instrumental in starting these regular adventures abroad in 2000, when the venue was Nepal. Usually accompanied by his wife, Elaine, who provides a welcome female presence, he has led trips to Peru, China, Kenya, Malawi and Morocco, among others. They have visited an Everest base camp, and during the 2011 trip to Borneo climbed the highest mountain in Malaysia as well as visiting and working in a kindergarten. In Kenya they stayed in a school for four days where they helped to install a water tank plus guttering and lavatories, funded by money raised through charitable events. As he says, the opportunity to do charity work is a major element in the expeditions, which help these relatively privileged young people to appreciate how others live, and to learn at first hand about other cultures, other religions and other ways of life. And there is, of course, a strong sense of adventure as they visit parts of the world which are different in so many ways from their homes.

uwesu
KUKRI
ROOTS
CANADA

PART 5:

The Clayesmore Community

Living, working and being educated at Clayesmore, at both prep and senior levels, seems inevitably to engender a huge loyalty and fondness for the school and all it stands for; the word 'family' is never far from the lips of those who talk about the warmth and the 'magnetic quality' of the school. That this was so in the earliest days too – presumably then inculcated by the extraordinary influence Lex had on his boys – is evident from letters, magazine articles and memorabilia now in the archives by and about Old Clayesmorians. Today it has its expression in the large number of activities carried out by OCs, both within their own organisation and for the benefit of the school as a whole, as well as parents, friends and current pupils.

In 2008 this huge wellspring of support and loyalty was formally constituted and united under a single banner – the Clayesmore Society. This body consists of Old Clayesmorians, parents of past and current pupils, the prep school parents' association, current and former staff, current pupils and friends of the school. The main function of the Clayesmore Society is to organise a programme of events throughout the year to keep people in touch with each other and the school. It is the umbrella over separate bodies; and it provides an overarching structure within which a large variety of different initiatives can flourish.

Old Clayesmorian Society

The Old Clayesmorians Club was founded in 1921 by Frederic St K Anderson who arranged the first Old Clayesmorian Dinner on January 16 1922 at the Café Royale. Material in the archives makes it clear that Clayesmore has always from the beginning enjoyed the continued support and interest of its old boys – though, inevitably, this support has experienced peaks and troughs through the decades, and has usually depended on the energy and willpower of individuals determined to keep themselves and their contemporaries in touch with the school and its doings. The present vigorous health of the society can perhaps be attributed to Robert Mash who, in the 1990s, gave it a new lease of life, acting as its secretary for many years and editing its newsletter. In 2007 the society entered into a new formal partnership with the school which bound the two institutions more closely together and setting arrangements between the two, both financial and administrative on a clear, firm footing.

A glance at the *Old Clayesmorian* – published annually and currently edited by OC SarahJane Newland (née Kennard, 1980–4), supported by OC Louise Smith (née Ross-Kellaway, 1994–8), the school's development officer – indicates how wide and varied the society's activities are. The annual dinner is now held in alternate years at the school after many years at Simpson's in London, and there are also local gatherings in some parts of the country. The OC cricket team, known as the Cormorants, hold an annual cricket week at the school, where they take on old rivals such as their equivalents at Canford, Bryanston and Sherborne in fixtures both home and away. They also take on the school team, usually during the OC weekend held in May, which also hosts musical events. Hockey and netball matches against the school are a feature of the spring term, and there are regular golf days.

The society presents prizes each year, of money or vouchers, to current pupils. The OC prize is awarded to up to three members of the Upper VI who have 'represented Clayesmore and taken its name to a wider audience'. Past winners include, for example, a musician who put on productions outside the school and sportspeople who have taken involvement in external competition to a wider area

Above left: Frederic St K Anderson (far right), founder of the OC Society.

Left: Prize giving, 1960. Charles Price receives the Bothway tennis cup, having beaten Piers Sabine in the final.

Below left: Old Clayesmorians meet in Sydney, March 2012.

Above: OC Society dinner, postwar.

Above right: The bust of Lex that sits in the school drawing room, given in 2003.

Below: OC Day, spring 2005.

than usual. The Scadding art prize goes to an artist who shows flair and originality, and there are two Luboff prizes, given for an outstanding contribution to drama at the school, one for acting and one for work backstage; they are funded by the Luboff family in memory of Andrew Luboff, who was at the school from 1940 to 1945 and died in 2005. In addition, many of the cups and prizes awarded to today's pupils bear the names of OCs of the past; and the winner of the annual Alan Pugh general knowledge quiz is given the Gawain Towler Shield to hold for a year. Gawain, who was at the school in the 1980s, won the competition every year during his school career; the shield was presented in 1986 by his parents.

A sub-section of the Old Clayesmorian Society is the Spinney Memorial Trust, a separately constituted charity set up in 1990 in memory of David Spinney. It provides bursaries and grants for the educational benefit of Clayesmore's pupils and is entirely funded by OCs. Pupils apply for it while still at the school, and it has mainly in recent years given grants to pupils embarking on gap year projects. As examples, recent beneficiaries have been funded to work with the National Youth Theatre, and others have attended the Global Young Leaders Conference, organised by the United Nations and held in New York.

At the 2003 Annual Dinner the OC Society presented, on behalf of OC Michael Gaskin (1948–52), a magnificent bust of Devine to the school which now presides over events in the drawing room at Iwerne. In recent times surplus OC funds have been used to purchase extras for the school, for example a plaque to commemorate Geoffrey Drummond and a new sound system for the school chapel. But the main aim of the society is to keep OCs in touch with each other and with the school in an enjoyable, fruitful and constructive way.

Friends of Clayesmore

The first event run by the Friends of Clayesmore was a concert on the terrace followed by a buffet supper in May 22 1992, and was the result of a conversation between Anne Beeby, the headmaster's wife, and Jenny Long, a parent, at the 1991 Christmas Fair. The idea was to organise social activities at the school, both as fundraisers and to encourage family feeling among parents and friends of the school. That first event had 160 people enjoying a superb performance by the school orchestra and the brass band on an idyllic spring evening, and the profit was enough to fund the purchase of a microwave oven for the tuck shop.

The first AGM approved the constitution, and in December 1992 the Friends held their first Christmas Fair, which raised a substantial amount both for charity and for their own coffers. By 1994 they were able to donate £1,000 to the refurbishment of the Social Centre and a further £1,000 to the Astroturf appeal. Their activities have waxed and waned over the 20 years of their existence, but have experienced a considerable resurgence in recent years, traceable back to the first Christmas Ball arranged by the Friends in the early 2000s, with the St Petersburg Winter Palace as the theme. The balls have continued very successfully ever since, always with a theme – 'Regency and the Romantics' in 2010 and '1950s Revival' in 2011. The annual Christmas Fair is run by the Friends, as well as musical and other events, for example clay-shooting competitions, throughout the year.

Apart from the very considerable social element, the main purpose of the Friends of Clayesmore is to fundraise for the school, for desirable extras rather than core needs. Some of their contributions go to substantial projects: they helped to refurbish the library, they funded a new kitchen in the Social Centre and they equipped a new gardening club. Other activities are more like the icing on the cake – a barbecue for one of the houses, for example.

Far left: Clayshoot.

Left: 'Revival!', 1950s ball, December 2011.

Left: Regency Ball, December 2010.

Above: Prep School Parents' Association Black and White Ball, summer 2009.

Below: Friends of Clayesmore Moulin Rouge Ball, 2006.

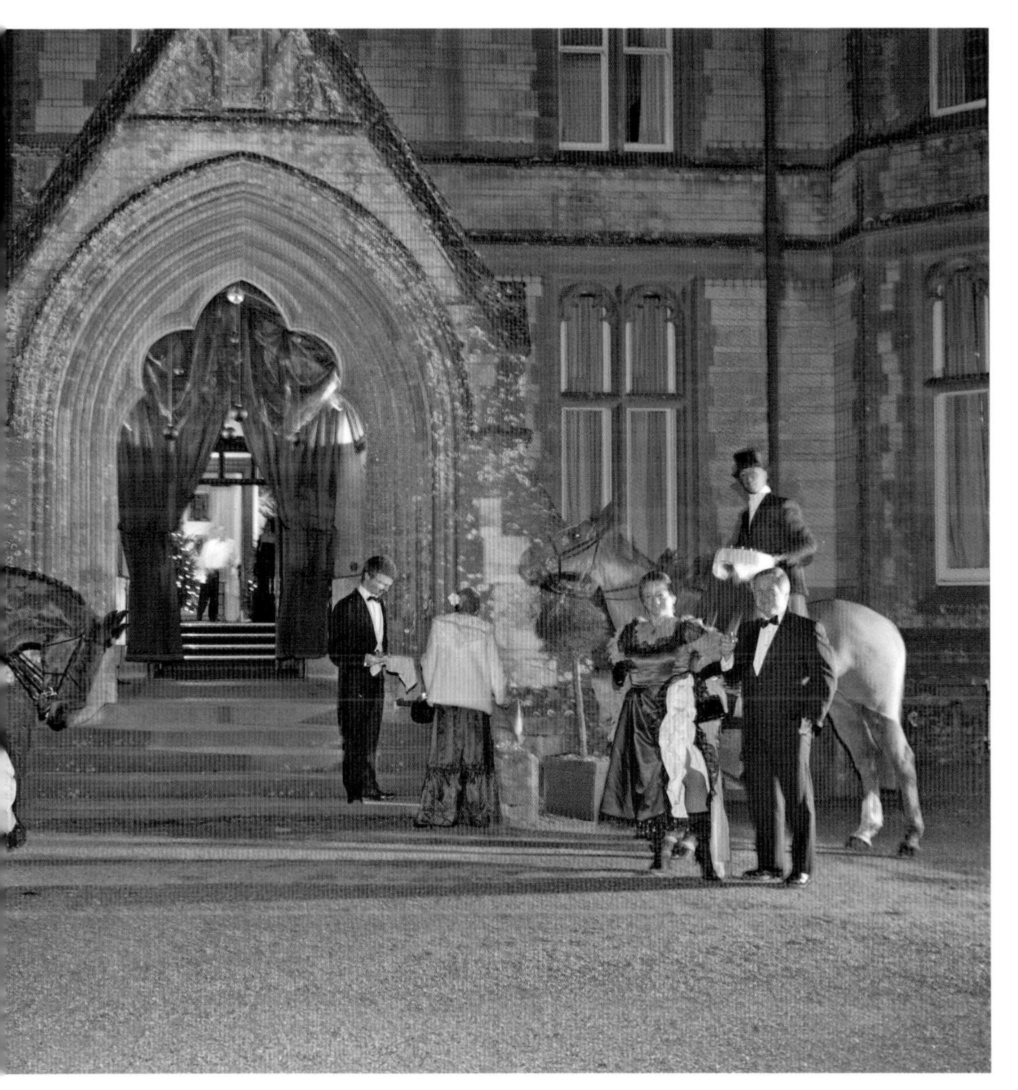

Prep School Parents' Association

The prep school parents have their own association and run their own quite separate activities. It has existed for well over 20 years and organises fairs at Christmas and in the summer and a jazz festival, as well as balls and other social events, including a monthly drop-in coffee morning. Their fundraising efforts have allowed the building of a new pre-prep playground, the purchase of staging, musical and lighting equipment and the upgrading of cricket nets, among other projects.

Governance

In the early days of the school Lex Devine maintained a fierce independence and ran everything himself. But his financial insouciance led, when the school was at Pangbourne, to the imposition of a board of managers and the appointment of a bursar. He hated these 'years of slavery', as he called them, and one can only imagine the merry dance he led his unfortunate bursars and governors who counted among their number in 1934 the poet Walter de la Mare and Major General LC Dunsterville (better known as Stalky in Kipling's *Stalky & Co*). By the time he died he was in full control again; but when Evelyn King took over, he rapidly established a limited company and a governing council, initially under the chairmanship of a Clayesmore parent, Sir Harold Bellman. King himself was to remain involved with the council long after he left, eventually serving as chairman.

The council has always enjoyed strong OC representation; past chairmen have included Roger Kingwill, John Brooke-Little and Ron Spinney, all OCs. Its influence on school affairs varied over the decades, until in the 1980s it was recognised that closer involvement, and a firmer hand, would be an advantage. This resulted in the appointment, first as a member and later as chairman in the mid-1990s, of Major-General Ward-Booth, followed by Ron Spinney. Both presided at difficult times when painful decisions needed to be made. Both exhibited strong leadership and management, resulting in substantial change and development in how the school was run and in a much leaner, fitter organisation.

The full School Council now meets three times a year, currently under the chairmanship of Dr Richard Willis, a

Crests and logos – the Clayesmore brand

Lex Devine would not have recognised the word 'brand' in its modern sense. But a school had to have a heraldic emblem. In a departure from his usual habit of insisting on the best, he did not apply to the College of Arms but made up his own: a lion rampant supporting (for no apparent reason) the flag of Sweden, with a motto in doubtful French – *Dieu premier, donc mes frères*. This served as the school's badge on blazers, caps, sports gear and stationery for decades, until an extremely belated application to the College of Arms put things right. As John Brooke-Little, then Norroy and Ulster King of Arms, wrote on College of Arms letterheading to David Spinney: 'What Lex did was to assume an illegal crest without adopting a coat of arms. Arms can exist without a crest, but the converse is not true; the crest is an accretion to a full achievement of arms, as are supporters. He therefore displayed a fundamental ignorance of heraldry so may possibly be exculpated from the sin of miserliness, pleading ignorance. I had not heard the theory that the lion came from the Enfield arms, but it sounds plausible. However, I cannot imagine why it holds the Swedish national flag nor do I know the provenance of the motto.'

Roy McIsaac's final Speech Day in 1979 was marked by the presentation to the Lord Lieutenant of Dorset by John Brooke-Little, in his then role as Richmond Herald, of a new, finally legal, coat of arms for the school; after presenting it, Brooke-Little promptly took off his badge of office and accepted it back on behalf of the school as chairman of the council.

The crest survives; but it is now accompanied by a new logo, designed as part of an entire new corporate identity for Clayesmore in 2007 by Picador Design. Richard Smith of the design team, who was a Clayesmore parent when this work was being done, writes: 'We started the process by designing the logo. Our inspiration was the magnificent Dorset landscape surrounding the school where Hambledon Hill literally meets the skyline and subsequently took the shapes formed by this fusion. This harmony permeates right through the ethos of both prep and senior schools, as anyone who knows Clayesmore will testify. We also introduced the county name Dorset as part of the brand so there could be no doubt as to the location and heritage of the school, which is extremely important when positioning the school to students and agents in the UK and overseas. Once the logo had been approved we set about inputting the brand across a wide range of applications: prospectuses, website, signage and minibuses, culminating in a complete set of guidelines which act as a blueprint for future marketing and promotional activities.'

former parent. Recruitment now relies to a large extent on a perceived need for a specific skill, allied with finding people willing to take on what can be a considerable commitment of time and energy. The council includes three sub-committees, one each for the prep and senior schools and one for the finances and general administration.

In Clayesmore as in other schools the last two decades have seen changes in the types of work undertaken by administrative staff. In 1993, David Beeby appointed Nikki Cheung as Clayesmore's first public relations consultant; her job was initially part-time and involved the considerable task of overseeing every level of external communication embarked on by both prep and senior schools. The job has expended considerably since those early days! Another new appointment, in 2008, was of OC Louise Smith (née Ross-Kellaway, 1994–8) to the new post of development officer; her role includes fundraising, facilitating relationships between OCs and the school, running events and looking after the Clayesmore Society. Alongside these new roles, the school continues to need a vibrant community of office staff. Many of those in post today have been there for years, and many of them, like the academic staff, are current or former parents of children at Clayesmore.

Clayesmore dynasties and marriages

The sense of family which Clayesmore embodies is perhaps best demonstrated through the countless siblings who have been educated at the school over the years. The first brothers were Alan and Douglas Ashton Henderson who entered the school in September 1895, register entries number 11 and 12 respectively.

It was 1916 when the first 'second generation' Clayesmorian joined the school. Noel Grosvenor Talbot Cliff joined in the September of that year at the age of ten; he is number 528 in the school register. His father, Grosvenor Talbot Cliff, was part of the first school intake in 1896, the ninth to join the fledgling school.

David Anderson (1938–45) was another 'second generation' Clayesmorian, joining in the autumn term of 1941 as the eldest of three sons of OC Frederic Anderson who had been at the school when it was at Pangbourne, joining in the Trinity term of 1908. Frederic Anderson was a founder member of the OC Society and for many years held various roles, eventually becoming president, as later did his son David, who was involved for over 50 years as a committee member, chairman and finally as president.

January 1995 marked the first instance of a third generation Clayesmorian joining the school, when Olivia Fangen followed in the footsteps of her father David (1961–6) and grandfather Stener (1932–5). Current pupil Emma Hamilton joined the school in September 2006, the second generation of her family to attend Clayesmore and the third generation of her family to be involved with the school.

At the time of writing there are close to 30 children at the school whose parents are former pupils of either the prep or senior schools or both. July 2011 marked the end of an era as the last member of the Trenchard family left. Mark joined the school in 1996, the youngest of three siblings to do so, following his father Tim (1974–7), sister Katie (1994–7) and brother George (1994–2008).

To date, some 13 inter-Clayesmorian marriages are known of, the latest between Francis Chan (1990–5) and Vicky Lam (1994–6) in the autumn of 2011. With the introduction of girls to the school inter-Clayesmorian marriage and children were something of an inevitability. The first children of an OC union are Oscar, Elliot and Ursula Perks, whose parents William Perks and Karen Ripper attended the school in the late 1970s, leaving in 1980.

Above: Grosvenor Talbot Cliff.

Right: The Trenchards.

Community Service and Charity Fundraising

A key element of the Clayesmore ethos has always been to encourage in pupils an awareness of the needs of others, setting these above personal needs, as well as awareness of the moral issues and responsibilities that surround them at school, both as members of a community and within the world at large. Lex set a precedent for this approach; in 1917, for example, he volunteered the services of the OTC to repair the road between Sparsholt and Winchester. Nowadays, this awareness is demonstrated in the school community service programme and in the substantial funds which are raised by pupils both past and present each year for charity.

Pupils from Clayesmore had been active in the local community for some years before the programme was formalised in 1992 by Stephen Byrne as an alternative activity to CCF for Lower VIth pupils. For one afternoon a week, pupil volunteers walked dogs and visited the elderly in Iwerne Minster, spent time in local primary schools and took part in a variety of other community-based activities. Matthew Corica was nominated for a Young Citizen Award for his involvement with the programme in 1998, and in 2000 the project was nominated as a whole for a Nationwide Award for Voluntary Endeavour.

The community service programme continues today, with a group of pupils each year volunteering for a week to help the National Trust tidy hedgerows and other tasks. A highlight is the cooking sessions run by Jane Hayes, head of home economics, in conjunction with the Forum School for autistic children which occupies the former home of Croft House School. Ten autistic sixth formers from the Forum come to Iwerne once a week to work with ten volunteers from the Clayesmore sixth form, all of them pairing off to cook a meal. The relationships that build are hugely valuable to both sets of young people.

Pupil power in fundraising for both the school and other charities is another feature of day to day life at Clayesmore. The Alex Appeal Day held in October 1988 raised £5,791 for the Hardy Roberts Ward at Middlesex Hospital, London, and the Macmillan Fund where pupil Alex Gunn was treated prior to his tragic death the following year. Methods used to raise funds have varied from sporting marathons to concerts, fashion shows (no one present will forget David Beeby in full leathers riding a Harley Davidson on to the stage in 1999) and the charity rag day in 1995 where 'gnoming' and other events for the NSPCC raised £1,895.88 and four members of staff and two pupils were gunged. This charitable spirit carries forward for many people into their lives after Clayesmore; every year the Old Clayesmorian Society website and magazine feature details of many former pupils' fundraising exploits in all corners of the world.

Both the prep and senior sections of the school have committees who are responsible for the fundraising activities among the pupil body in a particular year, which always include one local, one national and one international charity.

Clayesmore is a true community, embracing everyone within it from the smallest child in the nursery through to the chairman of the council and the headmaster, and taking along teaching staff, office staff, support staff both in the buildings and the grounds, very often the wives and husbands of those staff members, parents both past

Top: The 'Gunge Plunge', 1995.

Above left: 24-hour sports marathon, spring 2012.

Above: David Beeby on his Harley, 1999.

and present, friends of the school and of course the many boys and girls educated here over the years. Let the last word in this chapter go to Stephen Andrews, a parent, who offers his personal reflection on the spirit of Clayesmore in 2012:

'There is in Clayesmore a quiet power that enriches the lives it touches. If I did not recognise it, I certainly discerned it from the day when first I went there. Only later did I seek to understand how this subtle and compelling power ran through every design and thread of the fabric of Clayesmore life. It transcends, and yet draws upon, the beauty of Clayesmore's seat in Iwerne Minster. It was a power in the making and growing, surely, in Enfield, Pangbourne and Winchester.

'This is the spirit of Clayesmore, kindled by Alexander Devine. This spirit has been nurtured by, and has quietly blessed, every generation of the Clayesmore family. In 2012 it is strong and active. Were Lex to visit his school today he would see and feel the spirit of Clayesmore that is the enduring gift of his life's work. For Clayesmore is still *his* school; and yet today it is much more than a school. Here is a family and a community where all are welcome and where Alexander Devine could plainly see that all may belong and be valued for themselves. Lex would find young people, balanced and content in their learning and recreation, being educated not moulded. He would hear and sense in every strand of life his abiding words of encouragement and inspiration: "think for yourself".

'The half a generation I have belonged to the Clayesmore family is too short a time really to understand the spirit of Clayesmore. It is, though, quite long enough to see and to feel how that spirit has inspired the joy of every success; and revealed wisdom when plans have faltered. The spirit of Clayesmore is the lasting resonance of Lex's humanity and his profound understanding of the human condition. This book is a celebration indeed. At its heart is the spirit of Alexander Devine and the power that he bequeathed to Clayesmore.'

PART 6:

The Present and the Future

Martin Cooke

It was with a sense of trepid anticipation that I accepted the governors' invitation to take up the reins as headmaster of Clayesmore Senior School in September 2000. At the time, Eleanor and I were loving being at the helm of the prep school but we realised we couldn't stay there for ever, and the opportunity to return to working in a senior school was something that attracted and excited me a great deal after six years at the prep.

As we got to grips with things in the summer holiday it dawned on us just how much there was to do and there seemed to be considerable challenges at every turn.

I was fortunate in a number of key players at the time who gave me every possible support. Ron Spinney was chairman of the governing council and he was determined that we should be allowed to hit the ground running and make as swift an impact as possible. When I told him that we could identify several small projects which could make a difference to the lives and happiness of pupils and staff quite quickly, it was music to his ears, and he made £100,000 available upon which we could draw in our first year over and above what had already been budgeted. Bursar, David Little, and buildings and estate manager, Richard Tremellen, were unrelenting in their support of the plans and proposals that we put forward, with Eleanor drawing on all her experience learned at the prep school in making the very best of the facilities available.

In terms of the boarding houses, it was Gate House that seemed to need the most attention. It appeared to me that the sleeping arrangements were designed in a very poor way, whereby senior boys had to pass through younger boys' dormitories to get to their own study bedrooms. With no chance of an immediate solution, paint and new carpet would have to do in order to provide a fresh feel and hope for the future, and this served as a fillip both to the Gate boys and to their new houseparents, Christopher and Penny Middle. More permanent projects were possible in other areas of Gate – I am thinking of the clock tower wing which we remodelled almost immediately – and we were also able to get other refurbishment projects underway in Wolverton, in King's and later in Devine and Manor.

We learned very quickly that £100,000 doesn't go a long way, and we also learned that disappointments and opportunities often go hand in hand. When Dr Anne Jancis told me at Easter 2001 that she thought the moment had come for her to move out of Wolverton where, supported by her husband, Alan, she had been housemistress for several years, I was disappointed. Anne was held in very high regard as a housemistress, was tireless in her support and care of the girls and was much loved by them. Not only that, but she was the most experienced member of the house staff team and knew Clayesmore very well. I needed not only to find a replacement, but also to make sure that Richard Tremellen built into his summer redecoration plans the need to give the Wolverton flat a 'going over'. Next day, Richard was waiting for me. 'I know you're disappointed about Anne moving out,' he said, 'but this is a golden opportunity to redesign Wolverton completely – we should go for it!'

Within days, Richard was back with plans which moved the house staff flat from the centre of the house into lovely, spacious and new accommodation at the western end of the building, thus allowing for far greater cohesion and unity in the girls' accommodation. Getting all the work done in one summer holiday was a huge challenge for our maintenance team on top of all the other things that were planned, but we have never looked back. With days to spare, Stephen and Stitch Byrne and their two children, Tolly and Ophelia, moved in ready for the new term.

Science and provision for information and communications technology were at the top of my academic concerns list. Throw into the mix the fact that Clayesmore's highly reputable Learning Support Centre was accommodated in a wooden hut and several portakabins, and a large building project was inevitable. Chemistry and physics needed to be removed from the ground floor of Gate to enable Gate to become a successful and fully integrated boys' house. Biology and ICT would surely fall down if they were left in their two-storey wooden building for very much longer.

Above: Ron Spinney (right) with Baroness Warnock (second left), Martin Cooke and Clayesmore students, Speech Day 2003.

Right: Gate House refurbishment.

Below: Relaxing in the sixth form common room.

With the full enthusiasm and commitment of the governing council, we turned to Philip Proctor who had done such a splendid job with the new headmaster's house at the prep school, and he designed what later became the Jubilee Building, opened in the year of Her Majesty the Queen's Golden Jubilee, in 2002, and which was built for us by A Hammond and Sons, who had undertaken the building of the Sports Centre and King's House in the 1980s.

With Jubilee fully on stream that September (and formally opened a year later at Speech Day 2003 by Baroness Warnock), Clayesmore had new classroom and laboratory facilities of which we could be proud. Now Richard Tremellen and his team could crack on with our plans for the complete remodelling of Gate, taking over old laboratories for study bedrooms and fashioning smaller rooms for groups of two to four boys from the old large dormitories. A fine new entrance to the house was created on the southern side of the quad with a new hallway and grand staircase worthy of the building and its occupants.

What never really occurred to us at the time was that all of this would prove to be of colossal benefit in terms of pupil recruitment. Any head of a school our size bears the essential and very personal task of ensuring that the school is full each year, and nowhere can this be more true than at Clayesmore, as we have read, throughout our history. Following the recession of the early 1990s, the senior school had settled down to being a coeducational, family school of roughly 300 young people made up of 210 boarders and 90

day pupils. At no time did I ever set out to increase pupil numbers, but there is no doubt that we galvanised ourselves as never before to attract good new pupils. In addition to her other roles, Eleanor now became more involved in marketing, and until 2012 worked very closely with Nikki Cheung, our longstanding marketing consultant, in a very fruitful and creative partnership. Much attention was given to our printed materials and, of course, to our website – something that our son, Adam, has looked after for us since he was a pupil at the school. We worked very hard at our links with heads of all our local prep schools, building on the successes of the past and on the growing progress we were able to make at the school with new and refurbished facilities. Nikki's skill and experience in marketing has done untold good for the school over the 20 years she worked for us, and she identified very strongly with the School's vision and mission.

Our chief marketing tenet was, and remains, 'word of mouth' – I wanted happy and fulfilled girls and boys going back to their parents at the end of the day or at weekends or at the end of term, and wanted those happy parents to help spread the word of Clayesmore's increasing prowess. Clayesmore had, therefore, to be as busy and as exciting a school as it could be. I am sure that, early in my time, I said something like 'We must fizz and buzz' at a staff meeting. I must have said this, as I have often had the phrase repeated to me over the years. 'What are we doing today, Mr So-and-so,' I might say as I walked into a classroom. 'We're fizzing and buzzing, headmaster,' was often the reply!

Somehow or other, all these things came together; our sense of energy sped up and grew and Clayesmore grew with that energy. As I got to know the staff and the pupils, I came to realise more and more what a fantastic school Clayesmore was and that it is the relationship between the staff and boys and girls individually that makes all the difference, very much as Alexander Devine and others had felt and promoted over the years. As the *Good Schools' Guide* later put it, we were 'a school on a roll'.

Someone who very much enjoyed the excitement of all that was going on was Roger Denning, Clayesmore's long-standing deputy head and head of geography. Roger was a man of many talents with a huge enthusiast for his subject, for sport – cricket, especially – and he also relished in solving problems. As a deputy head, he could be fearsome; the very last thing that a pupil wanted was to be 'sent to Mr Denning'. If Roger grew tired of having to be formidable he didn't grow tired, it seemed to me, of administrative work, and he was very clever at getting things down on paper in an organised and planned way. This was crucial, of course, as I was becoming busier and busier on a daily basis seeing more and more parents and prospective pupils. In 2004, Roger relinquished his deputy head role but carried on as head of geography in a splendid way for some years, rejoicing in the greater freedom this gave him to be himself with the unofficial title of 'Uncle Rog'.

Above: Speech Day 2007.

Left: Roger Denning.

It became apparent in early 2003, with more and more interest being shown in the school, that far from struggling to reach our 300 pupil ceiling, we were going to find it quite hard to keep the lid on at this number. The refurbishment of the boarding houses and some migration into one or two other corners of the school meant that we could take a few more boarders (our capacity in 2012 is for 235 boarders) but it was the day market that really grew, and it wasn't completely clear how we should face up to this. It came down to two simple questions. Should Clayesmore now start to raise the stakes in Common Entrance, to keep numbers down? Or should we rise to this extraordinary new challenge, and allow the school to grow incrementally?

This was a critical moment, I feel, in the history of modern Clayesmore. We had long made a virtue of Clayesmore being a 'small family school'. Was there now a danger that we wouldn't any longer be a small school? We undertook a lot of work and self-examination at this juncture and, in the end, the governors, still led by Ron Spinney, went along with what I wanted to do, which was to increase the school numbers to just over 400 in the coming six years.

But there was one very difficult pill to swallow! We couldn't possibly do this without building a further new classroom block. Even Ron, a great optimist and a man who, in his everyday life as chief executive of Hammerson, juggled hundreds of millions of pounds, was unsure that further expensive development was necessarily wise. Of course, that's the story of independent schools the country over, throughout history. Every so often there are key, brave decisions to be made with no guarantee whatsoever that pupil numbers will remain constant or continue to grow.

Once again Philip Proctor and Hammonds were called upon, and the designs for what we now know as the Spinney Centre were drawn up. To begin with, they were much more elaborate, and one or two design features of Philip's needed to be curbed in order to keep costs down a little, but in the end the scheme presented to the governors for their final decision came to £1.4m. The decision went to the wire, as they say, and even at the November 2003 council meeting when their approval was granted, it was subject to Ron's further scrutiny of the scheme to satisfy himself that the plan stood up. It wasn't until after the end of the term that Ron finally gave permission to proceed, by which time, conscious that deadlines were pressing, Philip Hammond had already moved some of his plant on site ready to start, as it were, within the hour. I never told Ron!

And so another new building came to fruition with its wonderful new classrooms for history, geography, business studies and careers and the extensive new facilities for staff on the lower ground floor. It was the view of the staff that the new building should be named after Ron Spinney to mark the great progress that had been made during his period of office, and so it was Ron who came to open the building on Speech Day 2005 – an occasion marked by a fly-past by our friends at Compton Abbas airfield and another memorable day in Clayesmore's history. By now, pupil numbers had reached 360.

Right: The Spinney Centre under construction.

Below: A fly-past on Speech Day, 2005.

Claysemore Organs

As many readers will know, I am a keen organist and have done my best to support both prep and senior schools by accompanying choirs and services whenever possible. The chapel pipe organ has a story all its own, and the wonderful tale of its retrieval from St Jude's Church in Birmingham by Nicholas Zelle, OC and sometime director of music, and a group of enthusiastic boys is one of great determination and ingenuity. To cut a long story short, this venerable and large instrument served the school admirably, but its position at the west end of the chapel packed into quite a small chamber was a problem when it came to choral accompaniment. Clayesmore is proud of its choral tradition and over the years I have been called upon to play many of the finest choral works from the English cathedral tradition. The difficulty always was one of balance, with a choir at the east end and a mighty organ at the west. Inevitably young choirs need support, and yet, in the process of providing even a modicum of organ sound, the congregation, caught between organ and choir, couldn't hear the latter, and the latter couldn't hear the former! With electrical and transistorised components becoming increasingly unreliable, a major rebuild costing a lot of money was inevitable. It seemed to my mind that spending a lot of money on the pipe organ, while retaining it at the west end, was unwise.

And so in 2009 we installed a large digital organ with a mobile console and with most of the sound coming from speakers mounted in fine cases either side of the 'chancel'. This was built to my carefully constructed specification and was, I cannot fail to admit, one of the most exciting projects I have ever been caught up in. Built by Wyvern Organs, it is a stunning instrument with a very wide tonal palette including a battery of fanfare trumpets on the west wall which frighten the natives but remind them to sing lustily when they are deployed in a hymn. This is an ideal moment to mention Old Clayesmorian Tim Trenchard, who for many years looked after our pipe organ without, to my knowledge, ever submitting a bill. Tim is as staunch a supporter of Clayesmore as one will ever find as OC, husband of a member of the teaching staff, father of three Clayesmorians, adult member of prep and senior school choirs, tenor soloist and organ curator. His loyalty to the school is both immense and remarkable.

At about this time another very important event happened in the history of the school, namely our re-election to HMC – the illustrious Headmasters' and Headmistresses' Conference. Back in the 1970s Clayesmore had lost this important status, not because of there being a specific problem with the school or its headmaster but because we did not, at that time, meet the criterion about numbers in the sixth form. There is no doubting HMC membership as a kite mark, and in 2004, following an inspection, I was duly elected. To be honest, it is not a great deal to do with me personally and is much more due to the fact that staff and pupils bowled our inspectors over, that our exam statistics had improved and numbers in the sixth form corresponded with HMC's tough criterion. As a postscript, I would just say that the organisation to which Clayesmore has belonged since its inception – SHMIS, the Society of Heads in Independent Schools, or in its recently reborn guise the Society of Heads – has always been a delightful group of which to be a member, and I have greatly enjoyed and appreciated my association with it.

It has already been recorded that, in the middle of the last decade, the governors turned their attention in terms of development to the prep school, where a really delightful new pre-prep and nursery were created on the old swimming pool site. It had been a long time in the coming, and plans for it were well established even before I arrived as prep school headmaster in 1994. Of far greater magnitude, however, is the Everett building, very much in the Clayesmore/Iwerne Minster style, which crowns the whole prep school area with such a new feel.

But, of course, people are of much greater significance in places like Clayesmore than buildings and 'things'. As I write, I find myself rejoicing more than ever in the colleagues with whom I work, the governors who give us all such a wise steer, the delightful young people of Clayesmore today and their friendly and kindly parents.

In the latter part of the 'noughties', while we didn't contemplate any major new buildings, we undertook any number of small projects, a great deal of refurbishment and much renewal and repair. Two major projects are worthy of special comment – the first is the splendid new organ (*see opposite*). The other recent project has been the renewal of the centenary hockey pitch, the first item of major expenditure to be overseen by our new bursar, Mike Dyer. While this could so easily have been a rather lacklustre and uninspiring operation, we took the opportunity to

use our collective imaginations and I cannot help but feel we have taken a great leap forward. Spectators are at last afforded some shelter from the prevailing wind which now assails them from behind instead of blowing straight into their faces, and we have a proper warm-up zone and an excellent and much needed car park. We had been criticised from time to time for the very inefficient lighting units of 1996 which spilt luminescence across swathes of north Dorset, confusing wildlife into thinking night was day and lighting up the night sky in a most un-neighbourly way. All this has been put right, too!

The Clayesmore governing council has changed in style and membership very considerably over the years. The council that appointed me was made up almost entirely of retired professional people, whereas today almost all are working. All the governors that I have known here have served the school royally and we should all be hugely grateful for the time, wisdom and energy that they freely give. Eleanor's and my final interview in 1994 was conducted by the full council, chaired by Brigadier John Elderkin, OC, and it seemed all pretty formidable as we were shown into the corner of the main house drawing room to be confronted by 18 interviewers. I am bound to say that I was very relieved (having been extensively interviewed earlier in the week) that the Brigadier opened the batting against Eleanor for the first ten minutes or so!

From those early days two enduring friendships, both with us personally and with Clayesmore itself, are very special. Roger Kingwill, OC, served as a governor for many, many years including a long stint as chairman. His association with the school goes back to his boyhood, of course, and his love for and interest in it knows no bounds. His perspective and perspicacious insite into the issues that can bring themselves to bear on the life and work of a head in a place like Clayesmore have been of great benefit throughout the time I have known him. A visit from Roger and Judith is always something to look forward to, and his encouraging, beautifully handwritten letters that unfailingly arrive after any formal function have been greatly treasured.

Another great personal and school friend is Mrs Patsy Lidsey, who joined the council shortly before our arrival. Patsy, as a governor, was interested in everything except hot air and money and it seems to me that she brought a great breath of fresh air to the Clayesmore table. She rapidly became a much loved and respected figure and her involvement in the many projects that we undertook was always of great value. She spoke a great deal of common sense and was always able to keep our feet on the ground while at the same time encouraging all that we wanted to

do. I am delighted that Patsy has recently been appointed Governor Emerita, which marks the great esteem in which she is held by her fellow governors and by the whole Clayesmore community.

Dr Richard Willis took over as chairman of council in 2004 and has provided much friendship and support in this capacity. Despite running a busy private medical practice, Dr Willis is always ready to give help and advice and provide a listening ear. Under his chairmanship much has been achieved and he has carried on where Ron Spinney left off in terms of our building development, not being afraid to help steer us into exciting but much-needed new projects. The personification of Clayesmore governance is to be found to a considerable extent in vice chairman Malcolm Green, who leads both the schools' education committees. His wholehearted commitment to the school has been of inestimable value as a former head with detailed and personal knowledge and experience of how these places ought to run.

Mentioning names in a volume such as this is invidious, as it is impossible to include many who have played a significant part in things. We are blessed with a very talented and hard-working group of teaching staff at the school at the present time, for whom the needs of each of their pupils are the focus of their work as they seek to do more and more for them as each term passes. Their commitment and willingness to listen to new thoughts and ideas about how we want to do things, and then to adapt and to grow in all their different roles and capacities, is why we have been so successful. We have a very open-minded, thoughtful and creative common room and I believe that in a great many ways that means that Clayesmore leaves many other independent schools light years behind us. The determination of my colleagues to do their absolute best for our pupils in teaching them and caring for them is truly exceptional, as is their interest in planning intelligently and imaginatively for the future.

Richard Geffen runs a strong ship at the prep school. He and his wife, Ann, are doing wonderfully well and have built up an excellent team to teach and look after our youngest children. At the senior school the two deputy heads, James Carpenter and Mary Bailey, are very special. Both of them have worked tirelessly to support me fully and I have relied upon them each in their different ways completely. As we go to press the senior school has just undergone one of the first of a new breed of full inspections by the Independent Inspectorate. James Carpenter's indefatigable determination to prepare the way for this has reaped great benefits, and the fact that we have achieved 'Excellent' status in all areas of the school's work is very largely due to his hard work and optimistic enthusiasm. Mary Bailey, who is responsible for all welfare aspects of the school, oversaw the very important boarding component previously inspected by Ofsted, and she has ensured that, for the second time in three years, we have achieved the highest outcome. Mary and James have earned enormous respect from parents, pupils, staff and governors for their work at Clayesmore. We are also blessed with a very caring and able house staff team, in whom so much responsibility for our girls' and boys' happiness and welfare is vested.

Other members of the senior leadership team include Andrew West, Helen Farley, Tony Chew and, since 2011, Jamie Reach. Each in their different way contributes carefully, thoughtfully and enthusiastically to the life of the school. Tony is fondly remembered for his long stint as housemaster of Devine, since when he has served as senior master and head of sixth form, bringing great colour to these roles. As the complications of university entrance have grown in recent years, how fortunate we have all been to have had someone as wise as Tony to oversee each and every entry made by our pupils. Andrew West, as director of teaching and learning, has also brought a lot of wisdom to bear on our thinking and development, and the system of assessment that we use at the school, which has won considerable admiration from all who use it, is his brainchild. Helen Farley is also highly valued as head of learning support and contributes considerably. Her ability to make sense of our boys' and girls' learning difficulties to parents and colleagues is legendary and she will be much missed when she leaves shortly. Jamie Reach is the newest addition to the team as director of co-curriculum. He has reinvigorated the Duke of Edinburgh Award in the school, and now has oversight of and co-ordinates all non-academic activities.

Developing Clayesmore over the last 12 years has been about much more than taking in more and more pupils and putting up great new buildings to accommodate them all. We have developed our curriculum, no more so than in the sixth form, where in the recent past we have reintroduced economics and brought in new subjects such as music technology and travel and tourism, with psychology due to be introduced. Very shortly, we will be offering BTEC courses in sport, IT and hospitality, which will suit some of our senior pupils very well indeed and which will complement our A level programme. Some subjects have developed beyond recognition. Design and technology is one such subject which has made very exciting progress, and we now offer graphics as well as the trusty resistant materials D&T GCSE. Careers education and preparation for university have also changed beyond recognition, as has sixth form life generally with lots of new social and cultural initiatives. Pupils of all ages have become more and more involved in running the school: we train our prefects better than ever, we use pupils for interviewing new staff, there are pupil committees to advise on the social life of the school, a food committee, a peer mentoring scheme and, just recently, our own student union has come into being.

In earlier pages we have read of many men and women who are, or who represent, essential aspects of the support network that comes under the watch of the bursar. Nobody comes to Clayesmore without noticing the beauty of the gardens and grounds, the cleanliness of the buildings, the attention to detail in the decor and the quality of the buildings. If they taste the food, they are regularly astonished at its quality, and if they visit the school shop, they are charmed by the ladies who run it. Nobody wants to receive a bill each term, of course, but the bursary staff play an important role.

I spend much of my time with prospective parents and pupils, all of whom find their way to my door through the good services of the registrar's department staffed by Hilary de Bie and Margaret McCafferty, of whom special mention must be made. Margaret never misses a trick and works incredibly hard to help new parents who come to our website or who phone in wanting to know more. Easily distinguishable by her Scottish accent, she is very highly thought of by everyone who comes in contact with her and her patience knows no bounds. Clayesmore owes her a huge debt of gratitude. Parents frequently tell me how wonderful it has been to be able to email or phone Margaret and Hilary with queries and worries over the whole registration process and I could not be better served in all of this. 'Contact rhona@clayesmore.com' is a phrase that often pops up in newsletters going out from me to parents. This refers, of course, to Rhona Rutherford, school secretary, whose sense of fun and wicked laugh permeates much of the school's

administrative department. Hazel Horley sits opposite Rhona and is in charge of our ever-growing minibus operation and all the arrangements for pupils' travel needs at the beginning and end of term. Hazel is tireless in the pursuit of providing a tip-top service and works long hours to ensure parents' and pupils' needs are met.

When we set up the Clayesmore Society in 2009, it was essential that we were able to secure the services of exactly the right person to guide its work, especially with 'friend-raising'. Key in this respect was securing a new relationship with the Old Clayesmorian Society, which has been tremendously successful and beneficial. As an OC herself and with school marketing experience, Louise Smith has proved to be the very person we wanted and great progress has been made. Many Old Clayesmorians have commented on how much they enjoy hearing her friendly voice on the phone and meeting her at OC functions. Another OC who has made a most prominent contribution to the fostering of links between the School and its former pupils is Andrew Beaton, the current OC Society chairman who has recently become a governor of Clayesmore and chairman of our development committee. How fortunate we have been also in securing Debbie Geary as first chairman of the Clayesmore Society committee. After a lifetime's period of service at Clayesmore on the teaching staff of the prep school as senior mistress and ultimately deputy head, Debbie became a governor in 2007, and it is marvellous that we continue to benefit so greatly from her vast knowledge of the school and its people.

As I have picked my way through all my memories and reminiscences, the one group of people from which I have not singled out names for special mention is, of course, the fabulous boys and girls of the school, many of whom have grown through Clayesmore with us. There are hundreds I would want to mention – their parents too, of course – and it is just impossible! In thousands of different ways, young people have drawn themselves to my attention over the years, and my colleagues and I are so fortunate to be working with such delightful girls and boys. If anyone ever doubts the achievements, the quality, the sense of fun, goodwill and capacity for friendship that typifies the average modern Clayesmorian, you only need to meet a few of them or, perhaps, read a little of the 2012 inspection report which heaps praise upon them in abundance.

The final words of this chapter are being written as we near the end of an astonishingly busy and exciting spring term. As I write, pupils and staff have set out for an educational trip to Grenada, where they will stay with host families and attend lessons with their new Spanish friends. Another similar group leaves for France in a few days' time. The prep school has just staged another epic show in the theatre, while their junior girls and boys are putting the final touches to their end of term musical. In the senior school we look forward to our end of term spring concert with pupils playing concerto movements and the choir singing Fauré's Requiem. Meanwhile, a group of 12 pupils have been to participate in a Model United Nations experience with pupils from 14 other schools in Taunton for the first time, the CCF are out competing in the Dorset Cadet Challenge and the hockey players are getting ready to compete in the Bath Hockey Festival. During the holidays there will be a Duke of Edinburgh Gold Award practice expedition on Dartmoor and a group of enthusiasts will be setting off for Switzerland to visit CERN – the home of the Large Hadron Collider. How diverse a range of activities can one have?

With an excellent inspection behind us, with our staff and pupils doing more and more and with exciting developments creeping ever closer we remain a 'school on a roll'. As we look forward to celebrating 80 years in Iwerne Minster next year, as marked by this splendid publication, I am thrilled that Alexander Devine's vision for Clayesmore has served us so well and is proving so popular in its modern and colourful guise as lived, day in, day out, by everyone at the school today.

Above: Debbie Geary, long standing staff member, parent, governor and Clayesmore Society Chairman.

The 2020 Vision

As we come right up to date, what thoughts of the future? In 2011, we published our 2020 Vision, which sets out our building plans for the mid term. Now, with news of success in our 2012 inspection, with ever increasing demand for places – it seems likely we will grow to 460 or so in the next two years – and with a strong start to the fundraising campaign, the governors have just announced two important new buildings. The first will be the new Business Centre – a large classroom block which will be built on to the Jubilee Building of 2002. The second is a new boarding wing for girls on the site of the rather decrepit and run-down Hambledon House on the western side of the main house.

In the same way that other recent new buildings have enabled change and development in other blocks, so the Business Centre, which will become the home for economics, business studies, psychology, ICT and careers as well as providing two extra new science laboratories, will enable other subjects to expand elsewhere to take over three rooms that will be vacated in the Spinney Centre. The new girls' wing speaks for itself. Exciting times are ahead.

Above: Martin Cooke with Dr Richard Willis, Chairman of Governors and Andrew Beaton, OC Society Chairman.

Left: Artist's initial impression of the 2020 vision.

Below: The Jubilee Building with Business Centre extension.

List of Subscribers

This book has been made possible through the generosity of the following subscribers.
Dates indicate years of attendance.

Catherine Aalders **2011–**
Harry Aalders **2011–**
John Aalders **2011–**
Anthony Allen **2000–3**
David Anderson **1938–45**
Michael Anderson **1940–5**
Major General Stephen Andrews and Kim White
Rupert Angell **2011–**
Thomas Anwell **2010–**
Jack Armstrong **1995–2011**
Brian Arpel **1956–9**
Toby J Ashfield **2010–**
Ella Askew **2010–**
Jack Askew **2009–11**
Luke Askew **2010–**
Jacob Avon **1980–5**
Brian and Patricia Baggott
Giles Baggott **2002–8**
Ian Bailes **1941–51**
J B Bailey **1964–9**
Oliver Bailey **2007–12**
William Bailey **2009–**
Cherry Baker **2002–12**
Angela and Eric Balmforth
George E Banks **1963–6**
Katherine Barnes **2008–**
Emma Barrett-Hoey **1977–83**
Peter J Barrow **1960–4**
M Bassi
Harry Beardsley **2008–12**
Andrew Beaton **1964–9**
Ellie Beckett **2000–**
Bill Beesley **1949–55**
Jemima Belchambers **2011–**
Sophie Belchambers **2009–**
Edward Belford **2006–**
Jessica Belford **2007–11**
Michael Benka-Morgan **1949–53**
Joanna Bentley (née Mawby) **1983–7**
Maria Bernal Escribano **2011–**
George Bevan-Thomas **2011–**
H K Bhundia **1978–9**
Nigel Bill **1959–61**
Robert Blackwell **1974–7**
Nicholas Blake **1967–70**
Simeon Bleach **2007–12**
Sven Boehmert **2009–11**
Chettle Bogue **2010–**
Harry Bolger **2000–**
Julie Bolger **Staff, 2000–**
Alexander Boreham **2011–**
James Boyes **1958–63**
Jonathan Bradbeer **1952–5**
R L Bradbeer **1936–46**
The Bragg Family
Kathryn Breadmore **1981–7**
The Revd John William Bridgen **1953–8**
David Briggs **2001–6**
Stefanie Briggs (née Blomquist) **1999–2006**
Fenella Broomhead **2012–**
Jake Broomhead **2009–**
Julia Brown (née Green) **1979–81**
Mr and Mrs P Buckley
Miles W Burger **1960–4**
George Button **2003–10**
Carola C Campbell **Governor**
David Capel-Jones **1950–3**
Toby Casperd **2010–**
Michael Chadwick **1951–6**
Michael Anthony Chapman **1950–4**
William J Chennells **1952–6**
Joshua Cheung **1992–2011**
Olivia Cheung **1992–2008**

Wai and Nikki Cheung
Olivia Christopher 2004–9
Emily Clarke 2010–
Mark L Clarke 1985–8
Tim Collyer 1991–2001
James Comer 2006–
Olivia Cook 2011–
Katie Cook 2008–
Adam Cooke 1994–2005
Anna Cooke 1994–2008
Martin and Eleanor Cooke
Headmaster of Prep, 1994–2000
Headmaster, 2000–
Josie Cooper 2009–
Adrian Cornwell 1958–63
Alice Couling 2011–
James Couling 2008–
C A M Coxe 1949–53
Andrew Crabb 1985–8
Sarah Crabb 1984–7
Ian Crabbe 1967–72
Corinne E Cummings 2008–12
Joe Henry Cummings 2010–
Dr Frank Dall 1957–69
Dora Dane 2011–
Philip Davies 1951–3
Dominic R K Dawnay 2010–
Edward de Boehmler 2010–
George de la Perrelle 2007–
Abigail Dean 2011–
Eloise Dean 2010
Melody Dean 2010–
Susan J Dear
Ciara Deeker 2011–
Niamh Deeker 2011–
Richard Dibben 1961–9

Chloe Dixon 2010–12
Mr and Mrs R Dorrien-Smith
Malcolm Douglas 1968–73
Peter Ashford Down 1941–7
Harriet Duffell 2011–
James Dyer 2010–12
Bronwyn Ebsworth 2011–
John Elderkin 1938–43
Florence Elmberg 2010–
Tom Erbetta 2009–
Charlotte Emily Euridge 2005–10
Tristan William Euridge 2006–11
David J Evans 1952–6
Henry Fairfield 2010–
Geoffrey W E Faithfull 1945–50
David Ronald Fangen 1961–6
Mark Farrand 1978–81
Ambi Fensom 2009–
Ian Alan Ferguson 1940–3
Alice Fisher 1996–2009
Guy Fisher 1998–2011
Steve Flambert 1966–9
Peter Fleming 1958–62
Alexander Nicholas Ford 2002–10
Adrian Frost 1949–54
Megan Fry 2007–12
Alan Furneaux 1954–8
Franziska Ganz 2010–12
Deborah Geary **Staff,1975–2007**
Harriet Geary 1977–88
Luke Geary 1968–76
Mike Geary **Staff, 1964–97**
Rachel Geary 1969–74
Patrick and Sally Gent
Prep School Headmaster, 1988
Emily Gibbins 2006–

Jack Gibbins 2006–
Matthew Gibbs 2010–
Rosie Gibbs 2011–
Sindi Giles-Rowley 1998–2006
F David 'Ferdy' Gilson 1949–52
Edward Goates 2001–8
James Goates 1999–2004
Jack Goodman 2011–
Nicki Gray and Miles Kevin
1980–6
Elizabeth Green **Staff, 2010–**
Hannah Green 2000–10
James Green 2000–10
Paul and Sarah Haines
Emma Hamilton 2007–12
David G Hammersley 1954–8
Amber Hansmann 2011–
Stephen Hardie 1954–7
John Hardy-Smith
John Andrew Hardy-Smith
Steven Hare 1958–62
Richard Harman 1954–8
Archie Harris 1937–40
Robin Harrison 1944–8
Edward Hartwell 2003–6
Jeremy Hartwell 1999–2006
Toby Hartwell 2007–12
Anthony (Tony) Hawkins 1950–7
Dr Richard Hawley 1939–52
Jane E Hayes **Staff, 1998–**
Catherine Hayter **Staff, 2007–**
Jack Hayter 2008–12
Douglas Heap 1946–52
Adam Heaton 2007–11
Ben Heaton 2007–
Isabel Heaton 2012–

Christopher Helberg **2009–11**
Stuart C Henley **1960–3**
Brian Henson **1949–54**
Michael J Heyhoe **1945–8**
Mr and Mrs J B C Higgs
James Hill **2008–**
Simon A Hill **1953–8**
Nic Hillyard **1982–95**
Lauren Hinsley **2009–**
Barnaby Hitchings **2005–10**
Aimee Hockham **2009–**
Millie Hockham **2010–**
Mr and Mrs M Hocquard
George C Hodgson **1942–6**
Richard Hodgson **1953–8**
Victoria A Hofer **2011–**
Caitlin Holden **1999–2005**
Dominic Holden **2005–**
Luke Holden **2000–**
Rebecca Holden **2002–**
James Hole **1958–62**
Albert Ridley Holloway **1932–6**
Jeremy P Holroyd **2008–10**
Spencer Holtom **1947–52**
Molly Hopley **2010–**
Hazel Horley **Staff, 2002–**
George Hudson **2005–10**
Iain Hudson **2005–10**
Tom Hudson **2005–10**
David and Steffi Hughes
Sarah Jane Hutchins (née Allen) **1990–5**
Charlie Hutchinson **2011–**
Frederick Hutchinson **2010–**
Barnaby Huthwaite **2006–**
Toby Huthwaite **2007–**

Crispin Hutton **2005–**
Tristan Hutton **1994–2000**
Cdr David C V Isard RN (Retd) **Bursar, 1985–95**
Hannah Jackson **2006–**
James Jackson **2010–**
Dr A P G Jancis **Staff, 1992**
Grace Jarvis **1997–**
Rebecca Jefferis **1983–91**
Christopher Johnston **1958–60**
Asia Jones **2010–**
Colin H Jones **1951–6**
David D Jones **1961–6**
Kevin Jones **1981–5**
Lewis D L Jones **2007–12**
Xavier Jones **2010–**
Beth Judd **2009–12**
Jonathan Kemp **1960–5**
Jean and Robin Kennard
Louie Kerlogue **1997–2008**
Dara Khadjeh Nouri **1952–6**
Charles Kidner **2011–**
Paul Killik **1962–6**
Roger G Kingwill **1945–50**
Mr and Mrs Alan Kirkpatrick
Fiona Kirkpatrick **2003–**
Ross Kirkpatrick **2003–**
Sanchia Kirkpatrick **2003–4**
George Knight **2009–**
Sophie Knight **2009–**
The Knowldon Family **1979–85 and 2011–**
Jonathan Lambert **1987–9**
Feline Paula Leonore Lange **2011–12**
Andrew D Law **1975–8**

Joseph Lee **2005–10**
Max Lee **2008–**
Charles Stephen John Lees **1974–9**
Maksim Leonenko **2011–**
Amy Levinson **2002–7**
Stephen Levinson **1962–7**
Patricia Lidsey **Governor**
Benjamin Lindley-Start **2010–**
Jack Lindley-Start **2006–11**
Ned N Lindsay **2010–**
Kenneth E Lingwood **1935–41**
David Little **Bursar, 1998–2009**
Freddie Lobb **2011–**
Hamish Lobb **2011–**
Freddie Lodge **2010–**
Meg Lodge **2007–11**
Charles Lower **2011–**
Beatrice Maddison **2005–12**
George Maddison **2007–**
Charlie Magee **1975–85**
Alexander Male **2009–**
Isabella Marconato **2011–**
Jacob Marie **2009–**
Rebecca Marie **2004–12**
Samuel Marie **2006–**
Moritz Marschall **2011–12**
Imogen Robyn Marshall **2009–**
Robert Mash **1946–58**
Alec McCallum **1939–44**
Lewis McManus **2007–**
Alan F McMichael **1948–52**
John Brodie McMillan **1966–71**
Jonas Melbinger **2009–10**
Lauren Mellows **2007–12**
Eleanor Melluish **2010–**
Brian Merson **1958–63**

Polly Meyrick	2008–
The Miles Family	
Michael Millman	1980–90
Alice Mills	2002–09
Edward Mills	2002–10
Peter Mills	1953–62
Amelia Shani Mist	2009–
Charlotte Mitchell	2003–8
Emily Mitchell	2002–11
Marsha Mobey	1998–2004
Archie Moore	2011–
Abigail Morgan	2002–
Lauren Morgan	2000–
R V Morgan and A J Morgan	
Hugh D Morris	2005–10
Charles Newitt	2011–
Eric Newland	2007–
Mark Newland	Staff, 2009–
Rowan Newland	2003–11
SarahJane Newland (née Kennard)	1980–4 and Staff, 2002–
William Newland	2006–
J R Newnham	Governor
Rupert Nodder	
J Andrew Nurcombe	1951–4
Charles F Oliver	1973–8
James H Oliver	1973–8
W J Osmond	1947–51
Graeme Owton	1983–9
Clive Palmer	1959–64
So Chin Pang	2001–3
Polina Paniflova	2010–12
Alison Parnell (née Gent)	1975–80
Peter Parsons	1949–59
Hannah Patton	2009–
Kieran Patton	2010–
Perry Pearce	2006–11
Sebastian Pearce	2009–12
Vera Peevor	Staff, 2001–
Mark Pepper	1979–84
Michael Peters	1953–6
The Peters Family	
John Robert Petty	1948–50
Genevieve Phillips	1996–2004
Michael Phillips	1995–2000
Richard Phillips	2002–7
R H C Philllips	Governor
Ella Pickford	2002–
Thomas Piesinger	2008–
Michael J Pigott	1957–60
Lionel H Pimm	1938–41
Neill Pitcher	1957–62
Jennifer Pollock	1999–2005
Harry J Pontifex	2004–9
Joshua W Pontifex	2007–12
Charlie Potter	2010–
Charlie Pounds	2009–
Michael Poynor	1956–61
Peter D Preece	1939–42
Anthony F Prewett	1948–53
Charles Price	1956–61
Bryony Purdue	2003–11
Hugo Purdue	2003–8
Martin Quekett	1963–7
Colin Redston	1953–7
Douglas Reed	1961–5
Gary W Rees	1959–64
Joshua Richardson	2010–
Alexander B Roach	2000–11
Bree Roberts	2009–
Rebecca J Robertshaw	1995–2005
Edward Robinson	2012–
Lucy Robinson	2012–
Stuart and Hayley Robinson	
William Robinson	2012–
Alexander F Ross	2011–
April J Ross	2011–
Nicholas Ross	2000–5
Timothy Russell	1952–6
Piers Sabine	1949–60
Beth Sadler	1996–2011
Matthew Sadler	2000–
Cdr and Mrs D P Salisbury	
Dr Nigel S Salisbury	1949–54
Paul Sanday	1957–61
Fay Sandon-Allum	2008–10
Lucinda Sandon-Allum	2010–12
Iain H Savill	1962–7
Tana Maria Schäechtele	2002–3
Hugo Scott	2006–
Rosa Scott	2004–
Martin G Scovell	1952–6
John Stuart Seaton	1943–8
Amanda Sessions (née Farmer)	1986–8
Florian Shaflitzl	2010–
Mir Massoud Shahabi	1969–73
Andrew Shaw	1969–74
Neil Shelley	2011–
Bill Shephard	1963–7
Angus Shield	1978–83
William V Shields	1949–52
Alicia Short	2004–8
Gabi Skinner	2011–
Mark Skinner	1970–4
Oliver Bray Skinner	2011–
Clive Smith	1961–6
Ian F Smith	1958–62

Louise Smith (née Ross-Kellaway)
1994–8 and Staff, 2008–
Philip Paterson Smith **1949–53**
J D S Smithie **1941–9**
John Sparkes **1953–6**
Emma Spinney **2006–12**
Andrew J Stainer **1979–84**
J F N Stanier **Prep Pupil, 1950s**
Will Stevens **1951–5**
Tom Stilwell **Staff, 1994–2000**
Alexander Stocks **2011–**
Graham Stuart **1973–6**
Mitch Stuart **2010–**
Jack Sullivan **2007–**
Julia Sullivan **2007–**
Matthew Swarbrick **1991–5**
Emily Sykes **2010–**
A Guy Taylor **1945–9**
Jack Taylor **2008–**
Maggie Templeman **2005–**
Sam Templeman **2005–**
Gavin Tew **1989–97**
James Tew **1989–95**
Jo Tew **1989–97**
Sandra Tew **Staff, 1990–**
Tony Tew **Staff, 1993–8**
Fran Thomason **Staff, 1999–**
Zoe Threadgold **2008–**
Mr and Mrs Tim Trenchard
Tosco Troughton **2009–**

Gary Tuffy and Pamela Watson
Lewis H Twydle **2005–9**
Murray S Upton **1942–5**
Christopher Valenzia **1975–7**
Richard Vincent **1951–5**
Leon von Mulert **2011–12**
Moritz von Rosenberg **2011–**
William Choi Siu Wai **1967–70**
Richard Walker **Staff, 2003–**
Brian G Wallis **1959–63**
Georgina Wallrock **2007–10**
Richard (Charlie) Wallrock **1972–8**
George Wates **2005–**
Harriet Wates **2004–**
Tabitha Wates **2004–**
Alison Watkins **Staff, 1965–72**
Peter Watson **1956–60**
Andrew Weatherley **1970–4**
E Weatherley
Ben Weaver **2008–**
Emma Weaver **2008–**
Laura Webb **2008–**
Alister Webster
John Webster
Tony Webster
Natalie Weyland **2011–**
Conor White-Andrews **2001–12**
Fern White-Andrews **2009–**
Rory White-Andrews **1999–2008**
Ben White **2011–**

Peter Wightman **1944–8**
Nikita Wilkins **2009–**
C P Wilkinson **1955–61**
T Malcolm Y Wilkinson **1953–8**
Brian Williams **1946–50**
Dr Richard Willis
Chairmain of Governors, 2004–
Colonel H G Willmore **1951–5**
Harriet Wilson-Pinchin **2012–**
Alexander Wilson **1998–**
Dominic Wilson **1998–**
Guy Wilson **1998–**
Jamie Wilson **2002–7**
Jamie R Wilson
Daniel (Dan) John Wittleton
1963–8
Elliott Wood **1956–9**
Alexander Wood **2009–**
William Wood **2009–**
Harriet Wordsworth **2004–**
Joshua Wordsworth **2001–10**
Andrew Wright **1957–63**
Matthew Wright **1954–8**
Colin Young **1996–2004**
Emma Young **1983–7**
Graham Young **1994–2002**
Lucy Young **1997–2007**
E A C Zoephel **1973–8**

Index of Names

Bold = contribution
Italics = image / artist

Adam, James Graham 12, *12*
Ainscow, Arthur 30
Ainscow, Edith 30, *30*, 31
Alabaster, Maurice Cecil 14
Aldworth, Bill 67, 141, 142
Allen, Anthony 143, *143*
Allwright, Jackie 96
Ambert, Alexandre 28
Ambert, Henri 28
Ambert, Léon 28
Anderson, David 155
Anderson, Frederic St K **20**, 150, *150*, 155
Anderson, Michael 118
Andrews Sisters, the 118
Andrews, Rory 146
Andrews, Stephen **146**, 157
Anson, Eustace Arthur 14
Appleby, John 48, *50*, 51, 64, 66, 68, 74, 79, 106, 107, 116, 117, 127, 135, 141
Archer, Lady 80, *80*
Archer, Malcolm 114
Ardizzone, Edward 34, 61, 104, **105**, *105*
Armstrong, Lord 80
Arnolds, Michael 114
Arpel, Beryl *65*
Arpel, Brian *65*
Arpel, Lloyd *65*
Ashcroft, Peggy 120
Ashton Henderson, Alan 155
Ashton Henderson, Douglas 155
Atkinson, Richard *13*, 14
Attlee, Clement 63
Auden, WH 77
Austen, Jane 130
Ayckbourn, Alan 120
Ayrton, Michael 106

Bach, Johann Sebastian 110
Bader, Sir Douglas *95*
Badley, JH 15, 94
Baggett, Brian 64
Bailey, Mary 168
Balfour, Michael 118, *118*
Banfield, Charlie 57, 145
Banks, George **106**
Barber, Harriet 100
Barnes, Barbara 103, *103*
Barron, Mr 98
Beatles, the 110
Beaton, Andrew 170, *171*
Beeby, Anne 130, *131*, 134, 152
Beeby, David *80*, 130, *131*, 132, *133*, 134, 155, 156, *156*
Beethoven, Ludwig van 111
Beharry, Johnson 80
Bellman, Sir Harold 49, 64, 104, 153
Berg, Harry 14
Beynon, Matthew *127*
Bill, Michael 90
Bill, Nigel 90, **90**, **92–3**
Billington, Susan 86
Blaber, Angie 126
Black, Harry 18
Black, Jean 18
Blankers-Koen, Fanny 141
Blashford-Snell, John 80
Blomquist, Julia 101
Bluett 37
Bonnington, Chris 77
Booth, John 107
Boothby, Alice 31
Boothby, Geoffrey 30, *30*, 31
Bott, Oliver 51, **52**, 61
Bower, Thomas Bowyer 40
Brockhurst, Harriet 96
Brooke-Little, John 68, 78, *95*, 125, *125*, 153, 154
Brown, Gordon 60

Brown, Lord George 80
Brown, Sarah 142
Browse, Dan 102
Browse, Isobel 102
Burke, Peter 49, 63, *63*, 64, 65, 67, 68, 73, 77, 78, 81, 106, 109, 115, 116, 117, 118, 127, 141
Burney, Gilbert 29
Burnie, John 143
Butt, Ray 45
Butterworth, Peter 121
Button, George 137
Button, Lynn **137**
Byrne, Ophelia 160
Byrne, Stephen 156, 160
Byrne, Stitch 160
Byrne, Tolly 160

Cannon, Tommy 10
Carpenter, James 168
Carver, Lord 80
Carver, Miss 47, 48
Chadwick 106
Chan, Francis 155
Charles, HRH The Prince of Wales 125
Cheke, Marcus 36
Cheung, Nikki 155, 162
Chew, Tony **30–1**, **62**, **119**, **128–9**, 131, 132, 168
Chubb, Gordon 56, 57
Churchill, Winston 59, 63
Clark, Dudley 140
Clarkson, Richard Milroy 36, *36*, 132
Clay, David **76**
Clements, Paul 143
Cliff, Grosvenor Talbot 155, *155*
Cliff, Noel Grosvenor Talbot 155
Coates, Eric 114
Coke, Desmond 29, 35, 37, 49
Cole, George 121
Coles, Adlard 36
Coles, Alec 65
Colson, Miss 36, 37
Cook, Tracy 144
Cooke, Adam 162
Cooke, Eleanor 99, 102, 134, *134*, 136, 159, 162, 166
Cooke, Margaret 99
Cooke, Martin **6**, 45, 97, 98, 99, *99*, 101, 102, 134, *134*, 136, 146, **159–71**, *160*, *171*
Cooke, Trevor 97, 99
Corica, Matthew 156
Crabbe, Ian 110
Craig, Lawrence William Harvard 62
Craxton, John 104
Croft, Andrew 84
Crosby, Bing 118
Crown, Cyril 14, *14*
Crown, Roman 14, *14*
Cunningham, Capt 67
Curley, Carlo 112, 134
Curtis, Andrew 100

D'Allen, Neil 84
Daltrey, Roger 45
Dance, Charles 146
Daniell, Gilbert Lindsey *13*, 14
Daniels, Mr 51
Dave Clark Five 110
David, Billie 106
Davies, Rupert 121
de Bie, Hilary 169
de Fourtalis, Maurice *see* Alabaster, Maurice Cecil
de la Billière, Sir Peter 80
de la Mere, Walter 153
de la Warr, Earl (Herbrand 'Buck' Sackville, Lord Buckhurst) 26, *26*
de Selincourt, Anne 38, 48
de Selincourt, Aubrey 37, 38, *38*, 39, *39*, 47, 48, 49, 77, 109
de Selincourt, Guy ('Bob') 38, 39, 49
de Selincourt, Irene (née Rutherford) 38, 48
de Selincourt, Lesley 38, 48
de Selincourt, Martin 37, 39, 47, 48
Dear, Ruth Verling 48, 64, 66, *66*, 107, 115, *115*, 118
Dearmer, Dr 39
Denning, Lord 80
Denning, Roger 130, 162, *162*
Denny, Robyn 104, *104*, 107
Denny, Tom 107
Devine, Alexander (Lex) 6, 9, 10, *10*, 11, 12, 13, 14, 15, 16, 17, 18, 19, *19*, 20, 21, 23, *23*, 25, *25*, 27, 28, 29, 30, 31, 32, 33, 34, 34, 35, 36, 37, 38, 39, 48, 51, 86, 94, 105, 109, 120, *120*, 128, 132, 137, 138, 139, 146, 149, 151, *151*, 153, 154, 156, 157, 162, 170
Devine, George 120, *120*

di Balme, Count 29, 32, 35, 36, 37, 105
di Fragnito, David Maude-Roxby-Montalto 104
Dobie, George 48, *49*, 132
Dobie, Ivy 48, 132
Dodd, Edgar 29, 34, 35
Dollerson, Andrew 112
Dowling, Jeremy **81**, **116–17**
Drummond, Geoffrey Heneage *15*, 28, 29, 151
Dudley-Smith, Timothy 114
Duffy, Maureen 146
Dukes, John **64–5**
Dunsterville, LC 153
Dyer, General 70
Dyer, Mike 165

Eastman 36
Eastman, Mrs 27
Edwards *20*
Edwards, Maud 57
Edwards-Stewart, Ivor 79, 94, 95, *95*
Elderkin, John *133*, 166
Elena, Queen of Italy 32
Elizabeth II, HM the Queen 125
Elverson, Vendela 129
Epstein, Brian 106, 107, *107*, 118
Evans, Colin 146, 147
Evans, Edith 120
Evans, Elaine 147
Eveleigh, John 104
Everett, Dick 89, 90, 92, 93, 94, *94*, 102

Fairlie, Edward 28
Falcone, Shannon 143, *143*
Fangen, David 155
Fangen, Olivia 155
Farley, Helen 168
Farley, Robert 146
Farrow 70
Fauré 170
Fellowes, Julian 80, *80*
Ferguson, Ian **60**, *60*
Fernihough, Eric 36, 143
Finney, Albert 121
Fitzgerald, Robert 111, *111*, 112
Fletcher, Frank 50
Foot, Di 129
Frankiss, Charlotte 101, *101*
Fraser, Mark 121
Frink, Elizabeth 106

Garcia, Bettina 106
Gaskin, Michael 106, 151
Geary, Debbie 99
Geary, Deborah 102, 103
Geary, Mike 96, 98, 100, *100*, 103
Geary, Mrs 98
Geffen, Ann 102, *103*, 168
Geffen, Matthew 142
Geffen, Richard 102, 103, *103*, 167
Gent, David **96**
Gent, Patrick 97
Gent, Sally **96**
George VI, King 59
Gibb 53
Gielgud, John 120
Gilbert, WS 117, 118
Gill, Eric 68
Gillett 70
Gilmour, Alan 131, *133*
Gingold, Hermione 120
Glazebrook, Hugh 92
Glennie, Evelyn 112
Godfrey 68
Gold, John 51
Goldie, George 70
Goodman, Lord 80
Goodyear, Charles Edward 12–13
Gordon, General 10
Gordon, Malcolm 57
Gould, John **53**, 54
Green, Malcolm 167
Grun, James 21
Gunn, Alex 156

Hamer, Diana 102
Hamilton, Emma 155
Hammersley, David **74**
Hammond, Philip 163
Handley, Jonathon 86
Hannington, Robert Arthur George 12
Hardy, Thomas 42, *42*, 53
Hardyment, Tim 64
Harris, Jet 106
Harris, Keith Vivian Frank 62
Harris, Patrick Vivian 12
Hart, Michael 108, 118
Hart, Tony 60, *60*, 67, 106, 108, 118, 133, *133*
Harvey-Jones, Sir John 80
Hassall, Christopher 120
Hawardine, Archibald Stephen 12
Hawkins, Angela 127

Hawkins, Michael 123, *124*, 127, 134
Hawley, Richard **141**
Hayes, Jane 156
Hazledene, Miss 34, 104
Heap, Douglas 106, 107, 118, **118**
Heenan, Cardinal 80
Henbest, Mike 78, 79, *79*, 110, 124, 142
Hepworth, Barbara 106
Hicks, Tom 143
Hill, Rob 101, *101*, 132, *132*
Hillier, Mr 51
Hinchcliffe, John 101
Hitler, Adolf 59
Hodson, JL 39
Hogarth, William 53
Holmes, Richard 80
Homan, Bob 63
Horley, Hazel 170
Hughes 35
Humpage, Chris 144
Hunt, Dick 76
Hunt, Miss 145
Huntley, Gordon 56

Ingham, Bruce **76**
Isard, David 99, 119
Isherwood, Christopher 77
Isley Brothers, the 106
Ismay, Bruce 41
Ismay, James 41, 42

Jackson, Dr Francis 114
Jackson, Sir Mike 80, *80*
Jacobson, Neville *see* Jason, Neville
Jancis, Alan 84, 160
Jancis, Dr Anne 84, 160
Jason, Neville (formerly Jacobson) 106, 116, 118, **118**, *118*
Jenkins, Cerys 98
Jevons, John W 'Jack' **34**, 39, 144
John Paul II, Pope 100, *100*
John, Augustus 42
Jones, Canon of Chichester 19
Jones, Caron 96
Jones, Graham 99
Jones, Kevin **126–7,** *126*, *127*
Jones, Lewis 19
Joscelyne, V 54, 61
Joseph, Michael 120
Joseph, Stephen 120, *120*

Kardooni, Aadel 101, *101*
Karren, Mr 67
Katinakis, Francis Beresford *24*
Keating, Geoffrey 110
Keighley, Dick 101
Kelly 70
Kemp 110
Kerr *15*
Khan, Hussein Kuli *12*, 14
King, Evelyn 37, *37*, 43, 47, 48, 49, 50, 51, *54*, 61, 62, 63, 64, 66, 77, 78, 79, 80, 81, 89, 115, 120, 127, 131, 132, 139, 140, 153
King, Mackenzie 63
King, Mrs 145
Kingwill, Judith 166
Kingwill, Roger 66, 68, *80*, 81, 96, 153, 166
Kipling, Rudyard 153
Kirkby, RA 140
Knight, Jill 129
Koster, Martin 109
Koster, Raymond 109
Koster, Richard 109
Kuo, Chengi 65

Lam, Vicky 155
Lancefield, David 106
Lennon, J 56
Levesley, Guy Rutherford 13
Levinson, Stephen 136
Lewis, Alec 121
Leyton, John 106
Lidsey, Patsy 166, 167
Little, David 86, 102, 159
Lloyd, Richard 114, *114*
Lock, Laurie 35
Locke, Ivor King Harvey *13*, 14
Lole, Simon 114
Long, Jenny 152
Long, Mr *15*
Longdon, Mrs 98
Lorca 119
Lorimer, Elizabeth Scott 21, *21*
Lorimer, John Scott (Jack) 21
Lovelock, Joe 111
Luboff, Andrew 151
Lyndhurst, Nicholas 45
Lyttelton, Edward 11, *11*

Mac 142
MacAlister, JES 56
Macdonald, John 127
Macfarlane Watt, Miss 64
Mackenzie, Alister 37, 47, 48
Mackenzie, Mrs 54

Mackintosh, Kenneth 120
Macmillan *20*
Maer, Stephen 118
Mahon, Christopher 109, 114, 126
Mash, Robert 135, *135*, *146*, 150
Maughan, Daniel 101, *101*
Mawhinney, Catherine 102
May, Simon *112*
McCafferty, Margaret 169
McCallum, Alec **140**
McHardie-Jones, Ben 101
McIsaac, Roy 77, *77*, 78, 79, 81, *95*, 109, 123, 127, 135, 154
McKinlay, Valerie 86
McNeil, Anna 100
Mendelssohn, Felix 110
Mervyn, Graham **23**, 27, 32, **33**, 37, 138
Mi, Denny 67
Middle, Christopher 160
Middle, Penny 160
Miller, Richard 144
Miller, Tom T **33**
Miller-McCall, Freya 130
Mills, Andrew 64
Milne, Christopher Robin 48
Milner, Edward 43
Milton, Mrs 98
Mitchell, Moe 84
Moldung, Tore Jørn 76
Moore, Charles Hay Anzeley 14
Moore, Henry 106
Moore, Humphrey 48, 65, 72, 74, *74*, 110, 117, 135, 141
Morley, James (Jim) **38**, **74–5**
Mott, Phillip *126*
Moxham, Graham 99, 102
Mozart, Wolfgang Amadeus 109, 111
Munrow, Mr *15*

Neill, AS 89, 94
Neuberger, Julia 80
Newland, Mark 146
Newland, SarahJane (née Kennard) 124, 146, 150
Newman, Alan 99, 130
Nicholas I, King of Montenegro 31, *31*, 32
Norris, Ray 85, 130

Olby, Duncan 119
Osborne, John 120
Owton, Graeme 119
Panter, Howard 118, *118*, 121
Parfitt, Mrs 98
Parnell, Alison (née Gent) 96, **96**
Parry, Hubert 114
Patrick, David 119
Peevor, Vera 83
Penny, Giles 100
Perks, Elliot 155
Perks, Oscar 155
Perks, Ursula 155
Perks, William 155
Peters, Alan 107, 108, 121
Peyron, Michael **70–1**, *70–1*, 71
Pigot, Keith 112, 114
Pilcher, Sir Dennis **35**
Pimm, Lionel 56
Plamenatz, John 29, 32, 36
Plowright, Joan (Lady Olivier) 121
Pond, Maria 86, *86*
Poulenc, Francis 111
Powell, Enoch 80
Powys-Lybb *15*
Presley, Elvis 110
Price, Charles *150*
Priestley 56
Proctor, Philip 99, 161, 163
Pugh, Alan 151
Purseglove, Ian 112

Ransome, Arthur 38
Raphael 70
Rathbone, Julian 70, 71, **72**, *72*
Rattigan, Terence 100
Reach, Jamie 168
Reed, Douglas **110**, **142**
Richard, Cliff 110
Ridout, Alan 100
Ripper, Karen 155
Roberts-Wray, Andrew 102, *102*
Roberts-Wray, Charlotte 102
Rodney, Lord 78
Rogers 70
Rogers, Jeremy 143
Rolling Stones, the 106, 110
Roots, Martin 107
Ross, Anthea 96
Ross, Carolyn 108
Ross, Mark 96, 97, *97*
Rowse, AL 80
Rutherford, Rhona 169, 170

Sabine, Piers *150*
Saint-Denis, Michel 120
Salisbury, Bishop of 132, *133*

Salmond-Smith, Louise (née Thompson) 111
Sampson, Nigel 89
Samuels, Sarah 96
Sargent, John Singer *26*
Saunders 35
Scadding, Norris 66, 72, 74, 104, *104*, 106, 107, 108, 117, 118, 141
Scholefield, Ken 48
Scholfield, Charles *127*
Scott, Flora 141
Scott, George 146
Scott, Jonathon 98
Scott, Mike 121
Scott, Phylip 98
Seddon, Anne 96
Seddon, James 70, 71
Seddon, James 95, *95*, 96
Sedgley, EAE 56
Sessions, Reggie 48, 68, 109, 141
Shackleton, Ernest *19*
Shadows, the 110
Shaw, Andrew **110–11**
Shaw, George Bernard 116
Shaw, Glyn Byam 120
Shuttleworth, Dr 19
Simpson, John *58*
Sinatra, Frank 114
Skinner, John 124, *125*, 127
Skinner, Joy 124
Smith, Louise (née Ross-Kellaway) 150, 155, 170
Smith, Richard 154
Smith, Ronald 110
Smith, Stephen 146
Smuts, General 63
Snow, CP 80
Spinney, David 6, 10, 38, 48, 49, 50, 53, 65, 66, 68, 72, 74, 75, *75*, 78, 79, 109, 111, 115, 117, 132, 136, 138, 141, 151, 154
Spinney, Ron 102, 135, 136, *136*, 153, 159, *160*, 163, 167
Spittal 70, 71
Spoor, Jeremy 64
Stener 155
Stephenson, JHM 29, 34, 144
Stephenson, John 141
Stephenson, JWA 36, 141, 143
Stevenson, Barry 104
Stewart, Hugh 121
Stockton, Arthur 30
Stones, Darren 101
Stubbs, Miss 90
Sullivan, Arthur 117, 118
Sutcliffe-Hey 70
Swan 70
Sweetnam, Sir Rodney **58–9**, 132, 145
Swingle Singers, the 112
Sydney-Turner, CGR 13, 15, *15*

Tait, Tom 143
Tambling, Christopher 114
Taylor, John 64
Teed 68
Tew, James *109*
Tew, Sandra 86, 87
Tew, Tony 86
Thomas, KM 54
Thomas, Robert 89
Thompson, Frank 12
Thompson, Leslie 112
Thompson, Paul 98
Thorndyke, Sybil 37
Tilden, Jim 127, 145
Tippett, Michael 110
Todd, Duncan 119
Toksvig, Jenifer 119, 121
Towler, Gawain 151
Townsend, Sarah 96
Tremellen, Richard 86, 159, 160, 161
Trenchard, George 155, *155*
Trenchard, Katie 155
Trenchard, Mark 155, *155*
Trenchard, Tim 155, *155*, 164
Turner, Michael 63

Vaizey, George 138
Van Veen, Paul 106
Varcoe, Stephen 112
Venables, Stephen 77
Venour, VBH (Bruce) 62
Verrinder, Carl 38, 48, 56, 66, 74, 77, *78*, 79, 111, 115, 116, 117, 118, 139, 141
Verrinder, Eleanor 38, 77
Voss, Werner 38

Waller, Tony 112
Walmsley, Win 85
Walser, David *50*, 57, 114
Walton, David 64
Ward-Booth, Major-General 153
Warnock, Baroness *160*, 161
Warwick, Dionne 106

Warwick, the Countess of 17
Waterhouse, Alfred *40*, 41
Waterhouse, William 40
Waters, Joanne 98
Watkins, Alison **76**
Watkins, David 76
Watson, David 96, 97, *97*, 99
Watson, Gwyneth 97
Weatherall, Jonathon *127*
Weinholt, William Humphrey Meyrick 28
Wessex, the Duchess of *17*
West, Andrew 168
Whitbourn, Frank 39, 115
Whybrow, Ernie 63
Whyte, Robert Barbour 13, *13*
Wightman, Peter **59**, **67**, *67*, **145**
Wilkins 70
Wilkinson, Clive **141**
Willetts, Bill 85
Williams, Richard 100
Willis, Dr Richard 153, 167, *171*
Wilmot 70
Wilson, Allan 57
Wilson, Harold, of Rievaulx, Lord 80
Wilson, Woodrow 32
Wilter, Carl 34
Wolkonsky, Michael 14
Wolkonsky, Prince Peter 14
Wolverton, Lord 40, *40*, 41, 130
Wood, Mr 34

Yeats, William Butler 121
Yeomans 35

Zatopek, Emil 141
Zelle, Nicholas (Nick) 77, 107, 109, 110, 111, 164

Acknowledgements and Picture Credits

Acknowledgements

This book would not have been possible without the huge support offered in particular by Louise Smith who has been unstinting in her help and commitment to the project, Tony Chew, the school archivist, and, of course, Martin Cooke.

Others at the school were unfailingly generous with both time and material: Eleanor Cooke, Richard Geffen, Barbara Barnes, Mike and Deborah Geary, Mary Bailey, Thomasin Bailey, Julie Ann Murphy, Colin Evans, Vera Peevor, Keith Pigot, Ray Norris, Moe Mitchell, Bill Willetts, Win Walmsley, Anne Jancis, Chris Humpage, Andrew Croft, Sandra Tew, Richard Miller, Mark Fraser, Jane Hayes, Alastair Nye and Nikki Cheung.

Roger Kingwill was illuminating about the school both from his time as a boy there and through his later close involvement as a governor, parent and friend. And once again, the highly professional staff at Third Millennium have made producing the book look deceptively easy: designer Matt Wilson, production manager Bonnie Murray and overall coordinator Joel Burden.

Picture Credits

Unless otherwise noted, the illustrations in this book have been provided by Clayesmore School. Every effort has been made to contact the copyright holders of all works reproduced in this book. If any acknowledgements have been omitted, please contact Third Millennium Publishing:

Alamy 118; Brian Arpel 65; David Capel-Jones 100c; B Caulfield-Giles 59; Courtesy of The Photographer © British Council Archive 104l; Darlo2009 93b; James Drawneek 121; Ian Ferguson 60; Getty Images 56t, 63; Heritage Images 11bl; Imperial War Museum 57; Kevin Jones 126, 127bl;J R Keighley 97, 100; IC Murphy 66; National Portrait Gallery 40m; Pangbourne School 18b; M Peyron 70–1; Picador Design 154; Charles Price 140, 150; Alayne Pullen 72t; RIBA Library Drawings Collection, PA1954(1) 40; Salford Lads Club Archive 11m; Colin Simpson 58b; Louise Smith 52, 53; Arthur Stockwin / Parapress 30all; Paul Taylor 51b

Special thanks also goes to Roger Allen for the restoration work he has done to the photographs in the School archive.

Thirty-Odd Feet Below Belgium,
edited by Arthur Stockton, Parapress Ltd, 2005